Contesting the Crusades

Contesting the Past

The volumes in this series select some of the most controversial episodes in history and consider their divergent, even starkly incompatible representations. The aim is not merely to demonstrate that history is 'argument without end', but to show that study even of contradictory conceptions can be fruitful: that the jettisoning of one thesis or presentation leaves behind something of value.

Published

Contesting the Crusades
Norman Housley

In preparation

European Renaissance
William Caferro

Witch Hunts in the Early Modern World
Alison Rowlands

Reformations
C. Scott Dixon

The Rise of Nazism
Chris Szejnmann

British Imperialism
Jane Samson

Contesting the French Revolution
Peter McPhee

Origins of the Second World War
Peter Jackson

Vietnam
David Hess

The Enlightenment
Thomas Munck

German Empire 1871–1918
Matthew Jefferies

Contesting the Crusades

Norman Housley

Blackwell
Publishing

BLACKWELL PUBLISHING
350 Main Street, Malden, MA 02148-5020, USA
9600 Garsington Road, Oxford OX4 2DQ, UK
550 Swanston Street, Carlton, Victoria 3053, Australia

First published 2006 by Blackwell Publishing Ltd

1 2006

Library of Congress Cataloging-in-Publication Data

Housley, Norman.
    Contesting the Crusades / Norman Housley.
        p. cm. — (Contesting the past)
Includes bibliographical references and index.
    ISBN-13: 978-1-4051-1188-1 (hardcover : alk. paper)
    ISBN-10: 1-4051-1188-7 (hardcover : alk. paper)
    ISBN-13: 978-1-4051-1189-8 (pbk. : alk. paper)
    ISBN-10: 1-4051-1189-5 (pbk. : alk. paper)
    1. Crusades. 2. Europe—Social conditions—To 1492. I. Title. II. Series.

D157.H67 2006
909.07—dc22

                                                                                           2005021907
A catalogue record for this title is available from the British Library.

For further information on
Blackwell Publishing, visit our website:
www.blackwellpublishing.com

Contents

Preface

> Pilgrimage, military expedition, holy war, colonial war, a mighty movement of migration were all applied to the Crusades according to the temper of the historian or publicist and the climate of public opinion at the time of writing. Extolled or vituperated, the Crusades have been represented as a sinister plot of popery, a transparent cloak for material greed, a precursor of imperialism or a frenzied mass psychosis, but also as a gigantic enterprise to realize lofty ideals, the most articulate expression of collective contrition and a Messianic movement which ushers mankind to the Day of Judgement and the approaching Kingdom of Heaven.

Joshua Prawer's words ring as true today as when they were published three decades ago.[1] Few topics in medieval history have provoked as much controversy as crusading, and none has proved more enduringly popular among historians and public alike. So many scholarly publications relating to crusading and associated topics appear each year that it has become impossible even for historians actively engaged in research on the subject to read them all.

Hence both the purpose and the limitations of this book. It is a modest attempt to take a snapshot of crusading studies as they appear in the spring of 2005, to describe and account for the principal trends of research and publication. Restrictions of time and space have forced me to exclude two associated areas of research, the study of the Latin East and of the military orders. Of course both are intimately associated with the practice of crusad-

---

1 *The Latin Kingdom of Jerusalem. European Colonialism in the Middle Ages* (London: Weidenfeld and Nicolson, 1972), p. 4.

ing, but they are also thriving fields of study in their own right; including them would have more than doubled the length of the book. The focus is on research published in English, because those are the publications that most readily come to my attention, though I have done my best to incorporate work written in French, German, Italian and Spanish. For the most part I have not gone back more than about fifty years. This is not because I do not value the contributions of earlier generations, but because crusading is an exceptionally lively and fast-changing area of scholarship, and my principal aim is to show what is currently being done, rather than to set out in detail how we got here. The more remote historiography of the crusades has not yet received the attention it merits (and would amply reward). Readers interested in pursuing it should start with Jonathan Riley-Smith's chapter, 'The crusading movement and historians', in Riley-Smith, ed., *The Oxford Illustrated History of the Crusades* (Oxford: Oxford University Press, 1995), and the essay by Giles Constable cited in chapter 1, note 3. Benjamin Kedar's 'longitudinal examination' of the way historians have treated the massacre in Jerusalem in July 1099, in *Crusades* 3 (2004), sets new standards for the historiographical analysis of individual events during the crusades.

Chapter 1 is rather different from the other chapters, in so far as I not only set out the main schools of thought about the best way to define the crusade, but also offer my views as to how the impasse that has unfortunately come to characterize this complex and crucial debate might be resolved. It therefore moves beyond the description of contention towards a tentative proposal for its resolution.

Norman Housley
Leicester

Acknowledgements

I am grateful to Christopher Wheeler for the invitation to write this book, and to the Trustees of Dr Williams's Library, London, for their permission to make use of the text of the lecture that I gave to the Friends of the Library in October 2003, a modified version of which forms chapter 1. John France kindly commented on a draft of chapter 2, and the referees who read the typescript for Blackwell all made helpful suggestions for additions and changes. The grant of a semester's study leave by my university enabled me to complete the book.

Abbreviations

AHR	*American Historical Review.*
APC	M. Balard, ed., *Autour de la première Croisade. Actes du Colloque de la Society for the Study of the Crusades and the Latin East (Clermont-Ferrand, 22–25 juin 1995)* (Paris: Publications de la Sorbonne, 1996).
BEC	*Bibliothèque de l'École des Chartes.*
BIHR	*Bulletin of the Institute of Historical Research.*
CCBF	A. V. Murray, ed., *Crusade and Conversion on the Baltic Frontier 1150–1500* (Aldershot: Ashgate, 2001).
CCCCP	M. Goodich, S. Menache and S. Schein, eds, *Cross Cultural Convergences in the Crusader Period. Essays presented to Aryeh Graboïs on his Sixty-Fifth Birthday* (New York: Peter Lang, 1995).
CCM	*Cahiers de civilisation médiévale.*
CFCMI	N. Housley, ed., *Crusading in the Fifteenth Century. Message and Impact* (Basingstoke: Palgrave Macmillan, 2004).
CHR	*Catholic Historical Review.*
CIRCG	G. Airaldi and B. Z. Kedar, eds, *I comuni italiani nel regno crociato di Gerusalemme* (Genoa: University of Genoa, 1986).
CMTCS	M. Shatzmiller, ed., *Crusaders and Muslims in Twelfth-Century Syria* (Leiden: Brill, 1993).
CS	P. W. Edbury, ed., *Crusade and Settlement. Papers read at the First Conference of the Society for the Study of the Crusades*

	and the Latin East and presented to R. C. Smail (Cardiff: University College Cardiff Press, 1985).
CTS	J. France and W. G. Zajac, eds, *The Crusades and their Sources. Essays presented to Bernard Hamilton* (Aldershot: Ashgate, 1998).
DGF	M. Balard, B. Z. Kedar and J. Riley-Smith, eds, *Dei gesta per Francos. Études sur les croisades dédiées à Jean Richard* (Aldershot: Ashgate, 2001).
EC	M. Bull and N. Housley, eds, *The Experience of Crusading, Volume 1, Western Approaches* (Cambridge: Cambridge University Press, 2003).
FCJ	A. V. Murray, ed., *From Clermont to Jerusalem. The Crusades and Crusader Societies 1095–1500* (Turnhout: Brepols, 1998).
FCOI	J. Phillips, ed., *The First Crusade. Origins and Impact* (Manchester: Manchester University Press, 1997).
HC	K. M. Setton, gen. ed., *A History of the Crusades* (2nd edn, 6 vols, Madison: University of Wisconsin Press, 1969–89).
HH	B. Z. Kedar, ed., *The Horns of Hattin. Proceedings of the Second Conference of the Society for the Study of the Crusades and the Latin East* (Jerusalem: Yad Izhak Ben-Zvi, 1992).
HLHL	R. N. Swanson, ed., *The Holy Land, Holy Lands, and Christian History*, SCH 36 (Woodbridge: Boydell, 2000).
IHR	*International History Review.*
JCZK	A. Haverkamp, ed., *Juden und Christen zur Zeit der Kreuzzüge* (Sigmaringen: Jan Thorbecke, 1999).
JEH	*Journal of Ecclesiastical History.*
JMH	*Journal of Medieval History.*
MC	S. Ridyard, ed., *The Medieval Crusade* (Woodbridge: Boydell, 2004).
MFS	R. Bartlett and A. MacKay, eds, *Medieval Frontier Societies* (Oxford: Oxford University Press, 1989).
MSCH	B. Z. Kedar, J. Riley-Smith and R. Hiestand, eds, *Montjoie. Studies in Crusade History in Honour of Hans Eberhard Mayer* (Aldershot: Ashgate, 1997).
NCMH	*The New Cambridge Medieval History.*
OIHC	J. Riley-Smith, ed., *The Oxford Illustrated History of the Crusades* (Oxford: Oxford University Press, 1995).
OSHCKJ	B. Z. Kedar, H. E. Mayer and R. C. Smail, eds, *Outremer. Studies in the History of the Crusading Kingdom of Jerusalem presented to Joshua Prawer* (Jerusalem: Yad Izhak Ben-Zvi Institute, 1982).

P&P	*Past and Present.*
PCNAD	L. García-Guijarro Ramos, ed., *La primera cruzada, novecientos años después: el concilio de Clermont y los orígenes del movimiento cruzado* (Castelló d'Impressió, S.L., 1997).
PIW	J. C. Moore, ed., *Pope Innocent III and his World* (Aldershot: Ashgate, 1999).
PMC	H. E. J. Cowdrey, *Popes, Monks and Crusaders* (London: Hambledon Press, 1984).
RBPH	*Revue belge de philologie et d'histoire.*
RH	*Revue historique.*
SCC	M. Gervers, ed., *The Second Crusade and the Cistercians* (New York: St Martin's Press, 1992).
SCH	*Studies in Church History.*
SCSC	J. Phillips and M. Hoch, eds, *The Second Crusade. Scope and Consequences* (Manchester: Manchester University Press, 2001).
TISCAC	M. Gervers and J. M. Powell, eds, *Tolerance and Intolerance. Social Conflict in the Age of the Crusades* (Syracuse: Syracuse University Press, 2001).
TRHS	*Transactions of the Royal Historical Society.*
WGMA	J. Gillingham and J. C. Holt, eds, *War and Government in the Middle Ages. Essays in Honour of J. O. Prestwich* (Woodbridge: Boydell, 1984).

Chronology

1

Defining the Crusade

In the autumn of 2000 William Hague, the leader of the British Conservative Party, tried to cut to the essence of the polemic about the constitutional future of the European Union with the ringing declaration that 'if it looks like an elephant, talks like an elephant and walks like an elephant, it is an elephant'. Disagreement about what a crusade was has been a prominent feature of research into crusading for several decades now, so it is worth beginning our investigation of the subject by asking why Hague's brand of Yorkshire common sense cannot be applied to the issue. The answer is that no clear template or yardstick for a crusade exists against which we can measure the features of other expeditions to check if they 'qualify'. Some comparisons may help to illustrate how much this complicates things. In his recent book on the medieval economy of the British Isles, Christopher Dyer admitted that working out which settlements were 'towns' is hard because the difference between a town and a village is far from straightforward, while possession of a charter of self-government is not the help we might expect it to be. Yet we all have a rough idea of what we expect a 'town' to be like.[1] If the issue of definition arises in relation to settled communities of people, how much more so when the phenomenon being studied is a temporary but complex, and sometimes volatile, agglomeration of various groups of people whose own view of what they were doing differed widely? Nor have recent tendencies in historical scholarship helped. The current trend, driven by the growing

---

1 C. Dyer, *Making a Living in the Middle Ages. The People of Britain 850–1520* (New Haven, CT: Yale University Press, 2002), pp. 9, 58–70.

rift between history and the social sciences, is to dismiss all classifications as artificial and to question the validity even of such apparently well-established series of events as the Reformation and the Enlightenment. The very nature of crusading means that any definition is fragile, vulnerable to such an assault on its methodological foundations. But the search for a definition continues, and it is more than curiosity that drives it. For more and more we are discerning the role which crusading played in shaping both the internal development of medieval Europe and the relationship between Catholic Christianity and neighbouring faiths. Hence the paradox of contemporary crusading studies: an unprecedented richness of research, including now a dedicated journal, *Crusades*, set against a background of confusion in terms of definition which only seems to deepen the more we discover.[2]

Existing Definitions and their Problems

We have a good starting point in Giles Constable's recent review of the current definitions.[3] These may be described as traditionalist, pluralist, popularist and generalist, with the essential caveat that historians are usually far too individual to be readily sorted into schools of thought.[4] The first and second groups in Constable's list have been most prominent in recent debate. Traditionalists define the crusade as a campaign that was fought with the goal of recovering or defending Jerusalem. The cross that the crusaders (*crucesignati*) displayed indicated the common centrality of the holy places of Jerusalem, above all the Church of the Holy Sepulchre, to the devotional lives of crusaders and their military objectives. This was obviously true of the first three crusades, which marched or sailed to the Holy Land, but it also applied to the series of later expeditions whose destination was the Nile delta, since the strategy espoused by their leaders was that of assisting the cause of Jerusalem indirectly, by attacking the heart of Ayyubid and Mamluk power in Egypt.

---

2 This trend was pointed out by H. E. Mayer in *The Crusades*, trans. J. Gillingham (London: Oxford University Press, 1972), pp. 285–6, and in both respects the situation has become more extreme in the meantime, though Mayer deleted the remark in the 1988 edition of his book.

3 G. Constable, 'The historiography of the crusades', in A. E. Laiou and R. P. Mottahedeh, eds, *The Crusades from the Perspective of Byzantium and the Muslim World* (Washington, DC: Dumbarton Oaks Research Library and Collection, 2001), 1–22, esp. pp. 10–15.

4 Thus Constable has objected to being labelled a pluralist ('The historiography', p. 13), and J. Riley-Smith, *What were the Crusades?* (3rd edn, Basingstoke: Palgrave Macmillan, 2002), p. 102, sees Jean Flori as a popularist whereas I classify him as a traditionalist.

'The almost unbelievably obstinate simplicity of the believer's heart meant that these wars, the crusades, were directed again and again to the same goal: Jerusalem. This simplicity of thought, feeling and action must not be overlooked.'[5] These remarks by the German scholar Hans Mayer, a leading exponent of the traditionalist viewpoint, express the inductive reasoning behind such an approach in terms of an overall assessment of how crusading developed between the preaching of the First Crusade in 1095 and the fall of Acre in 1291. For Mayer, the response of the Catholic laity to the preaching of the Holy Land crusade, in the face of great expenses and obstacles, repeated defeats and overwhelming odds, showed that for them this was the only 'true' experience of crusade. The French medievalist Jean Flori reached the same conclusion as Mayer, but by a somewhat different route. For Flori, William Hague's elephant did exist and it was the First Crusade. That expedition established the synthesis of holy war and pilgrimage that constituted the quantum leap from holy war to something new that we have come to call 'crusade'. The goal of saving the Holy Sepulchre was therefore crucial: 'This objective alone permits and justifies the ideological fusion of holy war and pilgrimage that characterizes the crusade.' Flori has therefore offered a very simple definition: 'The crusade was a holy war that had as its objective the recovery of the holy places of Jerusalem for the Christians.' The best that could be said of expeditions that failed to match this definition was that they were holy wars (*guerres saintes*) or sacralized wars (*guerres sacralisées*), the latter comprising those conflicts that the Church attempted to raise to a higher level by granting them special status.[6]

Pluralists, by contrast, view crusading as a particular type of Christian holy war. Jonathan Riley-Smith has stated that 'A crusade was a penitential war which ranked as, and had many of the attributes of, a pilgrimage'. Given that Jerusalem was the pilgrimage destination *par excellence*, this seems at first glance similar to Flori's definition, but the very next sentence in Riley-Smith's text establishes the contrast: 'It manifested itself in many theatres of war: Palestine and the eastern Mediterranean region, of course, but also North Africa, Spain, the Baltic shores, Poland, Hungary, the Balkans and even Western Europe.'[7] What defined this penitential war was not its destination but its origins and characteristics. Participants were responding to an appeal to take action that was promulgated by

---

5 Mayer, *The Crusades*, pp. 283–4.
6 J. Flori, 'Pour une redéfinition de la croisade', CCM 47 (2004), 329–50, at p. 349. See too his *La Guerre sainte. La formation de l'idée de croisade dans l'Occident chrétien* (Paris: Aubier, 2001), p. 357.
7 Riley-Smith, *What were the Crusades?*, p. 87.

the pope and preached by the Church; some of them took crusading vows, they assumed the cross, incurring an onerous obligation that they could not easily evade, and they received valuable privileges of a temporal as well as a spiritual nature. Where crusaders fought depended on the wording of the vows they had taken, and their legal status and entitlements were predicated on the papacy's *magisterium* and on the Church's role as mediator in the bestowal of God's forgiveness to sinners. One of the most striking differences between the two approaches is the size of the field of study that emerges. The canvas addressed by pluralists expands geographically, as noted above, but also chronologically, for they have examined campaigns fought by *crucesignati* stretching from 1095 as far as the sixteenth and even the seventeenth century.[8]

As the name suggests, traditionalists are working within a well-established historiographical framework. To go no further back, the two best-known histories of the crusades that were written in English and French in the twentieth century, those by Runciman and Grousset, both adhered to it.[9] But where did pluralism come from? When Riley-Smith addressed this question in 1988 he pinpointed a number of major changes in the political and cultural climate of the late twentieth century that had led scholars to re-examine what he called 'ideological violence', in this case religious warfare. These were the juridical responses to the crimes committed against humanity in the Second World War and the proliferation of nuclear arms, new approaches towards the psychology of individual engagement in armed conflict, and most importantly, the development of a revolutionary Christian theology of violence in response to state terror.[10] Just as significant, however, were individual contributions and stimuli, above all the publications of Riley-Smith himself, notably his short but highly influential book *What were the Crusades?* (currently in its third edition), coupled with his ability to produce a cluster of topics about crusading for the doctoral students who worked with him at Cambridge and London.[11]

---

8 Riley-Smith, *What were the Crusades?*; idem, *The Crusades. A Short History* (London: Athlone Press, 1987, 2nd edn forthcoming); N. Housley, *The Later Crusades, 1274–1580. From Lyons to Alcazar* (Oxford: Oxford University Press, 1992).

9 S. Runciman, *A History of the Crusades* (3 vols, Cambridge: Cambridge University Press, 1951–4); R. Grousset, *Histoire des croisades et du royaume franc de Jérusalem* (3 vols, Paris: Plon, 1934–6).

10 J. Riley-Smith, 'History, the crusades and the Latin East, 1095–1204: a personal view', in *CMTCS*, 1–17, at pp. 5–8.

11 For an overview of Riley-Smith's contribution, see N. Housley, with M. Bull, 'Jonathan Riley-Smith, the crusades and the military orders: an appreciation', in *EC*, 1–10.

In the strictest sense traditionalism and pluralism are irreconcilable. Take for example the case of the Spanish *Reconquista*, to which the terminology, apparatus and rewards of crusading were extended at a very early point in the history of crusading. Mayer declined to accept the wars against the Moors in Spain as a crusade.[12] Flori was more forthright: those who fought in Spain were given spiritual rewards by the Church 'as if' (*comme si*) they had fought in a crusade. He saw Pope Innocent III's revocation of crusading status for the Spanish conflict in 1213 as proof that the extension of crusading practices to Spain was 'neither institutional nor permanent, but a product of circumstances [*conjoncturelle*] that could be revoked, which clearly could not have been the case with an authentic crusade'.[13] It is, however, possible to take up a stance as a 'modified' traditionalist and to argue that although crusading to the Holy Land was always the 'purest' and most popular experience of crusade, both campaigns which were conducted on other fronts, and expeditions which took place after 1291, were regarded by contemporaries as crusades and therefore must be treated as such. That Jerusalem was the prime but not the exclusive goal of crusading appears to be the position of the British historian Christopher Tyerman, who in his study *England and the Crusades* adopted a pluralist agenda while reserving a special place for Jerusalem.[14]

The other schools of thought identified by Constable were popularism and generalism. Constable referred to the influential work of the French scholars Paul Alphandéry and Alphonse Dupront, who saw crusading as essentially an eschatological act, inherently transcendental, the product of a surge of collective religious excitement experienced above all by the poor (*pauperes*). It was expressed primarily on the First Crusade, and thereafter was rapidly 'tamed' as crusading was institutionalized by the clerical *élite* and became the preserve of the fighting aristocracy.[15] Constable did not dub this approach 'popularism', writing rather of 'a spiritual or psychological definition that emphasizes the inner spirit and motives of the crusaders and their leaders'.[16] The term 'popularism', however, has

12   Mayer, *The Crusades*, p. 285.
13   Flori, 'Pour une redéfinition', p. 337. For the pluralist view of the *Reconquista*, a concept that naturally poses its own set of methodological issues, see J. F. O'Callaghan, *Reconquest and Crusade in Medieval Spain* (Philadelphia: University of Pennsylvania Press, 2003).
14   C. Tyerman, *England and the Crusades 1095–1588* (Chicago: University of Chicago Press, 1988); idem, *The Invention of the Crusades* (Basingstoke: Macmillan, 1998).
15   P. Alphandéry, *La Chrétienté et l'idée de croisade*, ed. A. Dupront (2 vols, Paris: A. Michel, 1954–9, new edn 1995 with postscript by M. Balard); A. Dupront, *Du sacré: croisades et pèlerinages, images et langages* (Paris: Gallimard, 1987).
16   Constable, 'The historiography', p. 13.

the advantage that it highlights the significance, not just on the First Crusade but into a much later period, of the association between crusading and a religious excitement experienced among society's disadvantaged. In the United Kingdom, Gary Dickson has made this something of a preserve, depicting crusading as one of a series of religious revivals that occurred throughout the Middle Ages.[17] One reason why it is important to keep the popularist approach in mind is Flori's recent restatement of the traditionalist viewpoint. This is based on the argument that reverence for Jerusalem's eschatological role, in terms of the events that would lead up to the return of Christ, played a major (though not exclusive) role in transforming holy war into crusade at the time of the First Crusade. This was particularly the case in those areas where Peter the Hermit recruited for the crusade, where there was 'a climate of apocalyptic effervescence'.[18]

Clearly, there are things in common between traditionalism and popularism. The main difference is that popularists see crusading losing its vitality as early as the time of the so-called 'Children's Crusade' in 1212; of all definitions it is the most restrictive.[19] 'Generalism', while sharing popularism's preoccupation with medieval eschatology, proceeds in exactly the opposite direction. It is possible to argue that the most significant event at Clermont in 1095 was the cry *deus lo volt* ('God wants it'). Once affirmed by the astonishing victory of the First Crusade, this belief in a world whose political and military ordering was not just notionally or sporadically, but intimately and constantly, shaped by God's will for his human creation, enabled crusading to persist. Defined as wars fought *deo auctore*, crusading extended to numerous theatres of military activity. Its incorporation into the Church's penitential system, its deployment by a self-confident and ambitious papacy, and its powerful association with the ideal of Christian knighthood, meant that crusading became axiomatic whenever medieval war was placed within an ideological context. From this perspective, even pluralism is too narrow to encompass the full breadth of what crusading meant for medieval Europe. In the most cogent recent exposition of this viewpoint, Ernst-Dieter Hehl concluded that 'each definition [of the

---

17 See, among other works, Gary Dickson, 'La genèse de la croisade des enfants (1212)', *BEC* 153 (1995), 54–102 [English version as 'The genesis of the Children's Crusade (1212)', in his *Religious Enthusiasm in the Medieval West: Revivals, Crusades, Saints* (Aldershot: Ashgate Variorum, 2000), study IV]; 'The advent of the *pastores* (1251)', *RBPH* 66 (1988), 249–67; 'Revivalism as a medieval religious genre', *JEH* 51 (2000), 473–96.
18 Flori, *La Guerre sainte*, pp. 348–51.
19 Werner Goez claimed that the last true crusade, or *passagium generale*, was the Third Crusade of 1189–92: 'Wandlungen des Kreuzzugsgedankens im Hoch- und Spätmittelalter', in W. Fischer and J. Schneider, eds, *Das Heilige Land im Mittelalter. Begegnungsraum zwischen Orient und Okzident* (Neustadt an der Aisch: Verlag Degener, 1982), 33–44, at p. 42.

crusade] runs the risk of detaching it as a specific war of the Church from the general development of medieval society, of making it an event [occurring] on the borders of Christendom, as opposed to locating its deep-rootedness in Christendom's central structures.'[20]

Let us turn to language. It is a truism that one reason for the difficulty of defining the crusade is the absence, until relatively late in the history of crusading, of a single word which can be translated as 'crusade'. Instead, we find clusters of words, of a more general nature, used to designate key aspects of what the crusader was doing or the process of which he formed part. For the journey we have such words as *peregrinatio*, *iter*, *via*, *expeditio* and (later) *passagium*; for the enterprise we find *negotium*, *bellum*, *causa*, *opus*, *voluntas*; for the collectivity we encounter *milites Dei* or *Christi*, *exercitus Dei*, etc.[21] Prominent here are words which sprang from the vocabulary long associated with pilgrimage, reflecting another big problem of definition, that in the twelfth century the boundary between crusade and pilgrimage was so thin as at times to be invisible. A new Christian devotional practice had come into being, that of taking the cross to engage in penitential warfare on behalf of Christ. But a distinctive crusading vocabulary was slow to emerge, possibly because it was not needed, and possibly because the Church felt uneasy about making it so apparent that it had embraced warfare. It was only around 1200 that the language used in relation to the launching of crusades, the preaching of the cross, and the status and obligations of the crusader, finally became distinctive. And for the following decades, there is no doubt that the pluralist position makes a good deal of sense. Because they were couched in terms of the individual sinner rather than the cause, the contents of the *ad status* or model sermons recently edited by Christoph Maier could relate to any of a number of crusading fronts.[22] So too could most of the careful consideration that was accorded the votive obligations of *crucesignati* by the decretalists.[23] The same approach underpinned the practice of commuting the vows of crusaders, as well as the procedure occasionally followed by the papal *curia*, of calling off crusade preaching for a particular front because it considered the needs of another to be more important or

---

20 E.-D. Hehl, 'Was ist eigentlich ein Kreuzzug?', *Historische Zeitschrift* 259 (1994), 297–336, at p. 333.

21 These examples are taken from Constable, 'The historiography', pp. 11–12. As he indicates, there is an extended discussion of the subject in D. A. Trotter, *Medieval French Literature and the Crusades* (Geneva: Droz, 1988), pp. 31–70.

22 C. T. Maier, ed., *Crusade Propaganda and Ideology. Model Sermons for the Preaching of the Cross* (Cambridge: Cambridge University Press, 2000), esp. pp. 51–68.

23 J. A. Brundage, *Medieval Canon Law and the Crusader* (Madison: University of Wisconsin Press, 1969), pp. 66–114.

urgent.[24] Working from vocabulary, preaching and liturgy, canon law and the implementation of papal policy, the pluralist case undeniably becomes a strong one in the thirteenth century.

From certain points of views, however, this strength is illusory. The devotional and juridical formulae, and the language in which they were couched, belonged to the clerical *élite* and their servants, popes and cardinals, prelates, canon lawyers and commentators, and there is an *a priori* risk involved in listening only to the *potentes*. They realized the danger of allowing the goals and apparatus of crusade to become detached from what the bulk of the laity wanted. The great canon lawyer Henry of Susa (Hostiensis) referred rather dismissively to the problem that 'the simple' (*simplices*) failed to agree with their superiors.[25] And in a letter to Charles of Anjou in 1266, Pope Clement IV commented with remarkable frankness on the issue. The new king of Sicily had asked for a crusade to be preached in support of one group of Greeks against another group. Clement replied that 'the indulgence cannot be granted in this manner to all and sundry, or what is intended as a means of salvation will be exposed to disbelief and derision'.[26] Within this pope's own lifetime the *curia* had suffered a rebuff when Gregory IX's attempt to divert a French *passagium* from the Holy Land to prop up the collapsing Latin empire at Constantinople had been turned down by the crusade's baronial leaders.[27] We should not deduce from this that there was a yawning chasm between the way the thirteenth-century Church viewed the crusade and the outlook of the laity. People took the cross to fight in all the numerous crusades that were proclaimed, but they did so in accordance with their own timetables, under their own terms, and for their own reasons. We shall see later in this book that the discovery of the 'lay voice' in terms of what crusading entailed has been an important and exciting feature of recent writings.

That lay people often had to be persuaded to take the cross, and that they held fast to views that the Church found it hard to accept, is not a severe threat to the pluralist position. A more difficult issue is that of contemporaries engaging in crusading enterprises who for various reasons operated outside or on the periphery of the established framework

---

24 M. Purcell, *Papal Crusading Policy 1244–1291. The Chief Instruments of Papal Crusading Policy and Crusade to the Holy Land from the Final Loss of Jerusalem to the Fall of Acre* (Leiden: Brill, 1975), esp. pp. 106–14.

25 N. Housley, *The Italian Crusades. The Papal-Angevin Alliance and the Crusades against Christian Lay Powers, 1254–1343* (Oxford: Oxford University Press, 1982), p. 37.

26 Housley, *The Italian Crusades*, pp. 34–5; Purcell, *Papal Crusading Policy*, pp. 94–5.

27 S. Painter, 'The crusade of Theobald of Champagne and Richard of Cornwall, 1239–1241', in *HC* 2: 463–85, at pp. 466–9. These events will be clarified in a forthcoming study by Michael Lower.

for taking the cross. This applies, for example, to the various 'popular' movements of the period, from the crusade of the *pueri* in 1212 through to the *pastoureaux* of 1320.[28] In the eyes of the popularists these were the only true crusades, but for rigorous pluralists there is the danger that they cease to be acknowledged as crusades at all: a conundrum readily explained by the popularist argument that the enforcement of clerical control over the crusade demobilized the *pauperes*, in the process robbing crusading of its vitality and leaving it a mere shadow of its former self. At the opposite end of the social spectrum, we have the plethora of raids which noble volunteers took part in against 'Saracens' in the decades between the fall of Acre in 1291 and the Nicopolis Crusade of 1396. For some of this military activity, such as Peter I's assault on Alexandria in 1365, there is evidence that people took the cross;[29] but on other occasions not. It has recently been pointed out that there is very little surviving evidence that the thousands of volunteers who flocked to Prussia to fight with the Teutonic Order in its *Reisen* against the pagan Lithuanians were *crucesignati*.[30] Nor is there any proof that the most zealous fighter against 'non-believers' (*infideles*) in the late fourteenth century, Marshal Boucicaut, ever took the cross.[31]

In fact once we pass 1291 the danger begins to loom that the pluralist approach remains fully coherent only when applied to the planning of a large-scale *passagium* to the east, as in the recovery treatises and in the negotiations between the French royal court and the papal *curia*. At these times it is overwhelmingly associated with the raising of sufficient funds to make the venture possible, as it became again in the middle decades of the fourteenth century in the case of the naval leagues against the Anatolian Turks.[32] On other occasions, when individuals or small groups can be witnessed embarking on warfare against non-believers, taking the cross ceased to be fashionable; on the other hand, the recurrence in sources for the *Reisen* of the word *peregrini* (pilgrims) for volunteers warns us not to view these conflicts as ventures that had been emptied of any devotional

---

28 See Dickson, 'La genèse de la croisade des enfants'; M. Barber, 'The pastoureaux of 1320', *JEH* 32 (1981), 143–66.

29 J. Smet, ed., *The Life of St Peter Thomas* (Rome: Pontificia Università Gregoriana, 1954), pp. 120–40.

30 A. Ehlers, 'The crusade of the Teutonic Knights against Lithuania reconsidered', in *CCBF*, 21–44.

31 This is an argument *ex silentio*, but his biographer, the anonymous author of D. Lalande, ed., *Le Livre des fais du bon messire Jehan le Maingre, dit Bouciquaut, mareschal de France et gouverneur de Jennes* (Geneva: Droz, 1985), lost no chance to praise Boucicaut, and surely would have mentioned it had it occurred.

32 See N. Housley, *The Avignon Papacy and the Crusades, 1305–1378* (Oxford: Oxford University Press, 1986), pp. 82–198.

meaning.[33] Perhaps taking the cross was considered to be inappropriate for certain contexts, or was shunned because of the obligations it carried (especially heritability), or was no longer regarded as necessary to gain the spiritual benefits which would accrue to those who fought Christ's enemies.

Pluralism is far from alone in raising methodological problems. Because of the wealth of evidence testifying to the extension of the crusade into areas far from Jerusalem, 'pure traditionalism' looks increasingly capricious. Thus the author of a recent study of the combatants in the Albigensian Crusade stated that although accepting the traditionalist definition, she would use the term 'crusade' because it featured in the contemporary accounts of the conflict.[34] Yet this is far from being solely a semantic issue: we are dealing with a whole fabric of religious, legal and cultural activity, ideas and feelings which can be seen at work in this and other crusades occurring hundreds of miles distant from the Holy Land.[35] It is a misreading of medieval religious thinking to regard the vow, the cross, the indulgence and the status and privileges of the *crucesignatus* as mere 'exterior signs' that were transferred to other locations than the Holy Land with the intention of 'sacralising' the conflicts that were taking place there.[36] 'Modified traditionalism' brings fewer problems, but it presupposes that the institutional uniformity of much thirteenth-century crusading could coexist with a kind of ranking system within the minds of contemporaries. It is hard to envisage how such a ranking system could function without a degradation of the spiritual benefit that accrued to the *crucesignatus* who fought on fronts other than the Holy Land. These other fronts then become 'substitute' crusades, pale imitations of the genuine article.[37] In other words 'modified traditionalism' is an attempt to square the circle, a concession to the pluralist challenge which when questioned closely views most crusades as purely ersatz ventures.

This applies *a fortiori* to the popularist approach. Its attraction resides partly in the fact that it slices through the Gordian knot of definition by judging later expeditions according to their ability to replicate the features

---

33   Ehlers, 'The crusade', pp. 30–5.
34   C. Woehl, *Volo vincere cum meis vel occumbere cum eisdem. Studien zu Simon von Montfort und seinen nordfranzösischen Gefolgsleuten während des Albigenserkreuzzugs (1209 bis 1218)* (Frankfurt am Main: Peter Lang, 2001), p. 4 note 7.
35   See, most recently, O'Callaghan, *Reconquest*, pp. 177–208.
36   Flori, 'Pour une redéfinition', pp. 340, 346 note 81, 349.
37   For a recent example see M. Menzel, 'Kreuzzugsideologie unter Innocenz III', *Historisches Jahrbuch* 120 (2000), 39–79, at p. 52, where Innocent III's promotion of both the *Reconquista* and the Albigensian Crusade in the period 1208–13 is viewed as a 'half-hearted' pursuit of *Ersatzunternehmen*.

of the First Crusade. This appears to capture the essence of crusading's appeal, its origins in the ferment of religious excitement that existed at the time of the Clermont Council. Its emphasis on an eschatological view of events is undoubtedly borne out by some of the sources for the First Crusade, which dwell on the plethora of 'signs, powers, prodigies and portents' sent by God 'to sharpen the minds of Christians so that they should want to hurry [to the Holy Sepulchre]'.[38] And it concurs with current interest in the eschatological convictions of many people not just in the eleventh century but throughout the Middle Ages. It is also in harmony with the 'new gothic' which Paul Freedman and Gabrielle Spiegel have characterized as a dominant feature of contemporary North American Medieval Studies, a lively interest in the bizarre 'otherness' of medieval life, partly in reaction against older trends that sought to justify the discipline by dwelling on reassuring similarities or precedents in government and law. Arguably, crusading fits the engaging model constructed by Freedman and Spiegel more than any other aspect of medieval life, so it is curious that they almost totally neglect it.[39]

Close inspection, however, soon reveals the weaknesses of the popularist approach. In the first place, there is an issue of style. Much of the work of Alphonse Dupront, one of the leading popularist scholars, is characterized by a tendency not to argue a case but to assert it, and to do so in a highly coloured prose full of rhetorical questions but lacking evidential support.[40] Dupront's work can be remarkably stimulating, but many of his arguments are vulnerable to critical questioning: one example is his claim that the revolutionaries of the nineteenth century were the true heirs to the crusaders.[41] Secondly, the popularist approach tends to be selective in the evidence examined. This applies even to the First Crusade, where it is at its strongest. Popularists largely ignore the substantial tranche of sources, such as monastic charters, that testify to a much less highly charged (though no less devout) view of what the first crusaders were doing.[42] It might be objected that the charters reflect the views of the cloistered religious and their well-off patrons, but even among the narrative sources for the expedition the popularist viewpoint is not exclusive.

---

38   'Historia peregrinorum euntium Jerusolymam', quoted by J. Riley-Smith, *The First Crusade and the Idea of Crusading* (London: Athlone Press, 1986), p. 33.

39   P. Freedman and G. M. Spiegel, 'Medievalisms old and new: the rediscovery of alterity in North American medieval studies', *AHR* 103 (1998), 677–704.

40   Dupront, *Du sacré*, pp. 264–312.

41   Alphandéry, *La Chrétienté*, 2: 273–89, at pp. 276–7, pages written by Dupront (cf. p. 274 note 1).

42   G. Constable, 'Medieval charters as a source for the history of the crusades', in *CS*, 73–89; M. Bull, 'The diplomatic of the First Crusade', in *FCOI*, 35–54.

Apocalypticism in particular, the expectation of an imminent Second Coming (*parousia*), is only patchily documented, and it is hard today to accept without heavy qualification the claim by Alphandéry and Dupront that 'throughout the west, the crusade set out in the grip of eschatological goals, the idea of the imminent arrival of Antichrist, the conquest of the Last Days, and the belief that the saints would dwell at Jerusalem'.[43]

Bernard McGinn has suggested that 'the crusade was not so much the result of apocalypticism, as it was a notable stimulus to the revival of apocalyptic themes', because Christian possession of Jerusalem highlighted its eschatological role within the religious thinking of twelfth-century Catholics.[44] This would lead one to expect eschatology to become more significant as we move into later crusading, and it is true that it continued to play a strong role, in particular during the crusades that were launched after the loss of Jerusalem in 1187. However, the eschatological features that we encounter on the big *passagia*, such as the Fifth Crusade, were less clearly associated with the tumultuous presence of the *pauperes*, and the view that crusading was their peculiar vocation as Christ's chosen was less frequently voiced. In other words, the popularist approach hinges on the mistake of focusing on one or two undeniably important and arresting strands in crusading thought and practice, and ignoring the rest.

Generalism, too, has certain attractions. If we apply the term 'crusade' to the whole spectrum of the medieval Church's acceptance of warfare, and its absorption of this violence into its own theological and juridical systems, then some of the problems referred to earlier in connection with the pluralist methodology fall away completely. Such an inclusive approach avoids the danger of leaving out important events and trends on the grounds of definition. It ceases to matter that the 'popular crusaders' of 1212 or 1320, for example, had not taken the cross in the prescribed manner from the hands of a cleric: the sources, hostile though they usually are, refer to individuals believing that they were engaged on God's business, which was communicated to them by alternative sources of authority, notably miraculous letters or charismatic leaders. In the same way, our inability to prove that volunteers in the wars of

---

43 Alphandéry, *La Chrétienté*, 1: 97. This judgement had a clear impact on the influential book of N. Cohn, *The Pursuit of the Millennium. Revolutionary Millenarians and Mystical Anarchists of the Middle Ages*, revd edn (New York: Oxford University Press, 1970), esp. p. 64: 'for [the poor] the Crusade was above all a collective *imitatio Christi*, a mass sacrifice which was to be rewarded by a mass apotheosis at Jerusalem.'

44 B. McGinn, ed., *Visions of the End. Apocalyptic Traditions in the Middle Ages*, Records of Civilization: Sources and Studies (new edn, New York: Columbia University Press, 1998), p. 89.

the Teutonic Knights were *crucesignati* is no longer a problem. They clearly subscribed to a chivalric ideology that placed a premium on fighting against non-believers, 'enemies of Christ', as was demonstrated by the fact that they gradually stopped going to Prussia once the conversion of the Lithuanians became a fact that could not be argued away.[45] By defining crusade as, in effect, the ongoing interface between an anxious and militant laity and a responsive Church, generalism carries through into the central and later Middle Ages an agenda of discussion that has proved immensely fruitful in the case of the 'pre-crusade' period.[46]

On the other hand, the wholesale acceptance of a generalist approach means that crusading loses any precise identity. Context becomes everything, the origins become the event. We cannot regard taking the cross as no more than instrumentality: that would be to fall into much the same trap that ensnared Carl Erdmann when he described the capture of Jerusalem as the *Marschziel* of the first crusaders as opposed to their *Kriegsziel*, i.e. the end of their march to the east rather than the reason they had taken up arms.[47] There exists a vast corpus of evidence testifying to the devotional lives and experiences of crusaders which was related specifically to the *imitatio Christi* of bearing the Saviour's cross, the working out by each individual and group of the full implications of the fusion of penitence and holy war which resided at the heart of crusading. This gets lost, or at most it is relegated to a sub-species of crusading, if we accept the generalist viewpoint.

Catching the Eel

Luther famously described Erasmus as 'the eel whom only Christ could catch'.[48] Luther was referring to Erasmus's notorious elusiveness, his ability to be all things to all men, but the eel analogy helps to clarify the problem of how best to define the crusade. Crusading is peculiarly hard to pin down both horizontally, in the case of each expedition, and vertically, in the ways the practice developed from generation to generation. Within each crusading host there were undoubtedly a number of different ways of envisaging the common venture, indeed the views both of individuals and

---

45 Ehlers, 'The crusade', pp. 43–4.
46 See C. Erdmann, *The Origin of the Idea of Crusade*, trans. M. W. Baldwin and W. Goffart (Princeton, NJ: Princeton University Press, 1977); Flori, *La Guerre sainte*; J. France, 'Holy war and holy men: Erdmann and the lives of the saints', in *EC*, 193–208.
47 Erdmann, *The Origin*, pp. 355–71, esp. p. 368.
48 T. G. Tappert, ed. and trans., *Luther's Works. Volume 54, Table Talk* (Philadelphia: Fortress Press, 1967), p. 19.

of the collectivity could change over the course of the campaign: witness the way the penitential aspect of the First Crusade became more prominent the closer the army got to Jerusalem.[49] But more important was the change that occurred over the *longue durée*. Crusading evolved, and its evolution was shaped by the interaction of a myriad of forces: social and religious change, the development of military techniques and organization, advances in the economy, the growth of governmental ambitions, all these and many more exerted an impact on the crusades. To refuse to accept this process of change, and to insist on defining the crusade by reference only to the First Crusade on the grounds that all subsequent developments were distortions, is methodologically unsound.[50]

One result of this constant change was that at various stages in crusading's evolution each of the four approaches outlined above achieves a close 'fit', only to lose it as things move on. We have already seen that the popularist definition arises from the view that the First Crusade was the 'purest', while the pluralist approach is most readily applicable in the case of much thirteenth-century crusading.[51] A strength of the traditionalist stance is that it communicates the viewpoint of the settlers in the east. But it also takes into account the aching anxiety that the Catholic west felt for the fate of the Holy Land once the Islamic counter-attack began, very soon after the initial conquests. Since all the great crusades to the east after the First were attempts to stave off the successive waves in this counter-attack, the traditionalist approach bestows on the development of crusading a certain coherence and unity, albeit of a responsive character. It is hard to deny that the juridical location of crusading within the just war tradition hinged on the fact that crusading in the Holy Land had become largely a defensive war.[52] Generalism, by contrast, comes into its own when the age of the great *passagia* draws to a close and crusading undergoes a period of fragmentation.

In recent years various attempts have been made by historians, especially in the United Kingdom, to make intellectual sense of this protean quality in the subject they are studying. All have emphasized the importance of the period around 1200, and above all the reign of Pope Innocent III (1198–1216), in the overall changes that took place. Jonathan Riley-Smith has used the biological metaphor of birth, adolescence, maturity, old age and death. This springs from his conviction that crusading oc-

---

49 Riley-Smith, *The First Crusade*, pp. 91–119.
50 Cf. Flori, 'Pour une redéfinition', pp. 336, 341–9.
51 In defence of the pluralist position, it should be noted that all of the features that it regards as characterizing a crusade were present in the First Crusade.
52 F. H. Russell, *The Just War in the Middle Ages* (Cambridge: Cambridge University Press, 1975).

curred within a movement that was susceptible to control (including its hijacking) while also possessing, as it were, a life of its own.[53] For my part, an interest in the mechanics of crusading has led to a focus on the issue of organization. Like Riley-Smith, I have divided crusading into three phases, characterized overall by the gradual consolidation of methods of control. Thus I have viewed crusading in the twelfth century as a relatively inchoate practice of 'armed pilgrimage', the 1200s as a century when the individual and governmental aspects of crusading were held in approximate balance, and the later crusades (c. 1300 onwards) as dominated by states, successful principally when the major governments of the day took a large hand in the mobilization of the resources required.[54] Most radical has been the approach of Christopher Tyerman. For him, everything that took place before c. 1200 consisted of variations on existing penitential practice and military service; the changes that then occurred were so fundamental in character that they effectively created crusading. The title of Tyerman's audacious essay was 'Were there any crusades in the twelfth century?' and his answer was no.[55]

Contemporaries themselves were often unsure what to make of crusading. We have already seen that this led to the deployment of a strikingly diverse vocabulary. It also affected their views on the status of the crusader. Medieval commentators were keenly interested in categorizing social groups, believing that order and stability on earth reflected that in heaven and made it easier for the militant Church to achieve its goals. Gerhoh of Reichersberg, for example, commented that 'every order and every profession...has a rule suited to its quality, under which it can reach the crown [of heaven] by fighting legitimately.'[56] Ironically, the 'God-willed' crusaders cut clean across accepted models. A man or woman of any status could take the cross, provided they acted with the permission of superiors in the case of clerics and, until a controversial ruling by Pope Innocent III in 1201, spouses in that of married lay people.[57] Assumption of the cross gave access to a group that possessed its own obligations and privileges but had no clear alignment with any other set of people. James Brundage remarked that '[the canonists] never really came to grips in a systematic way with the

---

53   Riley-Smith, *The Crusades*.
54   N. Housley, *The Crusaders* (Stroud: Tempus, 2002), pp. 9–52; 'The thirteenth-century crusades in the Mediterranean', in D. Abulafia, ed., *NCMH, Volume 5 c. 1198–c. 1300* (Cambridge: Cambridge University Press, 1999), 569–89; *The Later Crusades*, pp. 421–56.
55   Tyerman, *The Invention*, pp. 8–29.
56   Quoted by G. Constable, 'The place of the crusader in medieval society', *Viator* 29 (1998), 377–403, at p. 384.
57   Brundage, *Medieval Canon Law and the Crusader*, p. 77.

problem of clarifying [the crusader's] role in medieval society. While canonists treated the problems of numerous other groups and institutions of their society specifically and coherently in special treatises and commentaries, no treatise *De crucesignatis* has yet been discovered throughout the vast literature of the medieval canon law.'[58] Crusaders were predominantly penitential pilgrims, but they were also expected to fight, unless gender, advanced age or ordained status brought them exemption. And the traditional view of monks as a *militia spiritualis* meant that there was always a powerful temptation to view *crucesignati* as 'temporary religious'. One could say that this uncertainty over status extended beyond the grave, to the extent that crusaders themselves regarded their dead comrades as martyrs, while the Church exercised much greater caution on the matter.[59]

The same uncertainty attached to the operation of crusaders as a collectivity. Predominantly they formed an army, but it was one of penitents. On the Second Crusade the host was described as 'the entire army that wishes to walk in the way of Christ'.[60] In July 1099 the army could walk unarmed and barefoot in penitential procession around the walls of Jerusalem.[61] So tempting was it to associate crusading with a religious vocation (especially if you were a monk) that early historians of the First Crusade came close to depicting it as 'a military monastery on the move'.[62] On that crusade above all, participants can be witnessed wrestling with the issue of identity. Bishop Adhémar of Le Puy even made an attempt at improvising a tripartite functionalism, keeping the clerics in order and instructing the knights to look after the *pauperes* in exchange for their prayers to God.[63]

It is hardly surprising to encounter confusion and creative thinking of this kind during the First Crusade. What is more striking is its persistence throughout the period when crusading was exerting its greatest appeal. The legal situation was typical. When a juridical view of crusading at length emerged, a century and a half after the capture of Jerusalem, it was, as Frederick Russell put it, 'a *sui generis* synthesis of the pilgrimage, the vow, the holy war and the just war that has continued to defy attempts at neat analysis'.[64] Nor did contemporaries find it easy to

---

58 Ibid, pp. 189–90.
59 Riley-Smith, *The First Crusade*, pp. 114–16.
60 Constable, 'The place', pp. 385–6.
61 Runciman, *A History*, 1: 284.
62 The formulation is Riley-Smith's, in *The First Crusade*, p. 2.
63 R. Hill, ed. and trans., *Gesta Francorum et aliorum Hierosolimitanorum* (repr. Oxford: Clarendon Press, 1972), p. 74.
64 Russell, *The Just War*, p. 294.

place past crusades. The history of medieval views of the crusading past has yet to be written, but it already seems clear that in addition to the problem of gaining access to accurate information, there were two major obstacles in the way of contemporaries achieving an objective perspective on past events. The first was general acceptance of the fact that Jerusalem's recapture in July 1099 was an event of profound eschatological significance, which confirmed the covenant between God and the New Israel.[65] This inevitably distorted all views of what had happened in 1095–9.[66] Not just the first but also all subsequent crusades had to be placed within a framework which historically extended back to the wars of the seventh-century Emperor Heraclius and in an eschatological sense also comprised the conflicts of the Old Testament. In the case of both success and failure, this militated against any informed analysis of events: victory was attributed to the crusaders acting as true warriors of God, defeat mainly to their wicked behaviour, which rendered them unworthy of God's support. In both cases it was chiefly biblical precedents that were pressed into service. Crusading was 'the Lord's war' (*bellum Domini*), a 'special case', set apart from the mainstream of political and military events.[67]

The other factor which stood in the way of contemporaries building up a historically accurate and nuanced picture of past crusading which might have clarified its overall nature was the ongoing struggle against a powerful Islam. Previous crusades, and above all the great success story of the First Crusade, were referred to primarily for purposes of exhortation and encouragement. This functioned as a brake on any acknowledgement that the practice of crusading had moved on. Already at the time of the Second Crusade a tension had come into being between an aspiration to continuity and the real world of change. Reverence for the First Crusade is apparent in the opening phrases of the bull *Quantum praedecessores*, in which the pope called on the French to copy the example of their ancestors, the first crusaders; and it is well established that this had disastrous consequences for the management of the French and German expeditions.[68] But this emphasis on imitation concealed substantial innovations, including the crystallization of crusader privileges and the

65   Riley-Smith, *The First Crusade*, pp. 139–43.

66   See J. M. Powell, 'Myth, legend, propaganda, history: the First Crusade, 1140–ca. 1300', in *APC*, 127–41.

67   For example, J. Gilchrist, 'The Lord's war as the proving ground of faith: Pope Innocent III and the propagation of violence (1198–1216)', in *CMTCS*, 65–83.

68   P. Rassow, 'Der Text der Kreuzzugsbulle Eugens III', *Neues Archiv* 45 (1924), 302–5, trans. L. and J. Riley-Smith in *The Crusades. Idea and Reality 1095–1274* (London: Edward Arnold, 1981), pp. 57–9, no. 5; V. G. Berry, 'The Second Crusade', in *HC* 1: 463–512.

extension of military activity to other fronts.[69] Thereafter the past was constantly pressed into the service of the present in the hope of inciting contemporaries to replicate the piety and enthusiasm that, allegedly, had brought victory in 1099. For Humbert of Romans in the 1260s and Fulk of Villaret in c. 1305, the First Crusade remained a source of inspiration and hope.[70] Even in the mid-fifteenth century, when attempts were made to revive the crusade as a means of holding back the Ottoman Turks, the First Crusade was held up as an inspiring example by Italian humanists like Benedetto Accolti and Pope Pius II, though they must have been aware that in all respects except that of a shared Christian faith, the world of Godfrey of Bouillon and Peter the Hermit was as remote from their own as that of Julius Caesar.[71]

It would be wrong to press this argument too far. The past could be learnt from and viewed objectively. Geoffrey of Villehardouin reported a debate between the leaders of the Fourth Crusade in which it became clear that they had a reasonably accurate knowledge of the political errors made in Palestine during the early years of settlement there and were anxious to avoid repeating them.[72] And in the mid-fourteenth century the Florentine Giovanni Villani was able to compare the relationship between Moorish Granada and Islamic North Africa with that between Catholic Europe and its co-religionists in the Holy Land. This presupposed a fair knowledge of thirteenth-century crusading as well as the ability to assume a reasonably dispassionate viewpoint.[73] But we need to remember that by Villani's time the principal institutions of crusading had been well established for a century, and the chronicler was unusually detached in his worldview. Earlier generations had lived in a world where periodic upsurges of devotion for crusading coexisted with considerable uncertainty about the nature of the exercise.

Towards a New Definition

In 1988 the pluralist approach towards studying the crusades appeared so dominant that Riley-Smith could assert, somewhat hubristically, that

---

69 G. Constable, 'The Second Crusade as seen by contemporaries', *Traditio* 9 (1953), 213–79.

70 J. Petit, 'Mémoire de Foulques de Villaret sur la croisade', *BEC* 60 (1899), 602–10, trans. N. Housley in *Documents on the Later Crusades, 1274–1580* (Basingstoke: Macmillan, 1996), pp. 40–6, no. 8; P. Cole, 'Humbert of Romans and the crusade', in *EC*, 157–74.

71 R. Black, *Benedetto Accolti and the Florentine Renaissance* (Cambridge: Cambridge University Press, 1985), pp. 224–85.

72 Powell, 'Myth', p. 134.

73 Housley, *The Avignon Papacy*, p. 1.

it had 'won the day'.[74] But we have seen that the traditionalist approach retains its defenders, and for a number of reasons it is quite possible that it will reassert itself as the dominant methodology. The first reason is that the association of crusading with the series of great *passagia* to the Holy Land has not been uprooted from the public perception of crusading. It is enshrined in our day-to-day use of the word crusade to denote a programme of radical action dissociated from self-interest and driven by strong convictions, especially religious beliefs. It is extraordinarily hard to bring about a transposition of the word as used in modern parlance to other crusading fronts. Secondly, the traditionalist view lends itself to a conveniently 'closed' narrative, beginning in 1095 and ending in 1291. In the right hands the narrative can be delivered with panache, and it harmonizes with the contemporary trend in historical writing to favour such a mode of explanation. Thirdly, and perhaps most importantly, it seems to address one of the most urgent political issues of the early twenty-first century, the relationship between 'the West' and Islam. Even though we shall see that historians of the First Crusade have agreed for some time that the crusade's roots lay not in the east but in the west, given the current international climate a view of crusading that associates it closely with hatred for Islam is bound to exert a powerful appeal. This is ironic given that some of the richest recent work on the medieval encounter between Christianity and other faiths has been written about Spain rather than about the Latin East.[75] But of course Islam has all but vanished from Spain, whereas the problems of the Middle East are a constant feature of news headlines around the world. Thus in the same way that contemporary events played their part in stimulating the creation of the pluralist agenda, they have assisted the revival of the traditionalist approach: a nice illustration of the fact that whether they realize it or not, historians are prisoners of the times in which they work.

Yet traditionalism is a very confused methodology, because its leading exponents in France and the United Kingdom hold diametrically opposed views on when crusading began. As we have seen, Flori sees the First Crusade as the crusade *par excellence*, the breakthrough from *guerre sainte* (or indeed *guerre saintissime*) to something that was new; it is the template against which all later expeditions have to be measured to decide whether we should regard them as crusades. Tyerman on the other hand has argued that crusading only came into being a full

---

74 Riley-Smith, 'History', p. 10.
75 Notably D. Nirenberg, *Communities of Violence. Persecution of Minorities in the Middle Ages* (Princeton, NJ: Princeton University Press, 1996).

century later.[76] Is there an alternative way forward that would appeal to those of us who find any version of the traditionalist approach unacceptable? I believe that it must consist of a rather more nuanced application of the pluralist methodology. In the first place, it continues to make good sense to start from the essential attribute of crusading, the assumption of the cross with the intention of engaging in penitential combat, in response to a cause that was defined as holy by the pope and preached by the Church. A traditionalist might object that too much emphasis is being placed on procedure as opposed to purpose, but this is to underestimate the rich cargo of meaning that was attached to the cross as the link between the helpless sinner and the suffering, redemptive Saviour. The medieval laity was sophisticated enough to gain access to this cargo without requiring it to be anchored in the geographical Jerusalem. Granted that the devotional resonances released by the city and the Holy Land were of unparalleled richness,[77] a spirituality centred on the cross was far from being wholly dependent on those resonances.

Pluralism has proved to be a fruitful, indeed a liberating methodology, but its focus on procedures and formulae, on liturgical and devotional patterns, and on legal definitions, can become a hindrance because of crusading's protean character. There were expeditions in which the terminology of crusade did not feature, either because it had not been fully formulated, for example in the decades immediately following the First Crusade, or because it was not considered appropriate, as in some fourteenth-century fighting against non-believers. In our interpretation of these and similar events we have to be sensitive to the reactions of contemporaries, allowing our modes of description and analysis to flow from those reactions even at the cost of losing some precision. It is crucial not to become a prisoner of one's own methodology, and it seems perfectly reasonable to me to use phrases like 'crusading venture' or 'wars of a crusading type' provided that it is made clear what is meant by such terms, and that the sources are fully and professionally cited. In the case of the *Reisen*, for example, it is apparent that these were conflicts of a similar sort to those which at much the same time were being preached as crusades further south, against the Tatars and Lithuanians, and further north, against

---

76   See Flori's lengthy critique of Tyerman in 'De Clermont à Jérusalem. La première croisade dans l'historiographie récente (1995–1999)', *Le Moyen Age* 105 (1999), 439–55, at pp. 444–50.
77   See, for example, D. Bauer, K. Herbers and N. Jaspert, eds, *Jerusalem im Hoch- und Spätmittelalter. Konflikte und Konfliktbewältigung – Vorstellungen und Vergegenwärtigungen* (Frankfurt: Campus, 2001).

Novgorod.[78] Refusing to recognize the crusading character of the *Preussenreisen* on the grounds that, for what appear to be mainly organizational reasons, they were not preached as crusades, seems to be self-defeating. The historical pattern into which they fitted, the status and goals of the Teutonic Order, the language used to describe them, and the ways contemporaries treated them, point in a different direction.

This touch of generalism softens pluralism's edges, which seems essential to bring us as close as possible to how contemporaries seem to have made sense of their world. It brings context and perceptions more fully into the discussion alongside those areas that are pluralism's distinctive strengths: liturgy, canon law and papal policy. It should also clarify the relationship between crusading and the activities of the military orders. From a pluralist perspective *stricto sensu* the two ran on parallel but separate paths: the crusader and the professed member of a military order took vows and in practice they often fought side by side, but in other respects they were totally different. Yet this seems too surgical an approach. Giles Constable and James Brundage have recently addressed the status of the military orders and both have highlighted the degree of uncertainty which contemporaries experienced in categorizing them. Constable pointed out that for twelfth-century commentators the Templars in particular raised similar problems to crusaders in the way they seemed at different points to be warriors, monks and pilgrims.[79] Brundage described the struggles that academic canon lawyers experienced in finding a suitable legal pigeon-hole for members of the military orders. Eventually, Johannes Teutonicus declared in his *Glossa ordinaria* that they were 'ecclesiastical persons', neither monks nor laymen but akin to *conversi* in monasteries. 'Since they fitted into no existing category, the canonists' contribution was to create a new one for them.' Although something of a climb-down from the lyrical praise of earlier texts like St Bernard's 'De laude novae militiae', the adopted terminology proved acceptable because it enabled the orders' procurators and lawyers to defend their property and rights.[80]

This consolidation of the legal status of brethren in the military orders, which occurred at much the same time and for the same reasons as that of *crucesignati*, did not bring absolute clarity to the armies that fought in the east. Reading the sources for Louis IX's first crusade, above all Joinville's crowded and vivid pages, one receives the impression of a host which

---

78 Housley, *The Later Crusades*, pp. 322–50.
79 Constable, 'The place', pp. 395–8.
80 J. A. Brundage, 'Crusades, clerics and violence: reflections on a canonical theme', in *EC*, 147–56.

included crusaders, members of the military orders, pilgrims like the 453 persons who bought passage east on the *St Victor* and took its owners to court in Messina, servants and retainers, and professional fighters from the west or the Holy Land who enlisted for wages.[81] Possibly there were still some *milites ad terminum*, the term applied to knights in the twelfth century who went to the east to serve with the military orders for a specified period of time.[82] What was common to many of these people, though not necessarily all of them, was the hope of acquiring merit in God's sight by taking part in his war. A strictly pluralist view, which focused on the role of *crucesignati* and the professed members of the military orders, would not capture the full range of devotional timbre in this and similar expeditions.

When he preached what became the First Crusade in 1095, Urban II presented to Catholic society a form of holy war that for many reasons, both internal to that society and external to it, went on to enjoy an extraordinarily long life. It would be folly not to recognize a community of belief, purpose and identity linking those who responded to Urban II's appeal with, for example, the *crucesignati* recruited by Giovanni da Capistrano who relieved Belgrade three and a half centuries later.[83] This longevity of practice is not surprising given the deep-rooted propensity of Catholic Europe, in both the eleventh and the fifteenth centuries, to embrace the proposition that wars could be sanctified.[84] But so many changes took place in the practice of crusading that when we set out to interpret what contemporaries meant when they reflected on the experience, we have to use our empathy and intuition alongside our powers of analysis. In this respect William Hague's elephant analogy, with which this chapter opened, again becomes relevant. For we all know, a European super-state of the type feared by some Conservatives is nowhere near as easy to recognize as an elephant. It comes down to a reading of how powers such as legislation, taxation, the conduct of foreign policy and discretionary use of the veto are distributed. Experts in EU law will undoubtedly have a field day, just like their predecessors the canon

---

81 Housley, *The Crusaders*, pp. 95–137; B. Z. Kedar, 'The passenger list of a crusader ship, 1250: towards the history of the popular element on the Seventh Crusade', *Studi medievali*, 3rd ser. 13 (1972), 267–79.

82 Constable, 'The place', p. 402; G. Ligato, 'Fra Ordini Cavallereschi e crociata: "milites ad terminum" e "confraternitates" armate', in *'Militia Christi' e crociata nei secoli XI–XIII* (Milan: Vita e pensiero, 1992), 645–97.

83 N. Housley, 'Giovanni da Capistrano and the crusade of 1456', in *CFCMI*, 94–115, 215–24.

84 Flori, *La Guerre sainte*; N. Housley, *Religious Warfare in Europe, 1400–1536* (Oxford: Oxford University Press, 2002).

lawyers in the case of crusading and the military orders. Politicians have to cut through such complexities and interpret them in the way that suits them to an electorate that possesses neither the training nor the patience for in-depth analysis. Historians are in a much less difficult situation. We are not in a hurry. We can let the sources speak to us at length. On crusading, as we have seen, they do not speak with a single voice, but the more attentively and sensitively we listen to them, the more likely we are to get close to what crusading meant to its contemporaries.

2

The Origins and Character of the First Crusade

Origins

The ground-breaking nature of the First Crusade was arguably its most important feature and one of which contemporaries were deeply aware.[1] There was no precedent for these massive hosts of arms-bearing pilgrims taking the cross and making their way eastwards across hundreds of miles of unfamiliar terrain, much of it tenaciously defended by their Muslim enemies, to liberate the holiest of Christianity's many shrines. Monastic chroniclers, living out their lives under a regime that placed emphasis and value upon stability and tradition, reacted to such novelty by depicting the crusade as one of a handful of examples of divine intervention in the affairs of men.[2] Their stance was corroborated by the scarcely credible successes which the crusaders enjoyed, which in the eyes of the chroniclers proved divine initiation and support: Robert of Reims wrote that in these terms only the creation of the world and Christ's crucifixion could match the crusade.[3] It was natural to weave around this single, challenging idea an entire theology of crusading that depicted it above all as a new way to achieve salvation, in particular for society's arms-bearing elite.

---

1 For a recent bibliography of the First Crusade, concentrating on works published since 1945 but including some earlier publications, see A. V. Murray, comp., 'Bibliography of the First Crusade', in *FCJ*, 267–310.
2 Riley-Smith, *The First Crusade*, pp. 135–52.
3 Riley-Smith, *The First Crusade*, p. 140.

Guibert of Nogent, like Robert of Reims a member of the cluster of Benedictine chroniclers living in northern France who wrote up the First Crusade in the early twelfth century, wrote rhapsodically that 'God has instituted in our time holy wars, so that the order of knights and the crowd running in their wake, who, following the example of the ancient pagans, have been engaged in slaughtering one another, might find a new way of gaining salvation'.[4]

It is just possible that men like Guibert and Robert were correct, and that Pope Urban II experienced a revelation (divine or otherwise) that caused him to preach a wholly new way of earning salvation through pious violence in Christ's name, which preachers communicated without major change to an audience that both understood it and acted upon it. But such a scenario is hardly likely, presupposing as it does a uniformity of comprehension between these individuals and groups about a message that was so new. It is more probable that there were some differences, even if marginal ones, between what Urban II preached, what was subsequently disseminated across western Europe in 1095–6, and what people who took the cross understood and wanted. And since there is no sign that Urban or his entourage were shocked or disappointed by events, there must also have existed a cluster of core values, hopes and goals that were common to all who shared in the experience of 1095–9. These in turn were expressed in ideas, language and images that derived from a shared heritage and vocabulary. Only in this way can the paradox of the First Crusade, novelty conjoined with popularity, be explained. Marcus Bull, for example, has written of the way a series of motifs occurring in miracle stories would have attuned audiences at First Crusade sermons to what they heard.[5] This was more or less what Edward Gibbon meant when he wrote that in his Clermont sermon Urban 'touched a nerve of exquisite feeling'. The Catholic west was 'ready' for the First Crusade. So Urban II's call to arms was greeted not with incomprehension or confusion but with enthusiasm, and armies assembled with a speed which, given the social structures of the time, was remarkable. Following this reading, the innovative nature of the First Crusade was perfectly compatible with the existence of origins. The problem indeed is the number and diversity of these origins, so that historians of the First Crusade have had to be unusually careful in distinguishing between context and causes.

4 Quoted in Riley-Smith, *The First Crusade*, p. 149.
5 M. Bull, 'Views of Muslims and of Jerusalem in miracle stories, c. 1000–c. 1200: Reflections on the study of first crusaders' motivations', in *EC*, 13–38.

Perhaps the most striking shift that has occurred over the past fifty years has been a slackening of interest in a whole range of socio-economic and military factors that were once considered important. Steven Runciman portrayed western Europe as economically backward, plagued by high levels of violent behaviour at the level of village and lordship, and above all overcrowded.[6] This now reads like a caricature of a region that was undergoing rapid if uneven growth in agrarian production and trade, though it is true that substantially the same picture is painted by Robert of Reims in his account of Urban II's Clermont sermon.[7] By the time Mayer wrote on the same subject twenty years after Runciman, he was able to draw on work by Duby and Herlihy that focused on the problems of the lesser nobility, and Mayer argued that the enthusiastic response achieved by Urban II's preaching among this group was rooted in perceptions that here lay the answer to what to do with their younger sons.[8] In pure cost-benefit terms, this does not stand up to close scrutiny. The numerous examples of land reclamation, new villages and piecemeal expansion that characterized the twelfth century show that the First Crusade would have been a bizarre means of catering for surplus mouths. And the heavy expenses that aristocratic families had to shoulder in sending their members on the First Crusade reveal that it was the opposite of an easy option for them.[9] Attentive study of these mechanisms of family response is a more telling riposte to the reductionist demographic position than pointing to the inability of the early settlers to secure help from the west, since the latter point is vulnerable to the answer that their co-religionists had become aware of the many dangers that accompanied settling in the east. In chapter 4 we shall see that material motivations to take the cross certainly need to be taken into account at an individual level; but it has become very hard to argue the case for demographic pressure as a general explanation for the First Crusade, which is presumably why nobody has attempted to do so for some time.

Volume 1 of the collaborative American *History of the Crusades* contained essays on the rise of the Normans and of Italian sea-power,[10] and in

---

6 Runciman, *A History*, 1: 114.
7 R. Fossier, 'The rural economy and demographic growth', in D. Luscombe and J. Riley-Smith, eds, *NCMH, IV, c.1024–c.1198, Part One* (Cambridge: Cambridge University Press, 2004), 11–46; D. Keene, 'Towns and the growth of trade', ibid., 47–85.
8 Mayer, *The Crusades*, pp. 22–5.
9 Riley-Smith, *The First Crusaders*, pp. 106–43, esp. pp. 134–5; 'Early crusaders to the east and the costs of crusading 1095–1130', in *CCCCP*, 237–57; 'The motives of the earliest crusaders and the settlement of Latin Palestine', *EHR* 98 (1983), 721–36. Though note the comments of Flori, *La Guerre sainte*, p. 323 and note 62, in relation to cost-benefit thinking.
10 H. C. Krueger, 'The Italian cities and the Arabs before 1095', *HC* 1: 40–53; R. S. Lopez, 'The Norman conquest of Sicily', ibid., 54–67.

older histories of Europe in the central Middle Ages the First Crusade tended to feature alongside feudalism, the military and social dominance of the knights (*milites*) and the rise to power of the reform papacy, as salient features of Europe in the eleventh century.[11] Probably only the last of these continues to loom large in research terms, and we shall see that even its star is setting as the capacity of the popes significantly to influence the thinking of the population at large is questioned. Between all the others and the crusade there is no necessary causal link. It is perfectly possible to envisage the crusade taking place without Norman expansion into southern Italy or the burgeoning naval might and commercial ambitions of the Italian communes. Without the activities of the Normans the job of the crusaders might well have been easier, since Norman encroachments on the Byzantine empire encouraged suspicions at Constantinople about what the real intentions of the crusaders were. Without the help of Italian sea-power the First Crusade would have faced much greater difficulties. But it did not depend on either for its success.[12]

When it comes to broader trends of economic and social change the picture is a little murkier. The timing of the First Crusade appears to fit Marc Bloch's famed interpretation of the arrival of a 'second feudal age' around 1100.[13] In Bloch's view this was characterized by settled feudal relations, above all among the aristocracy, and these were starting to find legal expression. We shall see that the hosts which made their way east were structured according to the dominant social ties of the period, lineage and dependency, rather than relying on what we might regard as proto-states, the kingdoms. This view that the preaching of the crusade occurred at the 'right time' in terms of how western European society (above all Frankish or French) was developing harmonized well with the perception which Georges Duby, and to some extent H. E. J. Cowdrey, offered of the crusade as effectively the third stage in the consolidation of the peace movement. This movement originated in the late tenth century as a clerical response to the alarming proliferation of armed conflict at the local level in many parts of France, caused by lords striving to establish military control over districts. The argument ran that the attempts made

---

11 For example, C. Brooke, *Europe in the Central Middle Ages, 962–1154* (2nd edn, London: Longman, 1987).

12 John France disagrees, arguing that sea-power might have made the difference between survival and disintegration during the siege of Antioch. J. France, *Victory in the East. A Military History of the First Crusade* (Cambridge: Cambridge University Press, 1996), pp. 209–20.

13 M. Bloch, *Feudal Society*, trans. L. A. Manyon (London: Routledge, 1961). For more recent views see D. Barthélemy, *L'Ordre seigneuriale XIe–XIIe siècle* (Paris: Seuil, 1990); M. Bull, ed., *France in the Central Middle Ages* (Oxford: Oxford University Press, 2002).

by churchmen first to limit civilian suffering from such outbreaks of violence, through the Peace of God, and subsequently to place time limits on them, through the Truce of God, attained their natural culmination in the direction of that violence outwards, against the unbelievers. Duby thus wrote: 'The Crusade unquestionably carried the demands of the peace of God to its ultimate goal ... The ideal of the *reformatio pacis* was ... realized by the journey to Jerusalem',[14] while Cowdrey argued more cautiously that '[Urban II's] Crusade was the complement of the Peace movement'.[15] Jean Richard even viewed the First Crusade as an attempt to bring to the east the Christian peace that the 'peace leagues' were trying to enforce in the west.[16]

But this argument that the commitment of the first crusaders to their undertaking was shaped by an ideology centred on peace is hard to square with their behaviour before, during or after the crusade. Their own need to take part in an armed pilgrimage derived from religious anxiety caused by behaviour which was roundly condemned by the Church. Close examination of the operation of the First Crusade reveals numerous examples of competition, land-grabbing and selfish behaviour on the part of the *milites*. Ultimately, it is true, they were kept in check by the *maiores*, the lords and the small group of territorial princes who made key decisions, though it was no easy task, and at times these men behaved just as badly as their subordinates. And there was plenty of petty warfare and brigandage when the crusaders returned home, some of it indeed caused by former crusaders. In general it is hard to dispute the argument that the First Crusade could not have happened without both the revival of economic life and the arrival of more settled social relations in the late eleventh century, though the obvious problem behind the concept that the crusade was preached at the 'right point' is that it can be neither proved nor disproved. And while the 'export of violence' theme certainly featured in the various reconstructions that were made of Urban II's Clermont preaching, it is impossible to gauge how prominent it actually was in the pope's thinking. There is a problem of chronological disjuncture between the great age of the peace and truce councils and Urban II's preaching at Clermont, and no

---

14   G. Duby, 'Laity and the peace of God', in *The Chivalrous Society*, trans. C. Postan (London: Edward Arnold, 1977), 123–33, at p. 132.
15   H. E. J. Cowdrey, 'The peace and truce of God in the eleventh century', *P&P* 46 (1970), 42–67 (repr. in *PMC*, study VII), at pp. 57–8. For a more recent statement of Cowdrey's views, see 'From the peace of God to the First Crusade', in *PCNAD*, 51–61.
16   J. Richard, *Histoire des croisades* (Paris: Fayard, 1996), pp. 32–3. For the most recent treatment of the question see J. Flori, 'De la paix de Dieu à la croisade? Un réexamen', *Crusades* 2 (2003), 1–23.

correlation between those areas where the councils had been most active and those where crusade recruitment was most successful.[17]

What this leaves us with is the pre-eminence of religious beliefs and values in explaining the First Crusade. Such a broad statement demands some qualification. It does not amount to a naive acceptance of stated motivations, or to an attempt to prise religious thinking free of its social setting, which was unusually complex. It means rather that most participants would not have committed themselves to the crusade without the impetus of a worldview that set a premium on their spiritual health and above all on their chances of salvation. Like all generalizations this one can be countered with exceptions. If their spiritual health came close to being an obsession for some crusaders, for others it was capable of being overruled by other, more mundane drives. The point is that for the majority of the participants it is undeniable that the crusade proved to be a profoundly (though not obsessively) religious experience, and that its origins must be sought in the sphere of belief. This conviction has characterized much of the scholarship of the past fifty years and explains why it has been so fruitful and dynamic.

One advantage of stressing the religious origins of the First Crusade is that it accords with the picture presented in the sources, so the historian is working with the grain of his evidence rather than against it. And a major reason for the efflorescence of recent scholarship is the volume and richness of these sources.[18] They are detailed and varied, and they originated in many of the regions where the crusade was preached, though their overall concentration in France is undeniable. We have four eyewitness accounts of the expedition, by Fulcher of Chartres, Raymond of Aguilers, Peter Tudebode and the anonymous author of the *Gesta Francorum*. The last of these has long been a favourite of historians, in the eyes of some unduly so.[19] There are a cluster of other accounts written shortly after the end of the crusade, including those already noted by Guibert of Nogent and Robert of Reims. Their value has proved harder to assess, the reputation of Albert of Aachen's very detailed history in particular being exceptionally volatile.[20] Remarkably for this period we possess about twenty letters written either by crusaders or by others while the expedition was in

---

17 M. Bull, *Knightly Piety and the Lay Response to the First Crusade. The Limousin and Gascony, c.970–c.1130* (Oxford: Oxford University Press, 1993), pp. 21–69.

18 S. Edgington, 'The First Crusade: reviewing the evidence', in *FCOI*, 55–77.

19 J. France, 'The use of the anonymous *Gesta Francorum* in the early twelfth-century sources for the First Crusade', in *FCJ*, 29–42.

20 S. Edgington, 'Albert of Aachen reappraised', in *FCJ*, 55–67. Edgington's new edition and translation of Albert of Aachen (Oxford Medieval Texts, forthcoming 2005) will be the most significant publication in terms of evidence for many years.

progress. There survive also four letters written by Urban II between his preaching of the Clermont sermon and the end of the crusade in the east.

Obviously, the volume and variety of this evidence has had a considerable impact on the reconstruction of the crusade itself, but even allowing for the inevitable problems of hindsight its value for untangling the origins of the expedition should not be underestimated. We possess six versions of the pope's sermon at Clermont, though none can be regarded as authoritative, and it is arguable that the recorded council canon, for all its annoying brevity, comes closer than any of these reconstructions to being the most accurate record.[21] The biggest advance over the past two decades has been the revelation of how much monastic charters, compiled chiefly in relation to raising funds for the First Crusade, can teach us about the response of the laity as well as the religious to the preaching of the crusade.[22] Putting together the evidence for what occurred at Clermont itself and the spread of the pope's message over the course of the following four years or so, we have an impressive range of material.

But of course no historian has tried to argue that the origins of the First Crusade can be found by starting in November 1095 at the council of Clermont. The question is how far back it is necessary to go, and this brings us to the towering figure of Carl Erdmann. His *Die Entstehung des Kreuzzugsgedankens* (1935) was the first scholarly study of the crusade as a system of ideas about the proper practice of religion. He took the ideology of the crusaders seriously, rather than dismissing it as camouflage for people who were really engaged in a search for land and booty. In the forty years that followed its publication Erdmann's study became widely recognized as a landmark contribution to its subject. The publication of an English translation in 1977 coincided with the beginning of a new wave of research into the origins of the crusade, and to a large extent this took the form of a dialogue with the interpretation that Erdmann had set out. Erdmann died while serving in the German army in 1945, aged only 47, so he was unable to witness the extraordinary impact that his study enjoyed.[23]

Erdmann viewed the First Crusade as first and foremost a form of holy war, addressed to Christian knights in terms of their vocation by a pope who was fully conscious of what it meant for his authority. It represented a highly significant *rapprochement* between a militarized aristocracy and a Church that since its foundation had displayed strong ethical leanings

---

21 R. Somerville, 'Clermont 1095: crusade and canons', in *PCNAD*, 63–77.
22 Bull, 'The diplomatic'; Constable, 'Medieval charters'.
23 J. Riley-Smith, 'Erdmann and the historiography of the crusades, 1935–1995', in *PCNAD*, 17–29.

towards pacifism. At the heart of Erdmann's enquiry lay the questions when and how this *rapprochement* occurred. His answer was nuanced but firm: the major shift took place in the second half of the eleventh century, under the 'reform' popes Leo IX, Alexander II and above all Gregory VII (1073–85). The reform that they pursued consisted of two main objectives: first, that the Church must be set free from any secular control or interference (*libertas ecclesiae*); and secondly, that this liberated Church had a duty to intervene vigorously in the affairs of the lay world to ensure justice.[24] In the course of achieving both goals they embraced and broadcast the belief that armed service in the Church's cause could be spiritually meritorious for those who fought. In three chapters Erdmann examined in turn Gregory VII's radically bellicose ideas and policies, their expression in the bestowal of banners (*vexilla S. Petri*), and the pope's attempt to create a dedicated knighthood of St Peter (*militia S. Petri*). That Gregory's policies and instruments were contentious Erdmann recognized full well, and he followed these chapters on the pope with a review of the polemical literature that Gregory's actions generated. He then turned to Urban II, whom he characterized as the man who made Gregory's vision of the world practicable by couching it in terms of a goal that was universally acceptable, the healing of the breach that had opened up between Rome and Constantinople, and by tying the idea of a Christian knighthood (*militia Christi*) to the recovery of the holy places in Jerusalem.[25]

Erdmann thus linked the crystallization of the idea of crusade firmly to the radical views and aims of the Church reformers, but he accepted that while men like Gregory VII, Anselm of Lucca and Urban II either provided the intellectual concepts needed or reconciled them with traditional theology, the impact of their viewpoints on the laity could best be discerned in a group of conflicts (*précroisades*, as some French scholars have termed them) that appeared to anticipate or prefigure what took place in 1095–9. These included the wars that the Germans waged against the Slavs, the combats of the Normans in southern Italy and Sicily, the early campaigns in the Spanish *Reconquista*, and naval raids carried out by the Italian sea-powers. Among these there were a series of events that in different ways bore tantalizing similarities to the First Crusade. French knights who fought in Spain were thus granted by Pope Alexander II what looks very like an indulgence of their sins. In 1074 Gregory VII pursued a project that would have entailed his leading an army to the east to assist the

---

24   C. Morris, *The Papal Monarchy. The Western Church from 1050 to 1250* (Oxford: Oxford University Press, 1989), pp. 79–108.
25   Erdmann, *The Origin*. The foreword to the English translation reviews the reception of Erdmann's book up to 1977.

embattled Byzantines in the wake of their catastrophic defeat at Manzikert, and even going on to liberate Jerusalem. Pisans who took part in a raid on the North African port of Mahdia in 1087 were portrayed, in a poem written to celebrate their enterprise, in language which reads remarkably like that used for the First Crusade. In 1089 Urban II assured Catalans who wanted to journey to Jerusalem as pilgrims that they would receive the same indulgence if they helped instead to rebuild the city of Tarragona. In these and a number of other instances Erdmann portrayed a Catholic Church that appeared to be moving inexorably in the direction of the First Crusade. He depicted a steady accumulation of ideas, images and precedents that does not have the overall effect of extinguishing the radicalism of what Urban achieved in 1095, but does explain how the pope and his contemporaries could simultaneously understand a proposal that was new in so many respects.

One further aspect of Erdmann's study must be mentioned, which is his subordination of Jerusalem's role in Urban II's crusade plans. Erdmann was convinced that pilgrimage to Jerusalem, and the recovery of its shrines, played a merely instrumental part in the pope's thinking. It was an iconoclastic position to take up, but he was uncompromising. 'Jerusalem, to the pope, had been simply a recruiting device.'[26] And a little later: 'In sum, Urban II's idea of crusade did not arise from a concern for the Holy Sepulcher and pilgrimages. His original and primary basis was the idea of an ecclesiastical-knightly war upon heathens, and only in the course of bringing it about did he introduce pilgrimage as a subordinate theme. This conclusion is crucial to determining how to approach the origins of the idea of crusade – it has been central to the present book.'[27] The goal of the First Crusade, the pope's *Kriegsziel*, was the reunion of the estranged Churches. It was to be achieved through the military assistance that the crusaders brought to their fellow Christians in the east. Jerusalem and its shrines functioned only as their destination, or *Marschziel*.

Erdmann's views on Jerusalem were supported by Hans Eberhard Mayer.[28] Most other scholars, however, have parted company with him.[29] A major factor in bringing this about was the publication in

---

26 Erdmann, *The Origin*, p. 332.
27 Erdmann, *The Origin*, p. 333.
28 Mayer, *The Crusades*, pp. 9–40, 290–1 note 6. Mayer made little alteration to this in the 1988 edition of his book, apart from bringing the points made in note 6 into the main text on pp. 10–11.
29 On contemporary perceptions of Jerusalem see Bauer, Herbers and Jaspert, *Jerusalem*. A. H. Bredero, 'Jérusalem dans l'occident médiévale', in P. Gallais and Y.-J. Riou, eds, *Mélanges offerts à René Crozet* (2 vols, Poitiers: Société d'études médiévales, 1966), 1: 259–71, established the city's importance.

1970 of a seminal article by H. E. J. Cowdrey, in which he argued with great force that a man with Urban II's background could not have held such an attitude towards Jerusalem. As a former monk of Cluny, Urban shared its devotional world, in which Jerusalem had come to occupy a central place. Reconsidering the sources for the Clermont sermon, Cowdrey showed that the pope was in agreement with the crusaders, for whom Jerusalem was central from first to last in their view of their task.[30] Over the past thirty years or so Cowdrey has published a number of further essays that have amounted to a full-scale critique of Erdmann's analysis. They have dealt both with individual episodes such as Gregory VII's project of 1074, and the Mahdia *précroisade* of 1087, and more broadly with the way the Church reformers and the early canonists viewed warfare and the vocation of knighthood.[31] Cowdrey's life of Gregory VII, together with Alfons Becker's study of Urban II, have made it possible to assess the contributions of these two popes in unprecedented detail.[32] Few would dispute the importance of the two men, but in more general terms the change in Church thinking that Erdmann tried to chart is highly problematic. This is partly because key events like Alexander II's supposed indulgence for those who fought in Spain remain subject to debate,[33] and partly because the Church in this period was much less centralized than it later became. It is apparent that the early canon lawyers were far from united in their views about the legitimacy of violence,[34] and it has recently been suggested that even the thesis of the pre-reform Church being broadly opposed to war does not withstand close scrutiny.[35]

Most importantly, the entire debate about the *rapprochement* between the Church and the military aristocracy has recently proceeded in a fresh direction, with much more attention being paid to the relationship

---

30 H. E. J. Cowdrey, 'Pope Urban II's preaching of the First Crusade', *History* 55 (1970), 177–88, repr. in *PMC*, study XVI.

31 For example, H. E. J. Cowdrey, 'Pope Gregory VII's "crusading" plans of 1074', in *OSHCKJ*, 27–40, repr. in *PMC*, study X; 'The Mahdia campaign of 1087', *EHR* 92 (1977), 1–29, repr. in *PMC*, study XII; 'The genesis of the crusades: the springs of western ideas of the holy war', in T. P. Murphy, ed., *The Holy War* (Columbus: Ohio State University Press, 1976), 9–32, repr. in *PMC*, study XIII; 'Cluny and the First Crusade', *Revue Bénédictine* 83 (1973), 285–311, repr. in *PMC*, study XV; 'Christianity and the morality of warfare during the first century of crusading', in *EC*, 175–92.

32 H. E. J. Cowdrey, *Pope Gregory VII 1073–1085* (Oxford: Oxford University Press, 1998); A. Becker, *Papst Urban II* (2 vols, Stuttgart: A. Hiersemann, 1964–88).

33 For example, A. Ferreiro, 'The siege of Barbastro 1064–65: a reassessment', *JMH* 9 (1983), 129–44; J. Flori, 'Réforme, *reconquista*, croisade. L'idée de reconquête dans la correspondance pontificale d'Alexandre II à Urbain II', *CCM* 40 (1997), 317–35.

34 J. Gilchrist, 'The Erdmann thesis and the canon law, 1083–1141', in *CS*, 37–45.

35 Flori, *La Guerre sainte*; France, 'Holy war and holy men'.

between the religious houses and their lay donors in the period leading up to the crusade. This is a direct consequence of the realization of how much insight monastic charters have to give us. The charters are far from being unproblematic as evidence, but if treated with caution they do offer a window into the minds of eleventh-century aristocrats. The primary relationship that these men enjoyed with the Church was in most cases with the religious house or houses that they favoured with their patronage. Marcus Bull and Jonathan Riley-Smith have led the field in this area of research and it is a prominent feature of their arguments that they are supported by study of the sources for the expedition itself. The aristocracy that emerges from their work is riddled with tensions and contradictions: driven to pursuits they knew involved sin by their greed, ambition and honour, yet acutely aware of the spiritual dangers they incurred; respectful of their monastic *protégés*, but resentful of the costs which patronage entailed for family estates; attracted by the idea of abandoning the world for the cloister, but held back from doing so by responsibilities of lineage coupled with their own bellicosity, libidinous nature and energy. Spiritually anxious to an astonishing degree, restless and violent, it is obvious why such an aristocracy found the First Crusade an intensely appealing prospect. It is also apparent that Urban II, the son of a middle-ranking nobleman from Champagne, both understood and sympathized with the dilemma that they faced. Arguably his status as originator of the crusade is strengthened by this new approach, but with a concomitant shift from his role as the inheritor of Gregory VII's ideas, to his upbringing and earlier career as grand prior at Cluny, the French religious house *par excellence*.[36]

No monastic charters were written for the poor, so this revised view of the devotional origins of the First Crusade applies primarily to the nobles, the *milites* and their lords. This makes its emphasis on the spiritual anxiety of the participants, on the penitential drive behind the crusade and on its character as a pilgrimage, the more telling, in so far as these features applied *a fortiori* to the non-noble masses, who were not inclined by training, experience or social values to regard the expedition as a war.[37] The shift from Erdmann's position hardly needs emphasizing, and it has been accompanied in the case of Bull by a robust rejection of the importance of the *Reconquista* as a 'testing ground' for crusading ideas.[38] In Bull's opinion the emphasis should lie squarely on the penitential and

---

36 Bull, *Knightly Piety*; Riley-Smith, *The First Crusaders*.
37 For concise statements of Bull's approach see his 'The roots of lay enthusiasm for the First Crusade', *History* 78 (1993), 353–72; 'Origins', in *OIHC*, 13–33.
38 Bull, *Knightly Piety*, pp. 70–114.

the local: Urban's project of 1095 was 'an instinctive appeal to familiar religious values rooted for the most part in the localized experience of the dynast, lord and warrior shaping his piety through the intimate networks his family had forged with individual churches'. The First Crusade arose through 'a happy marriage' between Urban's hopes for the Church and 'the mundane preoccupations of thousands of discrete individuals'.[39]

It is not surprising that the contribution of French scholars to the study of a crusade which was proclaimed in France and achieved its most successful recruitment there has been distinctive.[40] Working at much the same time as Carl Erdmann, Étienne Delaruelle provided a study of the ideological origins of crusading.[41] As we saw in chapter 1, Paul Alphandéry emphasized the eschatological origins of the crusade, depicting it as an upsurge of collective religious excitement at what participants considered to be a unique moment in history.[42] Paul Rousset, in a study notable for its careful examination of the language used in the evidence, was perhaps the first scholar to approach the problem of origins through a close examination of the sources for the expedition; he provided a nuanced examination of the dual nature of the crusade as pilgrimage and holy war.[43] Most recently, Jean Flori has turned his attention to the First Crusade with a large number of publications. The most important to date is *La Guerre sainte. La formation de l'idée de croisade dans l'Occident chrétien*.[44] As its title suggests, this is Erdmann revisited, a bold attempt to reassert the origins of the First Crusade in the practice of holy war. But Flori provided two important variations on Erdmann's interpretation. First, as already noted, he denied that there was a major shift in the Church's thinking about violence in the mid-to-late eleventh century; on the contrary, the Church's readiness, at specific times, to sanctify combat can be traced back to the period preceding the advent of the reform papacy. And secondly, Flori argued that the factor that turned holy war into crusade was the special status of Jerusalem and its holy places. Far from playing

---

39 Bull, 'The roots', p. 372.
40 Cf. J. Flori, 'De Clermont à Jérusalem', reviewing publications in all languages, including those in French and Italian.
41 Delaruelle's 'Essai sur la formation de l'idée de croisade' failed to achieve the attention it merited because it was published in an obscure periodical, the *Bulletin de littérature ecclésiastique*, in six instalments between 1941 and 1954; by the time a more accessible edition of the text appeared in *L'Idée de croisade au moyen âge* (Turin, 1980), scholarship had largely moved on.
42 Alphandéry, *La Chrétienté*.
43 P. Rousset, *Les Origines et les caractères de la première croisade* (Neuchatel: La Baconnière, 1945).
44 *La Guerre sainte*. See its bibliography for Flori's many other publications.

down the role of Jerusalem, as Erdmann had done, Flori situated it at the centre of his interpretation; indeed, as we saw in the previous chapter, he focused his definition of crusade on the intention to recover or defend the city and its shrines.

Flori's account of the origins of the First Crusade is the longest to appear since Erdmann's. It is a remarkable development that after a period in which study of the devotional and above all the penitential origins of crusading have enjoyed prominence, a sustained attempt should now be made to swing the pendulum back towards holy war. The disagreements between Flori and Riley-Smith, who has played the leading role in the analysis of devotional origins, are countless. Of course, substantial changes have taken place in our view of eleventh-century French society since Erdmann wrote, in particular a thoroughgoing revision of how what used to be called 'feudal society' came into being and of the changes that occurred around 1000.[45] Even so, it is hard at times not to experience a sense of *déja vu* as Flori's book makes its stately progress through a series of episodes and key texts which, in the 70 years since Erdmann first set them out, have become all-too familiar. The law of diminishing returns has surely set in with this debate. Historians of the First Crusade appear to have got lost in an interpretative maze arising from the fact that while all agree on the two-fold nature of the expedition as both a pilgrimage and a holy war, they cannot agree which aspect was dominant. Why should one have been so? It is hard to see any resolution of the current impasse until a radically different methodology is adopted.

If there is one thing on which students of the crusade's origins are agreed, it is that events east of the Adriatic played at best the role of catalyst in producing the call to arms and the response that it achieved. The origins of the First Crusade lay in developments that took place within Catholic Christendom, and this explains the astonishment shown by the Greeks when the crusading armies first arrived, as well as the inability of the Byzantine court to grasp the character of crusading before the Fourth Crusade.[46] Moreover, the broad outlines of what occurred in the Middle East, from the arrival of the Seljuq Turks and their confrontations with the Fatimid regime of Egypt, through to the military disaster suffered by the Byzantine Greeks at Manzikert in 1071 and the resulting appeal by the Emperor Alexius I Comnenus to the pope, have not been subject

---

45   See the numerous works of D. Barthélemy, for example *L'An mil et la paix de Dieu: la France chrétienne et féodale, 980–1060* (Paris: Fayard, 1999).

46   J. Harris, *Byzantium and the Crusades* (London: Hambledon, 2003); R.-J. Lilie, *Byzanz und die Kreuzzüge* (Stuttgart: Kohlhammer, 2004).

to revisions anything like those that we have just examined.[47] While the casualties suffered by the Byzantines at Manzikert have been scaled down, the battle has not been reassessed as drastically as, for example, the battle of Myriokephalon in 1176; and Alexius I's despatch of envoys to the west in 1095 continues to be seen as part of a broader rescue package pursued by one of Byzantium's more capable rulers.[48] The harassment of western pilgrims by the Seljuq Turks was viewed in the older historiography as the trigger for Urban II's preaching, and it is true that it plays a large role in some of the attempts that were made to reconstruct his Clermont sermon. But the validity of this interpretation was successfully challenged some fifty years ago, and the sufferings endured by western pilgrims during the Seljuq conquests are now seen as a temporary phenomenon; it was soon replaced by a return to the order that had prevailed, with brief exceptions, throughout the period when the Fatimids had controlled the shrines.[49] What made the Seljuq occupation of Palestine and Syria intolerable to western sensibilities was not the radical change in the character of the Muslim power involved (it was, for example, Sunni rather than Shi'a), but a new sense of spiritual ownership of the Holy Land's shrines. This was expressed in a powerful rhetoric of pollution and the need for ritual cleansing that is conspicuous in the sources for the First Crusade and indeed for all subsequent crusading to the Holy Land. It was accompanied and bolstered by a belief in a demonic and dehumanized Islamic identity that shaped perceptions and conduct towards the Muslims, both soldiers and civilians, during the course of the expedition.[50]

Developments in the east did less to create the First Crusade than used to be thought, but there can be no doubt that events in the Islamic world on the eve of Clermont were crucially important in enabling the expedition to succeed, even if this was not appreciated in the west at the time. It has long been realized that the religious division and territorial rivalries between the Fatimids of Egypt and the Seljuqs, together with the location of the centre of Seljuq power in Iran, far to the east of Palestine and Syria, made a powerful contribution to the crusade's success. But Michael Brett and Carole Hillenbrand have recently emphasized the coincidence that

---

47 M. Angold, 'The Byzantine empire, 1025–1118', in Luscombe and Riley-Smith, *NCMH*, IV, *c.1024–c.1198, Part Two*, 217–53; M. Brett, "Abbasids, Fatimids and Seljuqs', ibid., 675–720.

48 J.-C. Cheynet, 'Mantzikert. Un désastre militaire?' *Byzantion* 50 (1980), 410–38; Angold, 'The Byzantine empire', pp. 238–9; M. Angold, 'The road to 1204: the Byzantine background to the Fourth Crusade', *JMH* 25 (1999), 257–78.

49 C. Cahen, 'An introduction to the First Crusade', *P&P* 6 (1954), 6–29.

50 P. Cole, "'O God, the heathen have come into your inheritance" (Ps. 78.1). The theme of religious pollution in crusade documents, 1095–1188', in *CMTCS*, 84–111.

death carried away virtually the entire upper echelon of the region's Islamic authorities in 1092–4. The Seljuq vizier Nizam al-Mulk and the sultan Malikshah both died in 1092, the Fatimid caliph of Egypt al-Mustansir, his vizier Badr al-Jamali and the Abbasid Sunni caliph, al-Muqtadi, in 1094.[51] Never again in crusading history would circumstances be so propitious for an invasion. Had they known, westerners would undoubtedly have seen this as yet another example of God's support for their task.

Character

As noted above, the First Crusade is one of the best-documented episodes of the central Middle Ages.[52] The main Latin narrative accounts take up an entire volume in the monumental *Recueil des historiens des Croisades*. It proved possible for the crusade's first serious historian, Heinrich Hagenmeyer, to produce a diary in which he set out the events of the crusade on a week-by-week and at times day-by-day basis,[53] and Sir Steven Runciman devoted an entire volume in his *History of the Crusades* to this single expedition (including, it should be added, its origins). Given the importance of the First Crusade it is not surprising that this large tranche of sources has proved attractive to historians, or that the events, personalities and character of the crusade have all generated debate and controversy.

Disagreement starts with the issue of how many took part in the crusade. Later crusades that went east by sea become susceptible to reasonably precise estimates, but the numbers in the armies that proceeded overland are inherently harder to assess. Can we trust the invariably substantial but very different figures that were provided by eyewitness chroniclers for those occasions when the various contingents gathered to form a single host? Since the writings of the German military historian Hans Delbrück, medieval historians have tended to discount large estimates on the grounds that they would have posed insuperable problems of command and supply, but in recent years this sceptical approach has been challenged. Some historians have suggested that

---

51   M. Brett, 'The Near East on the eve of the crusades', in *PCNAD*, 119–36; C. Hillenbrand, 'The First Crusade: the Muslim perspective', in *FCOI*, 130–41.

52   France, *Victory in the East*, pp. 374–82, surveys the sources from the point of view of the crusade's military history.

53   H. Hagenmeyer, *Chronologie de la première croisade (1094–1100)* (Paris: Ernest Leroux, 1902).

large (especially round) figures cannot simply be ignored in the case of the First Crusade. Jean Flori has argued that while we may decide not to accept some of the figures given by the chroniclers and letter writers, we should neither discount them as fantasy nor search for an allegorical or symbolic significance.[54] Bernard Bachrach went further and claimed that the figure of 100,000 effectives given for the start of the siege of Antioch, in October 1097, was not incompatible with the crusaders' logistical capabilities.[55] Others have pitched their estimates lower. At the end of a thorough analysis of the question John France concluded that the army probably numbered between 50,000 and 60,000 people when it assembled at the siege of Nicaea in May 1097.[56] Since some 20,000 had already perished on the Peasants' or People's Crusade, the total that set out may have reached 80,000. Jonathan Riley-Smith has suggested a total of 43,000 at Nicaea and 15,000 when the army arrived at Jerusalem.[57]

Much attention has been paid to the way the armies were organized. In this field the most significant recent work has been that of Jonathan Riley-Smith. In his *The First Crusaders 1095–1131* Riley-Smith combined a thorough reading of all the sources for the crusade, with the creation of a relational database comprising all the crusaders whom he managed to identify. As a result, Riley-Smith succeeded in recreating both the experiences and the relationships of the crusaders to a degree exceeding anything that had previously been possible. Analysing the preparations that crusaders made, Riley-Smith described the creation of an *ad hoc* infrastructure based on the appeal by crusaders to all the support mechanisms that existed, notably their ties of lordship and dependency, their lineages, and the backing of the religious communities with which they were affiliated. It was natural for all but the last of these to carry over into the crusade, so that individuals in the field who faced crises, whether they related to health, finance, mounts, food supplies or combat, relied on their friends, neighbours, kinsmen or lords.[58] In the case of one of the armies, that led by Godfrey of Bouillon, it has proved possible to recreate in considerable details its internal constitution and structure.[59] Over and above these

---

54   J. Flori, 'Un problème de méthodologie: la valeur des nombres chez les chroniqueurs du moyen âge. À propos des effectifs de la première croisade', *Le Moyen Age* 99 (1993), 399–422.
55   B. Bachrach, 'The siege of Antioch: a study in military demography', *War in History* 6 (1999), 127–46.
56   France, *Victory in the East*, pp. 122–42.
57   Riley-Smith, *The First Crusade*, p. 63. Riley-Smith has recently revisited the issue of casualty rates among arms-bearers: 'Casualties and the number of knights on the First Crusade', *Crusades* 1 (2002), 13–28.
58   Riley-Smith, *The First Crusaders*, pp. 81–143, and see also *The First Crusade*, pp. 58–90.
59   A. V. Murray, 'The army of Godfrey of Bouillon, 1096–1099: structure and dynamics of a contingent on the First Crusade', *RBPH* 70 (1992), 301–29.

individual ties of patronage, which John France has termed *mouvances*,[60] there were broader networks of authority and support: regional solidarity, focused on the persons and households of princes if these were present, the Church, and at times the lieutenants or agents of the Byzantine emperor. Because of the way crusader–Byzantine relations deteriorated over the course of the expedition, the role played by the latter is not easy to detect in the sources.[61]

The idea that crusaders responded to God's call to arms without either preparation or thought for those they left behind, based on the Gospel summons (Matthew 4:18–22; 8:19–22), has thus to a large extent been superseded by one of forethought and planning. This of course applied mainly to crusaders who had resources that they could mobilize, and property that needed safeguarding. About the poor (*pauperes*) we know much less, but one radical feature of Riley-Smith's overall reassessment is his argument that even the armies of the 'first wave', the People's or Peasants' Crusade of 1096, were not simple rabbles. Though most of their members had neither the time nor the resources to plan their crusading, these armies did contain knights as well as a number of middle-ranking leaders. They were less well-prepared than the armies that followed them, but the mistakes that they made, and their destruction at an early stage by the Turks in Anatolia, cannot be ascribed to their being totally disorganized.[62]

Building on the work of previous scholars like Rousset, Riley-Smith has also written extensively on the devotional lives of the first crusaders. He has pointed out that the group of Benedictine chroniclers who produced their polished accounts of the First Crusade some years after it concluded were not content to place the expedition within a theological framework which they considered appropriate; they also bestowed on the crusaders over-sophisticated views of what they were doing, and religious lives that verged on the ascetic. In sexual terms the latter was certainly a misinterpretation.[63] It is undeniable that the crusaders confronted exceptional dangers and sufferings, including famine, defeat, desertions and much squabbling among their leaders. They responded, unsurprisingly, by falling back on religious devices with which they felt comfortable, such as intercession, visions, and a range of penitential practices including fasting, prayers and processions; they also despatched westwards a stream of

---

60   J. France, 'Patronage and the appeal of the First Crusade', in *FCOI*, 5–20, at pp. 7–8.
61   J. France, 'The departure of Tatikios from the army of the First Crusade', *BIHR* 44 (1971), 131–47.
62   Riley-Smith, *The First Crusade*, pp. 51–7.
63   J. Brundage, 'Prostitution, miscegenation and sexual purity in the First Crusade', in *CS*, 57–65.

letters in which they beseeched their kinsmen and neighbours to support them with their prayers.[64] The crusaders placed unusual emphasis on relics, which was to be expected given that they garnered so many as they made their way southwards through Syria and Palestine. Among these the discovery of the holy lance in the cathedral of Antioch was of special significance because of the political role that it came to play, and the lance has long been a favourite topic for historians.[65] These expressions of lay piety were largely traditional.[66] But at the same time a new form of piety shaped by the crusading experience began to take shape. It was exceptionally volatile, oscillating between exultation and despair as the military situation changed. And after the capture of Jerusalem it became triumphalist in the extreme.

Although there is a general consensus on these points, the crusaders' views on martyrdom have been disputed. Martyrs were men and women who died witnessing their faith, so there was a natural tendency to depict those who died in a holy war as martyrs. Jean Flori has argued that this occurred in the case of the First Crusade, and constituted strong proof that both the Church and participants regarded the war as holy.[67] H. E. J. Cowdrey was not convinced,[68] and Jonathan Riley-Smith has noted that while references to the dead as martyrs certainly occur in the sources, there is silence on the matter in charters drawn up by their relatives and heirs.[69] Nor did the cult of any crusading martyr develop in the west. The resolution to this debate may lie less in any residual doubts on the Church's part about sanctifying violence than in a certain fluidity in the definition of martyrdom. When crusaders were described as martyrs the word was perhaps being used in a celebratory rather than a technical sense. It was a way of emphasizing the full measure of their personal sacrifice, and hence confirming the remission of their sins and their entry into paradise, rather than making a formal claim that these individuals should henceforth enjoy the status of martyr.

Part of the problem surrounding crusading martyrdom was that many crusaders died in combat, and it was impossible to know what their

---

64   Riley-Smith, *The First Crusade*, pp. 91–119, 135–52.
65   C. Morris, 'Policy and visions: the case of the holy lance at Antioch', in *WGMA*, 33–45; W. Giese, 'Die "lancea Domini" von Antiochia (1098/99)', in W. Setz, ed., *Fälschungen im Mittelalter. Internationaler Kongress der Monumenta Germaniae Historica 16.–19. September 1986* (6 vols, Hannover: Hahn, 1988–90), 5: 485–504.
66   B. McGinn, 'Iter sancti sepulchri. The piety of the first crusaders', in B. K. Lackner and K.R. Philip, eds, *Essays in Medieval Civilisation* (Austin: University of Texas Press, 1978), 33–72.
67   Most recently Flori, *La Guerre sainte*, pp. 334–43.
68   H. E. J. Cowdrey, 'Martyrdom and the First Crusade', in *CS*, 46–56.
69   Riley-Smith, *The First Crusaders*, pp. 72–4.

spiritual frame of mind was at the point of death. This is a useful reminder of the crusade's nature as a full-scale war. The particular difficulties posed by waging war in unfamiliar surroundings, in an intractable climate, and against a new form of enemy, have attracted many military historians to the First Crusade. The first to apply rigorous techniques to the subject was R. C. Smail, whose *Crusading Warfare* of 1956 has become a classic text.[70] Smail paid close attention to the various pitched battles of the First Crusade and he demonstrated the ingenuity with which the crusaders adapted their tactical methods to counter the fluid and demoralizing combat techniques used by the Turks, above all their adroit horseback archery. In his *Victory in the East* (1994) John France examined every aspect of the crusade as a war, combining a painstaking analysis of all the sources with close topographical study of each location where major combat occurred. France did not neglect the key role played by religious conviction in winning victory, as well as breaking the impasse that detained the crusaders at Antioch and came close to wrecking the whole enterprise. He agreed with Smail that the ability of the crusaders to learn and improvise was also crucial. To these factors he added others, some of which had been neglected: Byzantine assistance, Islamic divisions, the role of sea-power, and the exertion of sound leadership when it mattered most.[71] In the case of the 'follow-up crusade' of 1101, which some historians have interpreted as the last wave in the First Crusade, the absence of this last factor, linked to a well-managed response on the part of the Anatolian Turks, brought about the early destruction of the armies.[72]

France emphasized the importance of Byzantine advice and support, and this hinged on the establishment of a framework for co-operation when the crusade's leaders passed through Constantinople and its environs in the winter of 1096–7. Determined to secure the best terms that he could for his empire, Alexius Comnenus exerted considerable pressure on the crusaders through his control over their food supplies. Through patience, and at the cost of some good will, he managed to put in place juridical ties with all of the leaders, and due to their importance as well as disagreements between the sources, the nature of these ties has caused much debate. There is a

---

70 R. C. Smail, *Crusading Warfare (1097–1193)* (Cambridge: Cambridge University Press, 1956).

71 France, *Victory in the East*. See also his *Western Warfare in the Age of the Crusades, 1000–1300* (London: UCL Press, 1999).

72 This expedition has still received remarkably little attention, probably because its sources are not strong. See J. L. Cate, 'The crusade of 1101', in *HC* 1: 343–67; Riley-Smith, *The First Crusade*, pp. 120–34; A. Mulinder, 'Albert of Aachen and the crusade of 1101', in *FCJ*, 69–77.

general consensus that they were modelled on the feudal bonds that were most familiar to the crusaders, and which Alexius was happy to make use of. But this does not mean that his understanding of those bonds was identical to that of the crusaders. In addition, the weighting between the swearing of fealty and the performance of homage (which implied submission) was less than clear, as was the exact extent of the commitments that the emperor and the crusading leaders entered into. Byzantines and Franks could work together, but when acrimony arose the agreements that had been reached provided plenty of fuel for mutual charges of betrayal.[73]

Most of those who entered into these ties with Alexius went on to play especially prominent parts in the First Crusade, and their lives have attracted attention. Studies have been written about most of the main commanders, though they have varied in quality. Godfrey of Bouillon has aroused interest partly due to his later reputation as the leader of the crusade and partly because of the enduring puzzle of how he managed 'to come from behind' and grab the prize of being elected as first ruler of Jerusalem in 1099.[74] Raymond count of Toulouse remains an enigmatic figure, not least because of the difficulties attached to the eyewitness account written by his chaplain, Raymond of Aguilers.[75] Adhémar, bishop of Puy and legate for Urban II, was clearly a significant player up to his death in 1098, but it is hard to be sure how much of his authority derived from his legatine powers as opposed to his episcopal rank, his military following and his own abilities.[76] Bohemund of Taranto divides opinion sharply. For some, the most acute analysis of his agenda for the crusade is that of the Byzantine princess Anna Comnena, who considered Bohemund to be the arch-schemer and manipulator.[77] Other commentators

73 France, *Victory in the East*, pp. 110–21; W. M. Daly, 'Christian fraternity, the crusades and the security of Constantinople', *Medieval Studies* 22 (1960), 43–91; J. H. and L. L. Hill, 'The convention of Alexius Comnenus and Raymond of St Gilles', *AHR* 58 (1953), 322–7; J. Pryor, 'The oaths of the leaders of the First Crusade to Emperor Alexius I Comnenus', *Parergon. Bulletin of the Australian and New Zealand Association for Medieval and Renaissance Studies* ns 2 (1984), 111–41.
74 P. Aubé, *Godefroy de Bouillon* (Paris: Fayard, 1985); G. Waeger, *Gottfried von Bouillon in der Historiographie* (Zurich: Fretz und Wasmuth, 1969). Contention has arisen about what Godfrey was elected to: J. Riley-Smith, 'The title of Godfrey of Bouillon', *BIHR* 52 (1979), 83–6; J. France, 'The election and title of Godfrey de Bouillon', *Canadian Journal of History* 18 (1983), 321–9; A. V. Murray, 'The title of Godfrey of Bouillon as ruler of Jerusalem', *Collegium Medievale: Interdisciplinary Journal of Medieval Research* 3 (1990), 163–78.
75 J. H. and L. L. Hill, *Raymond IV, Count of Toulouse* (Syracuse, NY: Syracuse University Press, 1962).
76 J. Brundage, 'Adhemar of Puy: the bishop and his critics', *Speculum* 34 (1959), 201–12.
77 J. France, 'Anna Comnena, the Alexiad and the First Crusade', *Reading Medieval Studies* 10 (1984), 20–38; R.-J. Lilie, 'Der erster Kreuzzug in der Darstellung Anna Komnenes', in *Varia II: Beiträge von A. Berger et al.* (Bonn: R. Habelt, 1987), 49–148.

are much less willing to condemn Bohemund, accepting that his seizure of Antioch was self-interested but arguing that it possessed a strategic logic as well. What is widely accepted is that his brilliance as a field commander may well have saved the crusade.[78]

By far the most volatile reputation has been that of none of the *maiores* but of a mere hermit, Peter of Amiens. Some near-contemporary sources gave Peter the credit for initiating the First Crusade and this was enshrined in the work of the twelfth-century historian William of Tyre. In this respect Peter's reputation survived until his role was questioned by Hagenmeyer in the late nineteenth century on the basis of a critical examination of the full range of evidence.[79] It is not in dispute that Peter was a highly successful preacher of the crusade and that he led one of the contingents that met with annihilation in Anatolia in October 1096. Thereafter, as E. O. Blake and C. Morris put it, 'he appears in the chronicles in a variety of capacities: as a runaway, and an ambassador to the Moslems, as an adviser, as an associate with the popular element among the crusaders, and finally as a guide to the sacred sites at Jerusalem.'[80] They suggested that the sources referring to Peter's role in initiating the crusade constituted too strong a group to be easily set aside.[81] More recently, Jean Flori has made an ambitious and far-reaching attempt to reconstruct Peter's reputation; he has come close to reinstating him to the historical significance from which Hagenmeyer deposed him, as a co-promoter of the crusade alongside Urban II.[82] Riley-Smith has accepted that 'Peter must have been preaching some kind of religious expedition to Jerusalem before the council of Clermont', though he places this in the context of the 'waves of rumour' that anticipated the papal pronouncement.[83] It is safe to say that this debate will not be resolved quickly,[84] partly because Peter's most ardent near-contemporary supporter is the chronicler Albert of Aachen, the value of whose work is

---

78   R. B. Yewdale, *Bohemond I, Prince of Antioch* (Princeton, NJ: n.p., 1924). A new and comprehensive study of Bohemund's life would be welcome. For his military role on the crusade see France, *Victory in the East*, esp. p. 369.

79   H. Hagenmeyer, *Peter der Eremite: ein kritischer Beitrag zur Geschichte des ersten Kreuz-zuges* (Leipzig: Harrassowitz, 1879).

80   E. O. Blake and C. Morris, 'A hermit goes to war: Peter and the origins of the First Crusade', *SCH* 22 (1985), 79–107, at p. 79.

81   Blake and Morris, 'A hermit', esp. pp. 96–7. See also M. D. Coupe, 'Peter the Hermit – a reassessment', *Nottingham Medieval Studies* 31 (1987), 37–45.

82   J. Flori, *Pierre l'Ermite et la première croisade* (Paris: Fayard, 1999).

83   Riley-Smith, *The First Crusaders*, pp. 55–6.

84   The most recent contribution is J. Rubinstein, 'How, or how much, to reevaluate Peter the Hermit', in *MC*, 53–69.

unsettled; once Albert's reputation becomes stable so too may our evaluation of Peter's role and importance.

Going to the opposite extreme, we encounter the mass of pilgrims who remain nameless throughout the crusade yet who, at one crucial point in January 1099, exerted on their leaders the pressure that was required to initiate the final march on Jerusalem.[85] To some extent Riley-Smith's clarification of the crusade's infrastructure throws light even on these participants, who must have enjoyed some initial system of support and presumably lost it during the expedition as a result of death or desertion. We do have occasional glimpses of the leaders trying to make provision for the *pauperes*, including at one point the setting up of a treasury supervised by Peter the Hermit.[86] More intriguing are descriptions of some of them, the enigmatic *Tafurs*, electing their own leaders and even choosing a king. In the circumstances of famine that afflicted the crusade during its long central phase at Antioch some of the poor resorted to digging up and cannibalizing the Turkish dead, but the suggestion that this had a ritualistic as well as a nutritive motive has not been generally accepted. In any case, recently the *Tafurs* have been marginalized as a group on the crusade.[87]

This naturally brings us to the question of the crusaders' relations with other faiths. We shall consider this issue more fully in chapter 7, but two episodes located within the First Crusade are better handled here. These are the pogroms in the Rhineland in 1096 and the massacre in Jerusalem in 1099. Both are subject to complex problems arising from the nature of the evidence.[88] In the case of the pogroms, the historicity of the detailed accounts found in twelfth-century Hebrew sources has been challenged, particularly the striking assertion that in the face of unprecedented catastrophe Jewish women assumed the leadership of their communities. This

---

85 J. France, 'The crisis of the First Crusade: from the defeat of Kerbogah to the departure from Arqa', *Byzantion* 40 (1970), 276–308.

86 W. Porges, 'The clergy, the poor and the non-combatants on the First Crusade', *Speculum* 21 (1946), 1–23; C. Auffarth, '"Ritter" und "Arme" auf dem Ersten Kreuzzug. Zum Problem Herrschaft und Religion, ausgehend von Raymond von Aguilers', *Saeculum* 40 (1989), 39–55; R. Rogers, 'Peter Bartholomew and the role of "the poor" in the First Crusade', in T. Reuter, ed., *Warriors and Churchmen in the High Middle Ages. Essays presented to Karl Leyser* (London: Hambledon, 1992), 109–22.

87 L. A. M. Sumberg, 'The "Tafurs" and the First Crusade', *Mediaeval Studies* 21 (1959), 224–46; M. Rouche, 'Cannibalisme sacré chez les croisés populaires', in Y.-M. Hilaire, ed., *La Religion populaire. Aspects du Christianisme populaire à travers l'histoire* (Lille: Centre interdisciplinaire d'études des religions de l'Université de Lille III, 1981), 29–41; France, *Victory in the East*, pp. 286–7.

88 B. Z. Kedar, 'Crusade historians and the massacres of 1096', *Jewish History* 12 (1998), 11–31.

revisionism might necessitate some scaling-down of the loss of life that occurred.[89] As for the crusaders, Riley-Smith's new interpretation of the first wave that perpetrated these attacks on the Jews has removed their identification with uncontrollable *pauperes*, and bolstered the view that anti-Jewish beliefs and behaviour were, from the start of the crusades, deeply embedded within crusading ideas irrespective of social class.[90] Jean Flori has argued for the more traditional view that the pogroms resulted from the distinctive preaching of Peter the Hermit and his followers, who may have incorporated themes that were more overtly or implicitly anti-Jewish than the preaching that was conducted or organized by the pope.[91]

If anything, the massacre at Jerusalem is even more subject to debate. There is discussion about whether the crusaders were driven solely by some mixture of fury at the defenders' resistance and exultation at their achievement of final victory, or whether the killings also constituted an ideological act, a sacred purging of the holy city from the defilement caused by the Muslims, one that necessitated the shedding of their blood.[92] More recently, a debate has begun over the extent of the massacre, with the discovery since the Second World War of new sources that seem to contradict some of the excited claims of the Latin chroniclers and letter writers, and to demand a lowering of the high figures offered by later Muslim writers.[93] If the lower figures that are now suggested (perhaps as low as 3,000) stand up to scrutiny, the question is begged of why the crusaders themselves so crudely exulted in what they had done. One answer might be that they were conscious that their co-religionists in the west would expect the recovery of the holy places to be accompanied by a radical dispossession of the polluters, and that it was best to claim that this had occurred in order to secure the continuing military support that was necessary.

---

89 A. Malkiel, 'The underclass in the First Crusade: a historiographical trend', *JMH* 28 (2002), 169–97. See also R. Chazan, *European Jewry and the First Crusade* (Berkeley: University of California Press, 1987).

90 J. Riley-Smith, 'The First Crusade and the persecution of the Jews', *SCH* 21 (1984), 51–72. See also Chazan, *European Jewry*, pp. 63–4; F. Duncalf, 'The Peasants' Crusade', *AHR* 26 (1921), 440–54.

91 J. Flori, 'Une ou plusieurs "première croisade"? Le message d'Urbain II et les plus anciens pogroms d'Occident', *RH* 285 (1991), 3–27.

92 D. Hay, 'Gender bias and religious intolerance in accounts of the "massacres" of the First Crusade', in *TISCAC*, 3–10, 135–9; France, *Victory in the East*, pp. 355–6; K. Elm, 'Die Eroberung Jerusalems in Jahre 1099. Ihre Darstellung, Beurteilung und Deutung in den Quellen zur Geschichte des Ersten Kreuzzugs', in Bauer, Herbers and Jaspert, eds, *Jerusalem*, 31–54, at pp. 46–54.

93 B. Z. Kedar, 'The Jerusalem massacre of July 1099 in the western historiography of the crusades', *Crusades* 3 (2004), 15–75.

The point that emerges most clearly in relation to both the Rhineland and the Jerusalem massacres is that the emergence of a crusading ideology in 1095–9 had a highly significant impact on the Catholic Church's relations with the other two monotheistic faiths. In this respect it was ominous that the novelty of the entire crusading enterprise, which is where this chapter began, was accompanied by volatility. This has been emphasized by Riley-Smith, and one of his key insights, which underpins his entire approach to the subject, has been that the overall development of early crusading ideas did not follow anything like a straightforward course. The period running from Clermont to c. 1110 comprised at least four stages: the preaching of the Crusade, the response of the laity, the input of the crusaders themselves, and the hindsight reflections of the monastic chroniclers.[94] In such circumstances it was likely that the Church's acceptance and celebration of penitential violence would have implications for interfaith relations that Urban II could not foresee in November 1095 and probably would not have welcomed. Because of this, the editors and authors of the impressive group of volumes that arose from the commemoration of the First Crusade in the mid-to late 1990s, which have added a good deal to our understanding of the expedition, were fully aware of the sensitive nature of the subject that they were exploring.[95] Rather like the pope in 1095, they were overtaken by events, for what they could not foresee was that the events of 11 September 2001 would soon give their discussions and publications even more immediacy than they already possessed.

---

94 Riley-Smith, *The First Crusade*, pp. 153–5. This is one of the big question marks hanging over Flori's argument that the definition of crusade has to hinge on the First Crusade, given that, as he has himself suggested, there were not one but several First Crusades: Flori, 'Une ou plusieurs "première croisade"?'

95 *APC; FCJ; FCOI; PCNAD; Il concilio di Piacenza e le crociate* (Piacenza: Fida Custodia, 1996); *Le Concile de Clermont de 1095 et l'appel à la croisade* (Rome: École française de Rome, 1997); P. Racine, ed., *Piacenza e la prima crociata* (Reggio Emilia: Diabasis, 1995); M. Rey-Delqué, ed., *Les Croisades, l'orient et l'occident d'Urbain II à Saint-Louis (1096–1270)* (Milan: Electa, 1997).

3

The Development of Crusading in the Twelfth and Thirteenth Centuries

There is no evidence that Pope Urban II had plans to establish a practice of crusading when he preached the First Crusade, but he made it virtually inevitable that future crusading would occur by failing to make any clear provision for an alternative means of defending the recovered holy places. It is possible that the pope envisaged the extension of Byzantine power as far south as Palestine, or that he hoped the settlements formed there would assume the shape of Frankish marcher principalities, relying on Byzantine good will to counter the strongest attacks launched by the Muslims.[1] In practice relations with the Greeks deteriorated to such an extent in the later stages of the First Crusade that it became clear to Urban's successor, Paschal II, that 'follow-up' crusades would be needed. The first was the crusade of 1101, which was destroyed by the Turks in Anatolia;[2] and the second was the expedition recruited by Bohemund of Antioch, which was so hostile to the Greeks that it started its campaign by besieging the Byzantine port of Durazzo (Dyrrachion) in 1107.[3] It is arguable that with the launching of these expeditions the First Crusade had already ceased to be unique. The chronicler Orderic Vitalis described Bohemund's army as 'the third departure of people from the west for Jerusalem' ('tercia profectio occi-

---

1   R.-J. Lilie, *Byzantium and the Crusader States, 1095–1204*, trans. J. C. Morris and J. C. Ridings (Oxford: Oxford University Press, 1993).
2   See chapter 2 note 72.
3   J. G. Rowe, 'Paschal II, Bohemund of Antioch and the Byzantine empire', *Bulletin of the John Rylands Library* 49 (1966), 165–202.

dentalium in Ierusalem').[4] This numbering was not to stick, but it revealed a sense that things had already moved on. As the Muslims, Seljuqs and Fatimids alike, began to exert pressure on the newly established states of Jerusalem, Tripoli, Antioch and Edessa, a pattern set in. The settlers in the Latin East sent appeals for help to the west. And a combination of familiarity with the events of 1095–9, personal aspirations, and the devotional associations of the destination, propelled those people who responded to the appeals to shape their actions in the same mould as those of the first crusaders. They took the cross, made vows, and were assured by clerics that their pilgrimage in arms could stand instead of all penance for the sins that they had committed.

Historians who have studied the series of expeditions (*passagia*) that ensued have in general addressed two separate agendas. First, there has for long been a fascination with how the practice of crusading evolved in the course of the several generations which separated the first crusaders from those who accompanied Louis IX of France on the last 'general passage' in 1270.[5] Participants were united by the common bond of assuming the cross for penitential service in Christ's war, but in many other respects they differed. Secondly, each of the largest *passagia* quite naturally poses its own set of questions. Many of these remain fairly generic, relating to such issues as intention, leadership, strategy, the use made of sea-power and relations with the Byzantine Greeks; but some are more specific, creations of the particular circumstances of the day or the personalities of key players. It makes good sense to divide this chapter in terms of these two agendas.

The General Development of Crusading

Few historians would deny that around 1200 major changes took place in the way crusades were preached, organized and implemented, which were radical enough to constitute a watershed in the practice.[6] These changes have left plenty of evidence and as a result the *modus operandi* of crusaders in the thirteenth century is the subject of little contention; the debate shifts

---

4 M. Chibnall, ed. and trans., *The Ecclesiastical History of Orderic Vitalis, Volume III, Books V and VI* (Oxford: Oxford University Press, 1972), Bk 5, pp. 182–3.

5 S. Lloyd, 'The crusading movement, 1096–1274', in *OIHC*, 34–65.

6 J. Richard, '1187: Point de départ pour une nouvelle forme de la croisade', in *HH*, 250–60.

to the questions of whether the system had become corrupt, where the balance of power lay in the control of crusades, and how much popular enthusiasm crusading still commanded. In the twelfth century, by contrast, much simpler questions are hotly contended. These include what crusading consisted of and what was the exact nature of the crusader's spiritual reward, the indulgence.

The former problem derives from the close proximity as devotional practices of crusading and pilgrimage. When Calixtus II proclaimed a crusade in 1122–6, the affinity between his actions and those of Urban II was so strong that it is apparent that what occurred was a new crusade. . The importance of Calixtus's hitherto overlooked initiative was demonstrated by Jonathan Riley-Smith, who argued that among other things it generated the first crusading encyclical, or general letter calling Christians to arms.[7] But on many other occasions groups, some of them substantial, made their way to the Holy Land without leaving us a clear indication of their status: they were usually described as *peregrini* but were prepared to fight if the need arose. The devotional aspect of crusading remained well to the fore, and the growth in the popularity of the Jerusalem pilgrimage that naturally followed the recovery of the holy places makes the problem of identification greater. It is quite possible that some who went out to the east with the primary intention of fighting, such as the young Charles the Good, count of Flanders, did so without taking the cross; so neither all pilgrims nor all voluntary combatants who saw action in the Holy Land were *crucesignati*. As we saw in chapter 1, Christopher Tyerman has drawn on this fluidity to advance the argument that contemporaries perceived what we now regard as crusading as no more than a bellicose variant of pilgrimage, reserving the term 'crusade' for the fully formed institution that emerged at the close of the century.[8] E. O. Blake argued that the point of crystallization occurred 'from about the middle of the twelfth century', when 'the promulgation of the "crusade" in terms of ideas associated with the Jerusalem *iter* was met at the popular level by a capacity to recognize the allusions and accept the implications of it'.[9] Undeniably, the inchoate nature of much twelfth-century crusading presents its difficulties.

The shifting nature of the crusader's indulgence is no less problematic. What is at issue here is whether the process of undertaking an

---

7 J. Riley-Smith, 'The Venetian crusade of 1122–1124', in *CIRCG*, 337–50; Riley-Smith, *The First Crusaders*, pp. 169–88.
8 Tyerman, *The Invention of the Crusades*, pp. 8–29.
9 E. O. Blake, 'The formation of the "crusade idea" ', *JEH* 21 (1970), 11–31, at p. 30.

armed pilgrimage to the Holy Sepulchre was a penitential act of so exacting a nature that it purged the penalties that any sinning Christian incurred at the hands of a just God, or whether it fitted the technical meaning of the word 'indulgence' in the tighter sense of an activity which was considered so meritorious that it was deemed by the Church to replace all the penitential acts that would otherwise be required to purge the sinner. The most notable example of the former approach was the Second Crusade, which was promoted by St Bernard as a time of Jubilee (*tempus acceptabile*) on the basis that such a spectacular occasion for wiping out the consequences of sinful behaviour was not to be missed. 'I would call blessed', Bernard wrote, 'that generation that has the chance to obtain so rich an indulgence, blessed to be alive in this year of jubilee, this year so pleasing to the Lord.'[10] The latter approach, on the other hand, was theologically more conservative. It highlighted the mediating authority of the Church and tended to accentuate the role that the popes played. It has been argued that it was adhered to by the man whom many consider to have been the greatest twelfth-century pope, Alexander III.[11]

Prominent clerics were well aware that the crusade represented an important but sensitive link between the Church and the laity. In the past half century it has attracted the attention of some distinguished historians of the medieval Church.[12] The correspondence of the popes before 1198 was erratically preserved, but there are sufficient surviving letters to enable us to discern that approaches towards the crusade, and more generally towards the problems experienced by the crusader states, differed markedly between pontificates. The notorious 'fallow period' in crusading, which stretched from the failure of the Second Crusade in 1148 to the disastrous battle of Hattin in 1187, has been accorded particular attention. Sources are more abundant than for the first half of the century; there was a more frequent exchange of letters and envoys between the courts of Jerusalem, Constantinople and western Europe; above all there was a realization in the west of the threat posed by the

10   Mayer, *The Crusades*, 2nd edn, p. 97. I. S. Robinson, *The Papacy 1073–1198. Continuity and Innovation* (Cambridge: Cambridge University Press, 1990), pp. 341–9; J. Riley-Smith, 'The state of mind of crusaders to the east, 1095–1300', in *OIHC*, 66–90, at p. 82.

11   J. G. Rowe, 'Alexander III and the Jerusalem crusade: an overview of problems and failures', in *CMTCS*, 112–32.

12   For example, Robinson, *The Papacy*, pp. 322–66; E.-D. Hehl, *Kirche und Krieg im 12. Jahrhundert. Studien zu kanonischem Recht und politischer Wirklichkeit* (Stuttgart: A. Hiersemann, 1980); E.-D. Hehl, 'War, peace and the Christian order', in D. Luscombe and J. Riley-Smith, eds, *NCMH, IV, c.1024–c.1198, Part One*, 185–228.

gradual consolidation of power in the Muslim states which bordered the Latin East.[13]

Naturally clerical interest in crusading extended beyond the Roman *curia*. It was in this period that canon law reached maturity as a discipline, much of the credit for this being due to Gratian, the monk of Bologna who produced the first comprehensive corpus of canon law, the *Decretum*, c. 1140. We have already seen that the problem we face in defining crusading is reflected in the difficulties that canon lawyers faced when they attempted to categorize people who took the cross. Gratian himself did not confront it head-on, although much of his *causa* 23, in which he considered the precedents for and against clerical sponsorship of warfare, had a bearing on the subject. As James Brundage showed in his study of medieval canon law and the crusade, the decretists, those canon lawyers who applied Gratian's great text to the problems of everyday life, focused on what occurred when individuals took their vow. By the 1180s, on the eve of Hattin and the proclamation of the Third Crusade, the votive process had received a good deal of attention at their hands.[14]

Not surprisingly, high-ranking members of the secular Church, bishops and archbishops, played a major role in interpreting the crusading message and the complications that it raised. The most famous name, admittedly a somewhat special case, is that of William archbishop of Tyre. William was a key figure in the politics of the kingdom of Jerusalem and was very familiar with its relations with visiting crusaders and pilgrims; he left unrivalled insights into how the settlers themselves viewed crusading in his narrative account of the Latin East, one of the greatest histories written in the Middle Ages. William's career and writings have been much studied, and R. B. C. Huygens recently produced an up-to-date edition of his chronicle.[15] William's view of the struggle being conducted against the Muslims by the settlers has aroused particular interest. For R. C. Schwinges, his treatment of the Muslims in his chronicle shows that in the Latin East the crusading spirit was replaced by a more informed, sympathetic and balanced view of the enemy; William recognized, for example, that Muslims could entertain a sense of patriotism and fight

---

13   R. C. Smail, 'Latin Syria and the west, 1149–1187', *TRHS* ser. 5, 19 (1969), 1–20; Rowe, 'Alexander III'; J. Phillips, *Defenders of the Holy Land. Relations between the Latin East and the West, 1119–1187* (Oxford: Oxford University Press, 1996); G. Constable, 'The crusading project of 1150', in *MSCH*, 67–75; T. Reuter, 'The "non-crusade" of 1149–50', in *SCSC*, 150–63.

14   Brundage, *Medieval Canon Law and the Crusader*, pp. 30–65.

15   R. B. C. Huygens, ed., *Willelmi Tyrensis Archiepiscopi Chronicon* (2 vols, Turnhout: Brepols, 1986); P. W. Edbury and J. G. Rowe, *William of Tyre. Historian of the Latin East* (Cambridge: Cambridge University Press, 1988).

just wars. Schwinges argued that William's overall view constituted a form of medieval tolerance. This is contentious, but it is certainly true that the rulers of the twelfth-century kingdom faced the problem, which recurred throughout crusading history, of managing their relations with their enemies in ways which would reconcile their strong sense of identity as guardians of the holy places, dependent on western help, with the political and economic circumstances they confronted on a day-to-day basis.[16]

The role of secular prelates as interfaces and mediators is most apparent on the great expeditions. In 1147, when Bishop Peter of Oporto made full use of his rhetorical skills to persuade the crusaders making their way to the east to assist the Portuguese in assaulting Lisbon, while Bishop Godfrey of Langres argued for an attack on Byzantine Constantinople, their situations were different but they were exercising a similar role: their authority and pastoral duties as consecrated bishops meant that their audiences listened carefully, even if in Godfrey's case they declined to follow his advice. Of course, Adhémar of Puy was a clear precedent for this, and it is apparent that the lay leaders of the twelfth-century expeditions, like their predecessors on the First Crusade, were far from being docilely receptive to clerical words of wisdom. The difference is that the arguments of prelates in the field gradually became suffused by ideas about legitimate authority, just cause and right intention that reflected the more advanced juristic environment of their day.[17]

As Ernst-Dieter Hehl showed in 1980, the twelfth-century Church could not avoid contact with military activity in numerous respects, including its initiation, conduct and consequences.[18] From this viewpoint, the relative paucity of attention that was given to crusading by the theologians remains a puzzle.[19] There was naturally a theological element in the way crusading was presented in the opening flourishes, or *exordia*, of papal bulls of crusade, but for practical reasons it was kept concise. It seems that the closest thing we have to a sustained theological treatment is St Bernard's 'In praise of the new knighthood' ('De laude novae militiae') of c. 1128. Even this he wrote, possibly without great enthusiasm, not about crusading but as a form of publicity for the new military order of the

---

16   R. C. Schwinges, *Kreuzzugsideologie und Toleranz. Studien zu Wilhelm von Tyrus* (Stuttgart: A. Hiersemann, 1977); 'William of Tyre, the Muslim enemy, and the problem of tolerance', in *TISCAC*, 124–32, 173–6.

17   J. Phillips, 'Ideas of crusade and holy war in *De expugnatione lyxbonensi* (*The conquest of Lisbon*)', in *HLHL*, 123–41; Berry, 'The Second Crusade', pp. 488, 490–1; Cowdrey, 'Christianity and the morality of warfare'.

18   Hehl, *Kirche und Krieg*.

19   As noted by Russell, *The Just War*, pp. 252–7.

Templars.[20] But much of what Bernard wrote could be applied also to crusaders, especially his view of knighthood and his emphasis on the practice of charity.[21] For this reason, combined with the veneration in which its author was held, it is probable that *De laude* was cited more frequently than any other commentary that was written in relation to crusading.[22] Yet *De laude* contains more emotion and rhetoric than reasoned theology, and it constitutes a slight yield from what was surely the great age of medieval theology. Perhaps the reason for the silence was the unsettled nature of crusading, or academic distaste at such an open embrace of violence. Possibly too it was the shock induced by the failure of the Second Crusade. This caused St Bernard to write a reflective and measured theological response to the disaster, his *De consideratione*. He wrote this because of his sense of personal responsibility for what had happened; other theologians, not burdened with that guilt, may well have preferred not to handle the subject at all.[23] After Hattin, and the loss of Jerusalem, what was needed was not academic thought but the immediate mobilization of Christendom. In such a context the doubts that were expressed by such clerics as Ralph Niger were thrust aside.[24]

What made the thirteenth century different in many ways was the pontificate of Innocent III (1198–1216).[25] So much in crusading changes after Innocent that the danger exists of exaggerating his contribution. As in the case of all men whose actions seemed to have an extraordinary impact, it is possible to emphasize antecedents, to argue that events moved in Innocent's favour, or even to play down the effect of what he did. What is striking about Innocent III is that even when his reign has been subjected to all such balances, most of his achievement in crusading terms remains intact. With Innocent the magnificent series of Vatican Registers of papal letters begins, so that close study of his 'crusading policy' becomes possible to a degree that has no precedent for earlier popes; Innocent's early letters can now be read in a modern edition, though for the later ones we are still forced to consult Migne's *Patrologia latina*. In 1969 Helmut Roscher published a monograph on Innocent and the crusades

---

20 M. Barber, *The New Knighthood. A History of the Order of the Temple* (Cambridge: Cambridge University Press, 1994), pp. 38–63, esp. pp. 44–6.

21 For example, J. Riley-Smith, 'Crusading as an act of love', *History* 65 (1980), 177–92; A. Grabois, '*Militia* and *Malitia*: the Bernardine vision of chivalry', in *SCC*, 49–56; and the massive treatment of the theme of *militia Christi* in '*Militia Christi*' *e crociata*.

22 This is a personal impression: the subject would repay attention.

23 B. Bolton, 'The Cistercians and the Aftermath of the Second Crusade', in *SCC*, 131–40.

24 G. B. Flahiff, 'Deus non vult: a critic of the Third Crusade', *Mediaeval Studies* 9 (1947), 162–88.

25 For the pontificate generally see J. C. Moore, *Pope Innocent III (1160/61–1216). To Root Up and to Plant* (Leiden: Brill, 2003).

in which he systematically analysed the pope's approach. It was Roscher who first demonstrated how fundamental was Innocent's contribution towards crusading, and his findings have not been overturned, though in many detailed respects his picture of Innocent's policy and achievements has been modified.[26]

It is generally accepted that with Innocent III crusading was for the first time placed within a coherent ideological perspective. This revolved around the concept of a Christian community, *Christianitas*, or when conceived more juridically and politically, the *respublica christiana*. Crusading was seen as akin to the foreign policy of this community, and the role of the Roman *curia* in initiating and managing Christendom's crusading efforts was accentuated; it was no coincidence that Innocent formulated the doctrine that the pope was Christ's 'Vicar' or lieutenant on earth. The centrality of Christ in the devotional experience of crusading was thus to have its mirror image in the place that the Roman *curia* aspired to occupy, through its administrative offices, legates and bulls, in the organization of the crusading effort. And this was accompanied by a vigorous process of papal intervention in the secular politics of the Christian world with the goal of enforcing the internal peace that everybody recognized as the precondition for a crusade. We are long past the age when confessional animosity distorted historical writing, and nobody has recently suggested that this constituted an unscrupulous bid for power on Innocent's part. Rather, it sprang from the acutely difficult military situation faced by the settlers in the east throughout the pope's reign, to which he responded with extraordinary vision, ability and persistence. But the consequences were clear, and they were neatly summed up in a title on Innocent edited by James Powell, an American scholar who devoted much of his career to studying the pope: 'Innocent III, Vicar of Christ or Lord of the World?'[27] The secular rulers and indeed the episcopate of thirteenth-century Europe were fully capable of grasping the implications of accepting Innocent III's viewpoint. Much study of crusading in the thirteenth century has therefore taken the form of an implicit debate about Innocent's ambitions, focusing on their practicability and on the extent to which contemporaries found them acceptable.[28]

---

26 H. Roscher, *Papst Innocenz III. und die Kreuzzüge* (Göttingen: Vandenhoeck and Ruprecht, 1969). For material published more recently, see B. Bolton, ' "Serpent in the dust, sparrow on the housetop": attitudes to Jerusalem and the Holy Land in the circle of Innocent III', in *HLHL*, 154–80.

27 J. M. Powell, ed., *Innocent III, Vicar of Christ or Lord of the World?* (revd edn, Washington, DC: Catholic University of America Press, 1994).

28 For example, Menzel, 'Kreuzzugsideologie'.

The practice of transcribing and preserving outgoing papal letters was maintained after Innocent III's reign, and most of the registers for his successors through to the end of the thirteenth century were published, in full or calendared form, by academic members of the French School at Rome. This has made possible the analysis of the papacy's activities not just in relation to all the major *passagia* of the period, but also in the interstices between them, when an ongoing sense of the Holy Land's predicament created a virtually ceaseless pattern of negotiation, peace-making, preaching and financial activity.[29] The abundant material illustrating papal policy is complemented by much evidence about its application by bishops in many parts of Europe, as well as by an increasing volume of evidence left by the secular governments of the period. Every aspect of crusading, from taking the cross through to the management of the expeditions in the field, becomes clearer than had previously been the case. A good example is the clarification of the crusader's indulgence. The indulgence was finally settled by Innocent as a remission of sins (*remissio peccatorum*) achieved through the Church's mediation of God's grace. Theologically this rested for some time on the generalization that nothing could be dearer to God than his Son's cause; only in 1343 was it underpinned by Clement VI's invention of the 'Treasury of Merits', a kind of inexhaustible celestial bank account of good deeds on which the Church could draw to remit the sins of believers.[30]

In recent scholarship this greater clarity has been evinced in particular in three aspects of thirteenth-century crusading. The first was the status of the *crucesignatus* in canon law. In his 1969 study James Brundage used the collections of decretals (or definitive statements) of the thirteenth-century popes, together with their other letters, and the commentaries of the period's canon lawyers, the decretalists, to demonstrate how most major aspects of a crusader's commitment, duties and rewards were addressed and defined by the Church.[31] This was a more or less inevitable development given that so many of the popes who promoted the crusade keenly were themselves trained lawyers. As Brundage noted, the canonist Sinibaldo dei Fieschi even found time, when pope as Innocent IV (1243–54), to write 'a massive and incisive *Apparatus*' on Raymond of Penyafort's collection of Pope Gregory IX's decretals, the *Liber extra*.[32] In recent years

---

29 For example, Purcell, *Papal Crusading Policy 1244–1291*; B. Weiler, 'The *Negotium Terrae Sanctae* in the political discourse of Latin Christendom, 1215–1311', *IHR* 25 (2003), 1–36.
30 Riley-Smith, *The Crusades*, p. 121; D. Wood, *Clement VI. The Pontificate and Ideas of an Avignon Pope* (Cambridge: Cambridge University Press, 1989), pp. 32–4.
31 Brundage, *Medieval Canon Law and the Crusader*, pp. 66–190.
32 J. A. Brundage, *Medieval Canon Law* (Longman: London, 1995), pp. 225–6.

Brundage has revisited the subject on several occasions,[33] but the overall treatment he gave it in 1969 was so comprehensive that the legal position of crusaders has attracted remarkably little attention from others.

The second field that has been studied in depth is that of crusade preaching and devotional trends. In this field the most significant recent contributions are those of Penny Cole and Christoph Maier. We now enjoy a much fuller view both of the way preaching was arranged and monitored, and of the spectrum of devotional themes, scriptural exegesis and historical reference points that preachers habitually used.[34] In addition to a study of the important role that the mendicant friars came to play in preaching the cross, Maier has also provided an edition, with translation and commentary, of a group of model sermons from the thirteenth century.[35] More broadly, he has illuminated the involvement of the laity in the liturgical commemoration of the Holy Land in the period around 1200. Maier argues that one of Innocent III's most controversial measures, his policy that non-combatants who had taken the cross should be allowed to redeem their vows in exchange for simple cash payments, had its roots not solely in the pope's desire to retain crusading's 'democratic' character without prejudicing its military efficiency, but also in the deep sense of grief that the laity continued to express for the loss in 1187 of Jerusalem and the True Cross. Crusading had always been a deeply christocentric act, but the *imitatio Christi* involved had been external, indeed strenuously physical. Innocent's new emphasis on localized liturgical commemoration and intercession, situated above all in the mass, had the effect of placing the crusade at the centre of thirteenth-century religious life.[36] There is convergence here with work that Michael Markowski and Jessalyn Bird have published on the links between crusade preaching and the cult of poverty.[37]

The essential complement to the study of preaching, whose chief goal remained the recruitment of volunteers, is that of finance, and in

---

33   For example, J. A. Brundage, 'Holy war and the medieval lawyers', in T. P. Murphy, ed., *The Holy War* (Columbus: Ohio State University Press, 1976), 99–140; 'Immortalizing the crusades: law and institutions', in *MSCH*, 251–60.

34   P. J. Cole, *The Preaching of the Crusades to the Holy Land, 1095–1270* (Cambridge, MA: Medieval Academy of America, 1991); C. T. Maier, *Preaching the Crusades. Mendicant Friars and the Cross in the Thirteenth Century* (Cambridge: Cambridge University Press, 1994).

35   Maier, ed., *Crusade Propaganda*.

36   C. T. Maier, 'Crisis, liturgy and the crusade in the twelfth and thirteenth centuries', *JEH* 48 (1997), 628–57; C. T. Maier, 'Mass, the eucharist and the cross: Innocent III and the relocation of the crusade', in *PIW*, 351–60.

37   M. Markowski, 'Peter of Blois and the conception of the Third Crusade', in *HH*, 261–9; J. Bird, 'Reform or crusade? Anti-usury and crusade preaching during the pontificate of Innocent III', in *PIW*, 165–85.

particular taxation measures.[38] One of the most far-reaching changes initiated by Innocent III was his ruling that the Church must shoulder much of the escalating financial burden of crusading, and that it should do this by paying a form of income tax imposed by the pope and collected by clerics in the lead-up to *passagia*. The resulting structure and its operation were both studied in great detail by the American student of papal finance, W. E. Lunt.[39] Rather like Brundage in the case of canon law, Lunt's mastery of his material, much of it dauntingly technical, was so comprehensive that the subject of papal taxation for crusading has received little more recent study. Attention has shifted to individual taxes and the political tussles that so often resulted over access to the proceeds.[40] The association of a regular form of taxation with crusading carried implications in terms of the motivations of crusaders, while its impact on the economy was likely to be substantial: we shall return to both of these aspects in later chapters. For the moment, what needs noting is that taken together with the clarification of the crusader's legal status, and the more systematic preaching of the crusade, it made up a pattern. Crusading in the thirteenth century remained a devotional activity, hinging on each penitent individual's response to the call of the cross; and John Gilchrist has shown that a spiritual view of crusade lay at the heart of all of Innocent III's measures.[41] But winning these responses, then organizing them in order to achieve an effective military outcome, was handled with an attention to detail that was largely new, and it was complemented by an attempt to steer and manage the work of the crusading collectivity. On this there is a broad consensus.

There is, by contrast, no consensus at present on the issue of how long crusading retained its popularity in the thirteenth century. Nobody has denied that the Fifth Crusade arose from a broad-based commitment to crusading, one that affected all classes and most regions of the Catholic west. The 'Barons' Crusade' of 1239–41, and the two *passagia* of Louis IX, demonstrate that crusading retained a strong appeal for the French nobility, though the character of that appeal was changing in ways that have only recently begun to be explored.[42] Some historians would prob-

---

38 F. A. Cazel, 'Financing the crusades', in *HC* 6: 116–49.
39 W. E. Lunt, *Papal Revenues in the Middle Ages* (2 vols, New York: Columbia University Press, 1934); *Financial Relations of the Papacy with England* (2 vols, Cambridge, MA: Mediaeval Academy of America, 1939–62).
40 For example, S. Lloyd, *English Society and the Crusade, 1216–1307* (Oxford: Clarendon Press, 1988).
41 Gilchrist, 'The Lord's War'.
42 Riley-Smith, 'The state of mind of crusaders'. A forthcoming study by Caroline Smith will clarify this issue.

ably attribute Louis's ability to launch his expeditions primarily to the king's personal resolve, coupled with his command of French resources. Certainly, there exists a strong school of thought that views enthusiasm for crusading as having settled into a decline by the 1270s. In his *Criticism of the Crusade* (1940), Palmer Throop collected a substantial, albeit eclectic, volume of evidence testifying to the despair that many contemporaries felt at the failure of so many crusading expeditions in the past, and vociferous criticism of papal policy in many respects.[43] Despite being published at a highly inauspicious moment, Throop's book proved to be extraordinarily influential. In 1954 Steven Runciman drew heavily on its findings,[44] and in 1975, reviewing the reception that was accorded to papal policy, Maureen Purcell refined Throop's arguments but in large measure confirmed his conclusions.[45] The reason for the warm welcome given to Throop's book was that he appeared to provide an explanation for the most puzzling feature of the late thirteenth century, the discrepancy between the vast amount of energy that was clearly being poured into promoting the crusade, and the lukewarm if not feeble response.

Some historians have taken issue with Throop's pessimistic assessment. It was hardly surprising that in the wake of Louis IX's spectacular failure in Egypt, and his death while on crusade at Carthage in August 1270, attempts to mobilize fresh efforts should meet with increasingly stubborn resistance. This was recorded in some detail by contemporary preachers like Humbert of Romans. And the response to the ambitious crusading programme that Pope Gregory X tried to launch at the Second Council of Lyons in 1274 was certainly problematic. Yet we need to distinguish between fundamental disenchantment with crusading on the one hand, and despair caused by past failure, linked with scepticism about whether a new *passagium* would actually take place, on the other. Elizabeth Siberry has questioned how deep criticism cut in the thirteenth century, compared for example with the savage questioning of the validity of crusading that occurred after the Second Crusade.[46] And the plethora of recent publications about crusading in the period after 1291 suggests that the lack of response in the 1270s and 1280s may have been a temporary 'dip' which, unfortunately for the settlers in the east, came at the worst possible time. The issue remains undecided, but it seems increasingly likely, given the

---

43   P. A. Throop, *Criticism of the Crusade: A Study of Public Opinion and Crusade Propaganda* (Amsterdam: N. V. Swets and Zeitlinger, 1940, repr. Philadelphia: Porcupine Press, 1975).
44   Runciman, *A History*, 3: 339–42.
45   Purcell, *Papal Crusading Policy 1244–1291*. See too Mayer, *The Crusades*, 2nd edn, pp. 320–1 note 143; Brundage, 'Holy war', p. 137 note 148.
46   E. Siberry, *Criticism of Crusading, 1095–1274* (Oxford: Oxford University Press, 1985).

volume of research that is now being published on crusading in the late Middle Ages, that we shall have to devise a more sophisticated methodology to measure the state of enthusiasm in the later thirteenth century than has been applied in the past.

The Individual Expeditions

Historians agree that the Second Crusade was an expedition on a massive scale. Setting to one side the campaigns that were waged in Iberia and northern Germany, the French and German armies that marched overland to the east were both very large. So it is surprising that until recent years this crusade has attracted much less attention than its predecessor and successors; indeed, the last monograph written on it dates from 1866.[47] Historians may have been deterred by the relative paucity of original sources for the crusade, certainly by comparison with the First Crusade. The most important narrative account of Louis VII's French army, by Odo of Deuil, draws to a close before the end of the crusade, while in his account of the German march Otto of Freising confesses that the sufferings endured were so painful that he will leave it to others to provide details. Yet when these and other narrative accounts are supplemented by letters written home during the crusade, and when sources originating in Byzantium, the Muslim lands and the Latin East are added, there is enough primary evidence to make possible a detailed reconstruction and explanation of events.[48]

The crusade bristles with interpretative problems, and they begin with its faltering initiation by Pope Eugenius III. Notoriously, the pope's first attempt to arouse the Christian west to recover Edessa, the Mesopotamian stronghold captured by Zengi in 1144, fell flat. It was only after Louis VII had announced his plan to lead an expedition to the east, at his Christmas court at Bourges in 1145, that a second issue of Eugenius's encyclical, *Quantum praedecessores*, seemed to be a worthwhile venture.[49] Some scholars have also argued that Eugenius was seriously wrongfooted by his former teacher, Bernard of Clairvaux. Bernard used re-

47 B. Kugler, *Studien zur Geschichte des zweiten Kreuzzuges* (Stuttgart, 1866).
48 See *SCC*; *SCSC*, with select bibliography, comp. A. V. Murray, at pp. 201–18. A forthcoming study by Jonathan Phillips is eagerly awaited.
49 Mayer, *The Crusades*, 2nd edn, p. 93; A. Grabois, 'The crusade of Louis VII: a reconsideration', in *CS*, 94–104; J. G. Rowe, 'The origins of the Second Crusade: Pope Eugenius III, Bernard of Clairvaux and Louis VII of France', in *SCC*, 79–89; R. Hiestand, 'The papacy and the Second Crusade', in *SCSC*, 32–53, at pp. 35–8.

markable psychological pressure to persuade Conrad III to take the cross at December 1146, despite the fact that the pope relied on the German king to support him in his bid to control Rome. Not only did the pope lose his protector at Rome, but also the presence of both monarchs on the expedition was likely to generate rivalry and dissension. Recently, however, Jonathan Phillips has pointed out that the idea that Eugenius disapproved of Conrad's joining the crusade rests on thin evidence, and he has argued that German participation formed part of the pope's overall project.[50]

The orthodoxy has prevailed for a long time that the Second Crusade was St Bernard's creation, virtually to the extent that the First was Urban II's.[51] Bernard had strong views of what crusading meant, which he promoted with characteristic self-belief and stamina.[52] Apart from persuading Conrad to take the cross, Bernard's preaching was to a large extent responsible for generating a response whose extraordinary scale remains rather puzzling. It was after all not Jerusalem or Antioch that Zengi had captured, but a city far to the north of the Holy Land, strategically important but with no significant religious connotations. This being the case, it seems likely that the enthusiasm displayed arose from Bernard's message that the crusade constituted a Christian Jubilee, an opportunity for participants to gain heaven that it would be madness to refuse. The association of the crusade with Jerusalem was thus emphasized, and in *Quantum praedecessores* the pope made great play of the idea that this generation should aim to imitate the exploits of the first crusaders. In this way the seeds of disaster were sown: a controlled military response aimed at regaining Edessa and neutralizing Zengi was buried under a massive exercise in self-redemption, a counterproductive imitation of the heroes of 1099 by forces that were unmanageably large and diverse in composition.[53]

A second area of difficulties relates to the march eastwards, in particular the troubled relations that the crusaders had with the Byzantine Greeks. The difficulties that both kings encountered at Constantinople fitted the pattern that had been set out in 1096–7, with the difference that on this occasion the ill-feeling was sharper. In fact it was for long

---

50   J. Phillips, 'Papacy, empire and the Second Crusade', in *SCSC*, 15–31. For the traditional view see Hiestand, 'The papacy', p. 38.
51   For example, Mayer, *The Crusades*, 2nd edn, p. 95.
52   Grabois, '*Militia* and *Malitia*'; J. A. Brundage, 'St. Bernard and the jurists', in *SCC*, 25–33; J. Leclercq, 'Pour l'histoire de l'encyclique de S. Bernard sur la croisade', in *Études de civilisation médiévale, IXe–XIIe siècles. Mélanges Edmond-René Labande* (Poitiers: CESCM, 1974), 479–94.
53   Grabois, 'The crusade'; Hiestand, 'The papacy'.

thought that in 1149–50 the new crusade planned to bring help to the Latin East would start its work by attacking Constantinople. This idea has come under much attack in recent years, an important revision because it counters the thesis that the proposal for an attack on the Greeks had reached the stage of planning some fifty years before the Fourth Crusade, thus making the events of that expedition more understandable.[54] Even Odo of Deuil, who was no friend of the Greeks, at times showed some appreciation of the difficult position that the Byzantine court found itself in.[55]

In the summer of 1148 those remnants of the French and German armies that managed to reach the Holy Land after the catastrophic defeats they had suffered in Anatolia combined forces with the Franks of the kingdom of Jerusalem to lay siege to Damascus. This decision has long seemed strange: it was Nur ad-Din, Zengi's son and successor, who posed the most serious threat to the Franks, and he did not hold Damascus; in fact, alarm at Zengi's expansionist ambitions had caused the city's rulers to enter an alliance with Jerusalem eight years previously. The siege failed and Damascus fell to Nur ad-Din in 1154, enormously extending his grip over northern Syria. Not surprisingly both the decision to besiege Damascus and the failure to take it have been repeatedly analysed. Martin Hoch has established the full context of the campaign in terms of the internal politics of the kingdom of Jerusalem and its rulers' assessment of the strategic situation along their entire frontier from the Nile delta to northern Syria.[56]

Sandwiched between two expeditions that throw up considerable problems, the Third Crusade offers something of a contrast, for the contended issues are relatively few.[57] The crusade was preached intensively in England, France and Germany, and the richness of the sources, both for the process of preaching and for the way the recruits were organized, has made possible detailed reconstructions of the English and Imperial armies. The 'Saladin tithe', the unpopular tax that was imposed on income and movable property in France and England to finance the crusade, has attracted particular attention, because it has appeared to anticipate meas-

---

54 Constable, 'The crusading project'; Reuter, 'The "non-crusade" '.

55 J. Phillips, 'Odo of Deuil's *De profectione Ludovici VII in Orientem* as a source for the Second Crusade', in *EC*, 80–95, at pp. 85–9.

56 A. J. Forey, 'The failure of the siege of Damascus in 1148', *JMH* 10 (1984), 13–25; M. Hoch, 'The choice of Damascus as the objective of the Second Crusade', in *APC*, 359–70; M. Hoch, 'The price of failure: the Second Crusade as a turning-point in the history of the Latin East?', in *SCSC*, 180–200.

57 I am aware of no full-length study of the crusade; see the accounts given by Mayer, Richard, Riley-Smith and Runciman, and *HC*.

ures of national taxation.[58] Once the armies set out, attention has focused on why this enormous effort failed to achieve its objectives, namely the recapture of Jerusalem and the reconstitution of a kingdom of Jerusalem that would be viable over the long term. Rudolf Hiestand analysed Frederick Barbarossa's march to the east, showing that the meticulous care with which he controlled and led his army makes all the more telling the consequences of his death in the river Saleph in 1190. That was a bizarre accident that will presumably always remain unexplained.[59]

With the disintegration of most of Barbarossa's host, the fighting in Palestine was left mainly to the French and English armies. And since Philip II returned to France as soon as he decently could, this has entailed focusing on the rival leaders, Saladin and Richard I. Both were brilliant and charismatic men who have attracted biographical studies, including recent ones by M. C. Lyons and D. E. P. Jackson (Saladin) and John Gillingham (Richard).[60] The key questions are why Saladin was unable to complete the task of expelling the Franks, and why Richard failed to recapture Jerusalem. In each case the answer given has tended to be similar, that the resources to which each man had access were insufficient to give him absolute victory. In Saladin's case the issue revolved around the rather *ad hoc* military structures that he had at his disposal, which were not to improve until the inauguration of the Mamluk sultanate in the mid-thirteenth century. For his part, Richard was persuaded that Jerusalem was too isolated from the lands that had been recovered along the coast; even if the crusaders could take it, the city could not be held against a determined Muslim siege afterwards. A strikingly different assessment of Richard's strategy over Jerusalem has recently been offered by Michael Markowski. He has argued that the king was over-cautious in his approach to the issue. He lacked the religious conviction that in a similar strategic situation had driven the leaders of the First Crusade to press on

---

58   Tyerman, *England and the Crusades*, pp. 57–85; P. W. Edbury, 'Preaching the crusade in Wales', in A. Haverkamp and H. Vollrath, eds, *England and Germany in the High Middle Ages* (Oxford: Oxford University Press, 1996), 221–33; R. Hiestand, '"Precipua tocius christianismi columpna". Barbarossa und der Kreuzzug', in A. Haverkamp, ed., *Friedrich Barbarossa. Handlungsspielräume und Wirkungsweisen des Staufischen Kaisers* (Sigmaringen: Jan Thorbecke Verlag, 1992), 51–108; R. Hiestand, 'Kingship and crusade in twelfth-century Germany', in Haverkamp and Vollrath, eds, *England and Germany*, 235–65.

59   Hiestand, 'Precipua tocius christianismi columpna'.

60   M. C. Lyons and D. E. P. Jackson, *Saladin. The Politics of the Holy War* (Cambridge: Cambridge University Press, 1982); J. Gillingham, *Richard the Lionheart* (London: Weidenfeld and Nicolson, 1978). See also J. Gillingham, 'Roger of Howden on crusade', in D. O. Morgan, ed., *Medieval Historical Writing in the Christian and Islamic Worlds* (London: School of Oriental and African Studies, 1982), 60–75; J. Gillingham, 'Richard I and the science of war in the Middle Ages', in *WGMA*, 78–91.

and take Jerusalem by storm in 1099.[61] It is too early to tell whether Markowski's negative assessment will prevail. If it does, it will considerably dent a reputation for leadership that generally has been held to surpass that of any crusader in the east with the exception of Bohemund of Taranto and Antioch.

One of the key factors that enabled Richard I to reconstitute a Latin hold on the Levantine seaboard was the control of the sea-lanes by the fleets of the Italian trading republics. Sea-power had played a significant part in the First and Second Crusades, but it was only with the Third that the extent of its contribution becomes indisputable. The turning point in the crusade was Richard's reconquest of Acre in July 1191, and John Pryor has emphasized how disastrous a blow for Saladin was the Christians' capture of his fleet at anchor in the port: 'The capture of the fleet was as important as the capture of Acre itself; as was shown by the Crusaders' insistence that the surrender of the garrison would be accepted only if the fleet was not destroyed.'[62] This brought to an end the only sustained attempt made during the twelfth and thirteenth century by an Islamic ruler to challenge the Latin dominance of the eastern Mediterranean waters. The latter reaped the crusaders an incalculable harvest in military, commercial and logistical terms, helping to redress the underlying imbalance between the religions in demography, territory and military capacity.[63]

With the Fourth Crusade we reach the *passagium* that more than any other has generated fierce debate.[64] This was the first great crusade launched by Pope Innocent III to carry forward the job of restoring the kingdom of Jerusalem, which Richard I had been forced to leave incomplete when he returned to England in 1192. Yet the army, transported eastwards on Venetian vessels, was diverted first to Zadar in Dalmatia and then to Constantinople, which it captured and sacked. One big question hangs over this sequence of events: did the crusade follow that path because of a conspiracy that was formed before it sailed from Venice, or was the diversion the result of a sequence of accidents? Far from being

---

61 M. Markowski, 'Richard Lionheart: bad king, bad crusader?', *JMH* 23 (1997), 351–65.
62 J. H. Pryor, *Geography, Technology, and War. Studies in the Maritime History of the Mediterranean, 649–1571* (Cambridge: Cambridge University Press, 1988), pp. 112–34, with quote at p. 130.
63 See the essays in *CIRCG*.
64 For an up-to-date bibliography, with essays on the primary sources (by A. J. Andrea) and the literature, see D. E. Queller and T. F. Madden, *The Fourth Crusade. The Conquest of Constantinople* (2nd edn, Philadelphia: University of Pennsylvania Press, 1997). The proceedings of the conference of the Society for the Study of the Crusades and the Latin East held at Instanbul in 2004 will contain a number of essays on the Fourth Crusade.

manufactured by historians, the question was uppermost in the minds of contemporaries. The pope feared that his crusade would be hijacked by the Venetians; while the greatest narrative account, by Geoffrey of Villehardouin, has the overt agenda of proving the 'theory of accidents', or as Villehardouin construed it, the workings of providence. Villehardouin was a leading figure in the expedition and he benefited from the sack of Constantinople by becoming marshal of the Latin empire that was subsequently set up there. Hence much of the difficulty that besets the interpretation of what occurred revolves around his trustworthiness as a source.[65]

The essential features of the two conflicting interpretations are straightforward enough.[66] The main evidence that the conspiracy theorists possess consists of the personal ties that bound the exiled Byzantine prince Alexius with Philip of Swabia, the German magnate whose vassal, Boniface of Montferrat, was elected leader of the crusade when its original commander, Thibaut of Champagne, died unexpectedly in May 1201. In the eyes of the conspiracy theorists the Venetians, and in particular their remarkably able and ambitious doge, Enrico Dandolo, saw in these ties, and the crusade generally, a wonderful opportunity to exert control over a trading city that had long been crucially important to their prosperity but whose Greek rulers had become capricious in their behaviour towards western merchants. The conspiracy's leaders were able to engineer the diversion due to the financial quandary that the crusaders faced when insufficient numbers arrived to embark at Venice; they simply could not afford what they had offered for their transport to the east. First the Venetians offered a deferment of payment in exchange for the crusaders' help in taking Zadar, a Christian city that had rebelled against them. Then, when the debts again threatened to bring the crusade to a premature end, the pretender Alexius made the highly attractive offer that took the crusaders to the shores of the Bosphorus. Initially they helped Alexius to regain control of Constantinople for himself and his father; but when Alexius proved unable to provide what he had promised and renounced his pact, the crusaders and Venetians stormed the city and installed themselves as its rulers. The plan had been realized.[67]

The central problem with the conspiracy theory is that there exists no piece of evidence that shows Philip of Swabia, Boniface of Montferrat and

---

65 C. Morris, 'Geoffrey of Villehardouin and the Conquest of Constantinople', *History* 53 (1968), 24–34; P. Noble, 'The importance of Old French chronicles as historical sources of the Fourth Crusade and the early Latin empire of Constantinople', *JMH* 27 (2001), 399–416.
66 T. Madden, 'Outside and inside the Fourth Crusade', *IHR* 17 (1995), 726–43.
67 J. Godfrey, *1204: The Unholy Crusade* (Oxford: Oxford University Press, 1980).

Enrico Dandolo plotting this series of events. An alleged agreement between the Venetians and the Ayyubids, the dynasty established by Saladin in Egypt and Syria, which committed the city to diverting the crusade in exchange for payment, rests on no historical evidence, though it continues to be referred to by conspiracy theorists from time to time.[68] The evidence therefore has to be indirect, and it is of two kinds. First, there is the argument *ex silentio*, a good example being Villehardouin's failure to mention that he was familiar with Alexius's attempts to raise western support for his cause long before the prince appeared at the crusader camp at Zadar. This is one of the very few occasions when Villehardouin can be observed making an attempt to cover his tracks.[69] There is also the remarkable fact that no contemporary Venetian account exists of an expedition that brought the city such enormous conquests and commercial benefits.[70] In the second place, there is a cluster of circumstantial evidence. For example, it is striking that so many crusaders independently decided to embark for the Holy Land from ports other than Venice, showing, perhaps, that rumours of a conspiracy were circulating widely. Then there is the undeniable fact that the Venetians, who were so well acquainted with Constantinople, knew perfectly well that Alexius would not be able to meet the generous terms he agreed with the crusaders; arguably, therefore, they planned the Latin conquest of the city all along.

The chief arguments in favour of the theory of accidents relate to the nature of the crusade and the insuperable problems that its indebtedness entailed for both crusaders and Venetians. The Fourth Crusade was rather anomalous because, after two *passagia* that were led to the east by kings, who naturally took the major decisions after consulting with their barons, there was a reversion to the baronial leadership that had characterized the First Crusade; men like Thibaut of Champagne, Louis of Blois and Baldwin of Flanders could not hope to provide the well-stocked treasure chests of Barbarossa and Richard of England. Going by sea was known to be costly and the deal concluded by Villehardouin and the others sent to negotiate with Venice was not a particularly bad one. It did however hinge on anticipated numbers that were pitched too high, a mistake that could just as easily derive from human error as from a preformed master plan. Once that was appreciated, a remorseless logic set in. Both the crusaders and the Venetians, whose normal commercial activities had largely been suspended, had to do something dramatic to retrieve the situation. The

---

68 Queller and Madden, *The Fourth Crusade*, p. 51 and p. 235 note 84.
69 Morris, 'Geoffrey of Villehardouin', pp. 32–3.
70 D. M. Nicol, *Byzantium and Venice. A Study in Diplomatic and Cultural Relations* (Cambridge: Cambridge University Press, 1988), pp. 124–6.

diversions, first to Zadar and then to Constantinople, were natural choices to make.[71]

This is essentially the line set out by Villehardouin, who portrays the events of the crusade as a series of difficult decisions that were made in the hope of keeping the host together so that it could eventually reach its longed-for destination. Anguished debates about the legitimacy of what was proposed preceded each diversion. Villehardouin had little time for the opponents of diversion; in his eyes they were misguided because they were prepared to envisage the break-up of the host. Nonetheless, both he and others reported their arguments in detail, and it has become clear that far from being the readily acceptable, even predictable, outcome of more than a century of deteriorating relations between the Greeks and Latins, the capture of Constantinople by the Fourth Crusade came about only after much debate and anguish. It was also informed throughout by an awareness of the juristic context and implications.[72] This of course does not invalidate the conspiracy theory, but it does make it necessary for the exponents of that theory to make a very strong case, much more solid than the one that is usually advanced.

In recent years the theory of accidents has been in the ascendancy. A group of distinguished American scholars – Donald Queller, Thomas Madden and Alfred Andrea – have all advanced it.[73] They have been assisted by two broader trends. One is the collapse of the argument that anti-Byzantine feeling grew inexorably in the west throughout the twelfth century. Byzantinists such as Michael Angold and Jonathan Harris have shown that the situation was much more complex. Westerners had no fixed image of Byzantium at the time of the crusade, and certainly not one that was suffused by hatred and greed; 'the crusaders carried with them a blurred image of Byzantium, in which there jostled marvels, tyrants and disinherited princes'.[74] The trouble was that once the crusade entered Constantinople's 'force field' prejudices began to reassert themselves, and these included the ingrained belief that the Byzantines had failed to play their rightful part in defending the Latin East.[75] Secondly, historians of the

---

71 Queller and Madden, *The Fourth Crusade*.

72 R. Schmandt, 'The Fourth Crusade and the just war theory', *CHR* 61 (1975), 191–221; T. Madden, 'Vows and contracts in the Fourth Crusade: the treaty of Zara and the attack on Constantinople in 1204', *IHR* 15 (1993), 441–68.

73 Queller and Madden, *The Fourth Crusade*; A. J. Andrea, ed., *The Capture of Constantinople. The 'Hystoria Constantinopolitana' of Gunther of Pairis* (Philadelphia: University of Pennsylvania Press, 1997); Andrea, ed., *Contemporary Sources for the Fourth Crusade* (Leiden: Brill, 2000).

74 M. Angold, *The Fourth Crusade. Event and Context* (Harlow: Pearson Longman, 2003), pp. 70–1.

75 Angold, *The Fourth Crusade*; Angold, 'The road to 1204'; Harris, *Byzantium and the Crusades*, p. 184.

Fourth Crusade, in common with those of most crusades, have laid stress on the difficulty that the leaders of the *passagia* experienced in steering the great hosts that they were supposed to command; if men like Barbarossa and Richard I found the exercise of command a constant challenge, was it really likely that Boniface of Montferrat could divert the Fourth Crusade?

The difference, arguably, lay in the Venetian contingent, which was not only much more coherent but was led by their own doge.[76] Dandolo has always been the *bête noire* of the Fourth Crusade, and it is undeniable that one of Villehardouin's most naive passages is the one in which he describes, without irony, the rush of the Venetians to take the cross once the diversion to Zadar was agreed upon. Incidents occurred that throw a disturbing light on Venetian attitudes towards the crusade. For example, Robert of Clari, a relatively low-ranking participant, claimed that the Venetians kept the crusaders cooped up on the Lido and used their control over the supplying of the host to exert pressure on their leaders. On the other hand, such a pragmatic, even brutal approach was only to be expected from a city that depended on commerce to survive. A modern historian of Veneto-Byzantine relations, Donald Nicol, argued that Venice never really subscribed to the crusading spirit, but this seems to ignore or play down the Venetian tradition of involvement in the Holy Land crusades.[77] Nicol was an ebullient representative of the 'investigative journalist' school of history, which believes one of the historian's key jobs to be that of penetrating a fog of dissimulation created by wily contemporaries to cover their tracks. We shall return to this issue in the next chapter, but it is important to point out here that even if Venice's commitment to the Fourth Crusade could be shown to be based exclusively on cost-benefit analysis, a recent study by John Pryor of the shipping that the Venetians provided points towards their anticipation of the crusaders landing, not in the Bosphorus, but in the Nile delta.[78]

As it transpired, the first crusade to land in the Nile delta and attempt to implement the strategy of attacking 'the serpent's head' was the Fifth, which was launched by Innocent III in 1213, and preceded by the greatest of the medieval Church councils, Lateran IV, in 1215. Much of the scholarship of the Fifth Crusade has focused on its origins as a mature project of Innocent III. This has included its relationship not just to the Fourth Crusade, whose mistakes Innocent obviously planned to avoid

---

76 T. Madden, *Enrico Dandolo and the Rise of Venice* (Baltimore, MD: Johns Hopkins University Press, 2003).
77 Nicol, *Byzantium and Venice*, pp. 74, 79–80, 115, 124–47.
78 J. Pryor, 'The Venetian fleet for the Fourth Crusade and the diversion of the crusade to Constantinople', in *EC*, 103–23.

repeating, but also to the crusades that the pope had previously declared in Spain and southern France. Of particular importance were Innocent's attempt to ensure that the crusade was adequately funded by measures of clerical taxation, and his application of the radically new approach towards preaching the cross, allowing people who were not fit to fight to redeem their vows in exchange for cash payments.[79] It has even been suggested that the pope was content that the political situation meant that none of western Europe's monarchs could take part, and was hoping to make the crusade exclusively an enterprise of the Church, but this is not supported by the evidence.[80] In any case, this emphasis on Innocent may change as the crusading policy of Pope Honorius III (1216–27) starts to receive more detailed and sympathetic attention.[81]

Part of the Fifth Crusade's background, 'a prelude and a precondition' as Gary Dickson has put it, was the crusade of the *pueri* of 1212. This has generally ceased to be regarded as a 'Children's Crusade', which derives from a mistranslation of *puer*; like *miles* a century earlier, it is a difficult word to translate ('lad' or 'kid'?) but carries mixed connotations of poverty and rootlessness.[82] As Alphandéry noted, the crusade of the *pueri* was the most significant resurgence of 'popular crusading' since 1096, but on this occasion there was no participation by nobles.[83] Rather, as Dickson has shown, its background was the process by which the Church had fostered liturgical intercessions on behalf of the Holy Land since Hattin. The immediate context was highly complicated: it seems to have consisted of preaching for the Albigensian Crusade, processions organized to beseech God to assist the cause of the faith in Spain, and a continuing sense of grieving for the lost True Cross, expressed in the cry: 'Lord God, give us back the True Cross!' ('Domine Deus, redde nobis veram crucem!'). There was also a strong sense of innocence, a natural response to the association, so dear to Innocent III and his circle, between clerical and social reform and the mounting of a successful crusade.[84]

What took place during the Fifth Crusade, from the disappointing initial campaigns in the Holy Land, through the arduous siege and capture of the

---

79 J. M. Powell, *Anatomy of a Crusade 1213–1221*, The Middle Ages (Philadelphia: University of Pennsylvania Press, 1986), pp. 13–120.

80 Mayer, *The Crusades*, 2nd edn, p. 217; Powell, *Anatomy*, pp. 108–9.

81 For example, R. Rist, 'Papal policy and the Albigensian Crusades: continuity or change?' *Crusades* 2 (2003), 99–108.

82 P. Raedts, 'The Children's Crusade of 1212', *JMH* 3 (1977), 279–323.

83 Alphandéry, *La Chrétienté*, 2: 115–48.

84 Dickson, 'La genèse'; G. Dickson, 'Stephen of Cloyes, Philip Augustus, and the Children's Crusade of 1212', in B. N. Sargent-Baur, ed., *Journeys Towards God. Pilgrimage and Crusade* (Kalamazoo: Medieval Institute Publications, Western Michigan University, 1992), 83–105.

port of Damietta, to the disastrous march inland from Damietta, has probably attracted less recent scholarship than the events of any of the preceding crusades to the east.[85] This is surely not because of the absence of problems in explaining how such a massive investment of resources could fail; rather, it is due to the paucity of the sources, for the only detailed narrative account is that of Oliver of Paderborn, the versatile *scholasticus* of Cologne, who in addition to being a chronicler was an effective preacher and a skilful engineer. Attention has tended to focus on the leadership issue, in particular on the controversial role that was played by the Portuguese legate, Pelagius, cardinal bishop of Albano. In 1950 Joseph Donovan laid most of the blame for the crusade's failure at the door of Pelagius, 'a man of driving energy but hopelessly shortsighted, autocratic, self-satisfied, and uncommonly pigheaded', as Mayer described him.[86] James Powell attributed the disaster more broadly to the inadequate machinery that was set up for making effective decisions in the field.[87]

In June 1228 the Emperor Frederick II sailed with forty ships to Acre. His expedition is traditionally given the name the Sixth Crusade, though recently it has been plausibly suggested that it would be more accurate to regard it as the last act in the Fifth.[88] Certainly, one reason for the Fifth Crusade's failure was Frederick's delay in leading an army east, which he had sworn to do at the time of his coronation as king of Germany in 1215. His expedition in 1228–9 managed to be both anti-climactic and highly controversial. Leading a comparatively small force, all that the emperor could achieve was a truce whose terms secured most of the holy sites of Jerusalem for the Christians, but without a defensive perimeter and largely cut off from the land held by the Christians along the coast. As the sole achievement of a ruler whose lands stretched from Sicily to the Baltic, this was bitterly disappointing, but at the same time the months Frederick spent in the Latin East proved to be intensely divisive due to his strenuous pressing of his dynastic claims in Cyprus and the kingdom of Jerusalem, and his status as an excommunicate. Study of these events has concentrated first on the political and constitutional issues involved, and secondly on the place that crusading and the kingdom of Jerusalem held within Frederick's own view of his role. The trend in recent scholarship has been

---

85 Powell, *Anatomy*, pp. 121–204.
86 J. Donovan, *Pelagius and the Fifth Crusade* (Philadelphia: University of Pennsylvania Press, 1950); Mayer, *The Crusades*, 2nd edn, p. 223.
87 Powell, *Anatomy*, pp. 107–20.
88 Powell, *Anatomy*, pp. 195–203; J. M. Powell, 'Crusading by royal command: monarchy and crusade in the kingdom of Sicily', in *Potere, società e popolo tra età normanna ed età sveva (1187–1230)* (Bari: Centro di studi normanno-svevi, University of Bari, 1983), 131–46.

to argue that Frederick took his crusade vow seriously and intended that his expedition to the east should be an impressive one. The emperor was interested in prevailing eschatological ideas that associated the imperial office with Jerusalem, and it is likely that his wearing of his imperial crown in the Church of the Holy Sepulchre was a richly symbolic act, despite the dismissive comments of his critics.[89]

The 'Barons' Crusade' of 1239–41 was a very different type of expedition from Frederick's. Consisting of two separate armies recruited by Thibaut of Champagne and Richard of Cornwall, it began life as an attempt by the papal *curia* to anticipate the end of the ten-year truce sealed by Frederick II in 1229. The campaigns conducted by Thibaut and Richard in Palestine were lacklustre: like Frederick before them, they had comparatively few troops, and had to reckon with the wishes of the resident Franks, who ever since Saladin's death had grasped that their survival hinged on their playing off the rival branches of the Ayyubid dynasty in Egypt and Syria. The 'Barons' Crusade' has therefore largely been studied in terms of the interplay of politics in the Holy Land,[90] though recently Michael Lower has used it as a test case to study how far Pope Gregory IX's ambitions to 'manage' the crusading efforts of Christendom were compatible with the wishes and goals of the lay nobility.[91]

In 1244 Jerusalem was recovered by the Muslims and the sultan of Egypt won a decisive victory at Harbiyyah (Gaza, La Forbie) over his kinsman the sultan of Damascus, who was allied with the Franks. This disastrous situation persuaded King Louis IX of France to take the cross in thanks for his recovery from a serious illness, and the crusade that followed, traditionally termed the Seventh, proved to be the biggest exertion of military power since the Fifth Crusade. Harbiyyah made it clear that Muslim power must be confronted in the Nile delta, and Louis imitated the strategy of the Fifth Crusade by landing at Damietta in 1249. He quickly captured the port, but as in the case of the earlier crusade, it was managing the march inland that confounded the westerners. Louis and the whole of his army were captured in 1250 and had to be ransomed, Damietta itself forming part of the price. Sailing not back

---

89   R. Hiestand, 'Friedrich II. und der Kreuzzug', in A. Esch and N. Kamp, eds, *Friedrich II. Tagung des Deutschen Historischen Instituts in Rom in Gedenkjahr 1994* (Tübingen: Max Niemeyer Verlag, 1996), 128–49; D. Abulafia, *Frederick II. A Medieval Emperor* (London: Allen Lane, 1988), pp. 164–201.
90   P. Jackson, 'The crusades of 1239–41 and their aftermath', *Bulletin of the School of Oriental and African Studies* 50 (1987), 32–60.
91   Painter, 'The crusade'. Michael Lower's study is forthcoming.

to France but to Acre, Louis spent four constructive years in the Latin states before returning to France in 1254.[92]

For many reasons the Seventh Crusade has been a favourite of historians, especially of French ones. It was predominantly a French enterprise,[93] led by the ruler whose reputation persists as medieval France's most brilliant and charismatic king. Moreover, Louis's period in the east was described in considerable detail by his friend and biographer Joinville, whose *Vie de saint Louis* is an immensely attractive text.[94] In recent years Louis's life has been the subject of two substantial studies. Jean Richard placed crusading central to Louis's reign and his conception of his kingship, while Jacques Le Goff accorded it less significance.[95] What is certain is that the preparation of Louis's attack on Egypt, which was reconstructed in the fullest of detail in 1979 by W. C. Jordan, showed how impressive the administrative reach of the Capetian monarchy had become, while at the same time acting as the stimulus and justification for a significant exertion of royal demands across the kingdom.[96] In turn, for all the personal humility he showed while on crusade, Louis IX acted not just as a particularly important crusader, but also as king of France. Jean Richard has shown that he regarded captured Damietta as annexed to the royal domain, and while in the Holy Land any infringement of his perceived majesty as king of France was severely punished.[97] The shock of Louis's failure was so great that it generated a further 'popular crusade', the crusade of the *pastoureaux* (shepherds) in France in 1251.[98]

It was during Louis IX's captivity in Egypt that the Ayyubid dynasty was toppled by a clique of its own Mamluk slaves, who inaugurated a new regime based on an oligarchy of officers.[99] They quickly extended their power into the former Ayyubid lands in Syria, and there is general agree-

92   J. R. Strayer, 'The crusades of Louis IX', in *HC* 2: 487–518.

93   Though not exclusively: see, for example, S. Lloyd, 'William Longespee II: the making of an English crusading hero', *Nottingham Medieval Studies* 35 (1991), 41–69; 36 (1992), 79–125.

94   J. Dufournet and L. Harf, eds, *Le Prince et son historien. La vie de saint Louis de Joinville* (Paris: Honoré Champion Éditeur, 1997).

95   J. Richard, *Saint Louis. Crusader King of France*, trans. J. Birrell (Cambridge: Cambridge University Press, 1992); J. Le Goff, *Saint Louis* (Paris: Gallimard, 1996).

96   W. C. Jordan, *Louis IX and the Challenge of the Crusade. A Study in Rulership* (Princeton, NJ: Princeton University Press, 1979).

97   J. Richard, 'La Fondation d'une église latine en Orient par saint Louis: Damiette', *BEC* 120 (1962), 39–54.

98   M. Barber, 'The crusade of the shepherds in 1251', in J. F. Sweets, ed., *Proceedings of the Tenth Annual Meeting of the Western Society for French History* (Lawrence, KS: Western Society for French History, 1984), 1–23.

99   R. Irwin, *The Middle East in the Middle Ages. The Early Mamluk Sultanate 1250–1382* (London: Croom Helm, 1986).

ment that their first great leader, Sultan Baybars, posed the gravest threat to the Franks since Saladin.[100] Baybars pursued his campaigns with ruthlessness and urgency because of his fear that the Mongols, who had overrun Iran and Iraq, might join forces with a new crusade from the west to crush the Mamluk lands. In 1267, reacting to news of Baybars's conquests, Louis IX took the cross for a second time. The resulting expedition has received much less attention than the king's first crusade. In part this is because the sources are disappointingly patchy. Joinville refused to accompany his king on this new venture, and although we have indications of intensive preparations, such as the contract for service that was made with the future Edward I of England, most of the records seem to have been lost.[101]

The biggest problem surrounding the crusade is Louis IX's decision to lead his army in the first instance to Tunisia. Landing near the ancient site of Carthage, the king fell ill in the summer heat and died in August 1270. This Tunisian diversion used to be seen as the outcome of leverage exerted by Charles of Anjou, Louis's younger brother. Charles had recently been crowned king of Sicily and he wanted to re-establish the protectorate over Tunisia exercised by his Norman predecessors; the comparison with the Fourth Crusade and the role supposedly played by Doge Dandolo is apparent. But as with the earlier crusade, clinching evidence is lacking. It would also have been curiously out of character if Louis had allowed himself to be duped in this way; unlike the Fourth Crusade this was an army under strong central command. The king's decision to incorporate a landing in north Africa into his plans is more satisfactorily explained in terms of the contemporary report that the emir of Tunis had secretly converted to Christianity; this was made known to Louis and he wanted to do all that he could to facilitate the conversion of the Tunisians.[102] Whatever the reason for it, the Tunisian diversion proved fatal not just for Louis but for his crusade. As Joseph Strayer put it, 'the age of the great crusades, led by the kings of the west, had ended'.[103] Most of the king's companions returned home in sorrow, though Edward of England and a small force progressed to the Holy Land.[104] Edward could do little to

---

100 P. Thorau, *The Lion of Egypt. Sultan Baybars I and the Near East in the Thirteenth Century*, trans. P. M. Holt (London: Longman, 1987).

101 Jordan, *Louis IX*, pp. 214–17; Richard, *Saint Louis*, pp. 293–329; Le Goff, *Saint Louis*, pp. 290–7.

102 Richard, *Saint Louis*, pp. 320–4; J. Longnon, 'Les Vues de Charles d'Anjou pour la deuxième croisade de Saint-Louis: Tunis ou Constantinople?' *Septième centenaire de la mort de Saint-Louis. Actes des colloques de Royaumont et de Paris* (Paris, 1976), 183–95.

103 Strayer, 'The crusades of Louis IX', p. 518.

104 B. Beebe, 'The English baronage and the crusade of 1270', *BIHR* 48 (1975), 127–49; S. Lloyd, 'The Lord Edward's crusade, 1270–2: its setting and significance', in *WGMA*, 120–33.

counter Baybars's attacks, and further attempts to organize a *passagium* to stave off disaster proved unsuccessful.[105] In 1291, when they stormed the port city of Acre, the Mamluks finally extinguished the Frankish settlements in the Holy Land.

---

105   V. Laurent, 'La Croisade et la question d'orient sous le pontificat de Grégoire X (1272–1276)', *Revue historique du sud-est européen* 22 (1945), 105–37; Throop, *Criticism*, pp. 214–82. As noted earlier, Gregory X's crusade plans need to be reinvestigated.

4

The Intentions and Motivations of Crusaders

'Men hold different opinions about the way [of God]. Some say that the wish to go has been aroused in all pilgrims by God and the lord Jesus Christ; others that it was through lightheadedness that the Frankish magnates and the multitudes were moved.'[1] Albert of Aachen's comment on the First Crusade shows that a fascination with what caused people to take the cross has existed almost from the first point at which they did so. This is not hard to explain. As had long been the case with pilgrimage,[2] the reason for the fascination with intention resided in the voluntary nature of the act and the range of reasons that might lie behind it. There has always been a natural curiosity about what fuelled the *voluntas* and triggered the decision; why particular individuals or groups were susceptible to the appeal of crusading, as they had been to that of pilgrimage, and what tipped this into commitment. Since crusades were preached in terms of religious faith, a perception existed that individuals and groups might feign devotion to conceal ulterior motives for action. This too had characterized criticism of pilgrimage,[3] but it applied with greater force in the case of crusading because of the opportunities for personal gain that the practice opened up. From the start contemporaries did not shrink from condemning crusaders when

---

1   Quoted in Riley-Smith, 'Early crusaders', pp. 244–5.
2   D. Webb, *Medieval European Pilgrimage, c. 700–c. 1500* (Basingstoke: Palgrave, 2002), pp. 44–77.
3   G. Constable, 'Opposition to pilgrimage in the Middle Ages', *Studia Gratiana* 19 (1976), 123–46.

they thought their actions called for it, as when Orderic Vitalis stated that Bohemund's expedition of 1107 deserved to fail because it was unjustly attacking Byzantine lands.[4]

Taking the First Crusade as an example, there is no doubt that the cluster of narrative accounts that were written very soon after it came to a close owed their existence not just to the expedition's extraordinary success in regaining Jerusalem for Christianity, but also to a fascination with why so many thousands of individuals had responded to Pope Urban II's summons. For the sake of comparison, if Jerusalem had been captured by a Byzantine army bolstered by large numbers of western mercenaries raised with the help of the pope, the interest aroused by the event would surely have been much less. As for the issue of 'right intention', it arose in two contexts. For its part, the Church was always conscious that what was being promoted as a holy war carried the possibility of material gain for those taking part, which could create unworthy motives. In theological terms, the devil, who was constantly striving to undermine the Church's mission of saving souls, could cause it to place the laity in greater danger of damnation by encouraging them not just to dissimulate, but to engage in activity that was sinful. Hence the strong emphasis on pure intention found in the recorded decree of the Clermont Council: 'Whoever for devotion alone, not to gain honour or money, goes to Jerusalem to liberate the Church of God can substitute this journey for all penance.'[5] There is evidence in the early history of the Templars that such concerns afflicted thoughtful fighting men as well as clerics.[6] On the other hand, those who had good reasons to be hostile to or wary of the crusaders seized on the idea of false motivation to discredit their opponents or explain their actions. Islamic historians such as Ibn al-Athir and Ibn Taghribirdi dismissed crusading piety as gullibility that was exploited by the greedy or ambitious;[7] and Anna Comnena made a distinction that was very likely commonplace at Constantinople by the time she wrote her account of her father's exploits: 'The simpler folk were in very truth led on by a desire to worship at Our Lord's tomb and visit the holy places, but the more

---

4 M. Chibnall, ed. and trans., *The Ecclesiastical History of Orderic Vitalis, Volume III, Books V and VI* (Oxford: Oxford University Press, 1972), Bk 5, pp. 182–3.

5 L. and J. Riley-Smith, ed. and trans., *The Crusades. Idea and Reality, 1095–1274* (London: Edward Arnold, 1981), p. 37. See also Somerville, 'Clermont 1095'.

6 J. Leclercq, ed., 'Un document sur les débuts des Templiers', *Revue d'histoire ecclésiastique* 52 (1957), 81–91. Cf. the qualms of no less a figure than the patriarch of Jerusalem some decades later: J. Leclercq, 'Gratien, Pierre de Troyes et la seconde croisade', *Studia Gratiana* 2 (1954), 583–93; Hehl, *Kirche und Krieg*, pp. 154–8.

7 C. Hillenbrand, *The Crusades. Islamic Perspectives* (Edinburgh: Edinburgh University Press, 1999), p. 314.

villainous characters (in particular Bohemund and his like) had an ulterior purpose, for they hoped on their journey to seize the capital itself, looking upon its capture as a natural consequence of the expedition.'[8]

Following the lead set by contemporaries, nearly all historians of the crusades have accepted that the exploration of intention lies within their brief. Words like 'intention' and 'motivation' are not easy to define with precision, but the agenda that they somewhat clumsily seek to delineate is clear enough, consisting of the spectrum of goals, hopes, beliefs and fears that first impelled people to take the cross and later sustained them while they were on crusade. So integral is a grasp of this spectrum to the work undertaken by historians of crusading that none have isolated it as a separate topic for analysis. No book, and relatively few articles or essays, address the issue of intention head-on, but this is far from indicating a lack of interest; rather, such interest is all-pervasive in the corpus of work written about crusading. This makes a chapter like this one unusually challenging to write. It seems best to handle the issue in two parts; first, we shall consider some general questions relating to it, then we shall review the lines of enquiry that have been pursued with regard to each of the major groups that participated in the crusades. The latter approach does not imply a determinism based on group identity: it is simply a methodology suggested by the nature of the evidence.

General Issues

We saw in chapter 2 that a distinctive feature of recent writing on the First Crusade has been a retreat from a materialist explanation of its causality, and the same applies to the whole span of crusading to the east. With one exception, no structural explanation of crusading in economic terms exists.[9] On the whole, Marxist historians did not engage with the subject. There are only passing references to the crusades in Perry Anderson's ambitious *Passages from Antiquity to Feudalism* (1974).[10] Rodney Hilton's treatment of crusading, written at much the same time as Anderson's, is revealing because, taking his cue from the popularist

---

8   E. R. A. Sewter, trans., *The Alexiad of Anna Comnena* (Harmondsworth: Penguin Books, 1969), p. 311.
9   The exception is G. M. Anderson et al., 'An economic interpretation of the medieval crusades', *Journal of European Economic History* 21 (1992), 339–63, but this is crude and eccentric methodologically. See L. García-Guijarro Ramos, 'Expansión económica medieval y cruzadas', in *PCNAD*, 155–66, at pp. 162–6.
10   P. Anderson, *Passages from Antiquity to Feudalism* (London: NLB, 1974), pp. 151 note 7, 193, 244.

school, he emphasized the eschatological beliefs that impelled the 'people's crusades'. Hilton took it as read that the lords were 'land-hungry' and 'acquisitive', but he accepted that non-noble participants had a primarily religious motivation.[11] The surge of interest in crusading studies that has occurred since Anderson and Hilton wrote has been conducted largely by historians who are sympathetic (in no naive sense) to a primarily religious interpretation of what occurred. For the most part this is a positive development, but one result has been a disturbing imbalance in the literature. It is not helped by the bifurcation that has arisen between historians who study the nature of settlement in the Latin East, the development of east–west trade, and the politics and military affairs of the settlers, on the one hand, and those who focus on the series of crusading *passagia* on the other. This bifurcation is far from total: there are leading historians, such as Rudolf Hiestand and Jonathan Riley-Smith, who have illuminated both the crusading expeditions and the history of the Latin East. But a certain fragmentation has taken place, partly because the sheer volume of published work has made it increasingly difficult to keep up with developments in both areas of study.

In practice this means that there is a danger of crusading being 'westernized', of the practice being explained mainly if not exclusively in terms of what was happening within the 'heartlands' where crusaders were recruited, and largely with regard to the religious and social lives of those who took the cross. In recent studies of the First Crusade, for example, irrespective of the interpretative line that their authors follow, events that took place in the lands east of the Adriatic have become less and less prominent. Similarly, research into the Second and Third Crusades has been conducted with comparatively little reference to the commercial activities of the Italian communes;[12] this is all the more striking given that Genoese interest in Spain has begun to attract interest with respect to early crusading there.[13] It is possible that the links between the great *passagia* and commercial expansion in the central Middle Ages actually were circumstantial, and that this detachment between the two will persist. But it seems more likely that new relationships will be discovered and explored. As for the settlers in the Latin East, there are

---

11   R. Hilton, *Bond Men Made Free. Medieval Peasant Movements and the English Rising of 1381* (repr., London: Routledge, 1986), pp. 97–102, with quotes at p. 98. Hilton dismissed poor harvests as a factor and referred instead to population pressure, 'if a socio-economic foundation for these events is sought': ibid., p. 99 and note 6.

12   With some exceptions, notably the papers in *CIRCG*.

13   For example, J. B. Williams, 'The making of a crusade: the Genoese anti-Muslim attacks in Spain, 1146–1148', *JMH* 23 (1997), 29–53.

already signs that their role in the generation and control of crusading is attracting fresh attention.[14]

There is a big difference, however, between establishing an appropriate balance between the roots and expression of crusading in east and west, and attributing it primarily to economic or indeed political causes. It is unlikely that the emphasis placed by recent research on devotional motivations will be overturned and that a materialist interpretation will be put forward with authority. This is not because it is inherently misguided to explain crusading in materialist terms; we shall see in the next chapter that historians of the Baltic crusades remain alert to the association of their subject with a process of conquest, subjugation and extraction that was more overt, and often cruder, than in the Latin East. Rather, it is because the devotional motivations that have been put forward are both appropriately nuanced and firmly embedded in broader contexts, cultural as well as economic and social. That is to say, there is no question of a simple choice between a 'genuinely religious' motivation and one that was 'profit-based', the first unhelpfully vague and the second overly precise, and both anachronistic. We have seen that the contemporary emphasis was on 'intention', and this is much more useful as a methodological tool. It required participants to engage in a dialogue with their consciences; like the comparable demand that anybody who was to receive the crusader's indulgence should be both contrite and confessed, it placed on individuals the onus of self-examination, in the knowledge that God saw all that they thought and did. It would be folly to assume that all did so or that those that did were incapable of self-deception, but there is much evidence to back up the view that people who took the cross were far from being the unreflective and greedy fanatics of one stereotypical view that still, regrettably, persists.

The retreat from a materialist interpretation has been accompanied by some attempts to enter the minds of crusaders, to read a psychology that by common assent was very different from our own.[15] This brings with it a whole group of problems, of which the most glaring is the comparative scarcity of surviving evidence. Take, for example, the extension of the crusader's indulgence that occurred from the late twelfth century onwards to a whole spectrum of groups, including clerics who preached the cross and collected money for it, and the wives of those who set out.[16] Common sense would lead us to suppose that this was a form of debasement, in so far as spiritual reward was prised free from the context

---

14   Phillips, *Defenders*; Riley-Smith, *The First Crusaders*, pp. 169–88.
15   Notably Riley-Smith, 'The state of mind'.
16   Brundage, *Medieval Canon Law and the Crusader*, pp. 154–5.

of exacting *imitatio Christi* that had given rise to it. We would expect a dilution of devotion; yet we cannot support this with evidence because so little exists. The abundant reports submitted by papal collectors, in particular, are uninformative about the responses that they encountered, nor is there any reason to expect otherwise.[17] Also in the thirteenth century, there is evidence for royal lawyers and administrators registering discontent with *crucesignati* who were not embarking for the east to fulfil their vows, but in the mean time were enjoying the legal benefits, notably stay of justice (*essoin*) and a moratorium on the payment of interest on debts, to which canon law entitled people who had taken the cross. This points to an abuse of the crusade and an underlying attitude that was lacking in reverence, but because we possess only the complaints, not the replies of the *crucesignati*, we can rarely be confident about such judgements.[18]

Nor is the situation much clearer in the case of those who did set out. We have a good deal of evidence for the quotidian lives of crusaders on campaign, and naturally it has received some attention. But it points in contrary directions. On the one hand, we witness an impressive array of devotional activities, much penitential zeal, and ascetic practices that display considerable ingenuity.[19] On the other hand, it is quite clear that every crusading army was accompanied by prostitutes, who were expelled (though never very far) when God's wrath seemed to manifest itself.[20] Gambling in the form of dice was also popular, and blasphemy was common. These two images may be considered as complementary rather than opposites. No army in the field could be expected to maintain the level of behaviour depicted in the first image, but during crises the nature of the enterprise took pride of place, creating a heightened religious ethos that approximated to it. None the less, if behaviour on campaign fluctuated in this way, can we learn anything useful from it about underlying intention? It can even be argued that the constant stresses imposed by campaigning, especially the incessant demands of safety and subsistence, constitute barren soil for ascertaining what took participants there in the first place. So behaviour may not be a reliable guide to motivation, a point to which we shall return. Given that so much of the evidence that purports to spell out motivations is located in narratives that were com-

---

17   The fullest published series is for Italy: P. Guidi et al., eds, *Rationes decimarum Italiae nei secoli XIII e XIV* (13 vols, Rome: Vatican City, 1932–52).

18   Brundage, *Medieval Canon Law and the Crusader*, pp. 159–90.

19   McGinn, 'Iter sancti sepulchri'; Riley-Smith, *The First Crusade*, pp. 91–119.

20   For sex-workers on the First, Third, Fifth and Seventh Crusades see Brundage, 'Prostitution' (Alan Murray is currently re-examining the issue); Tyerman, *England and the Crusades*, pp. 62–3; Powell, *Anatomy*, p. 185; J. Monfrin, ed. and trans., *Joinville, Vie de saint Louis* (Paris: Dunod, 1995), ch. 171, pp. 84–5.

posed once campaigns had drawn to a close, this makes life difficult. Where can we hope to discover what impelled crusaders?

A partial answer to that question may lie in two bodies of evidence that have recently begun to attract attention. Most of the sources for the First Crusade derive from the clerical *élite*, though it is possible that the *Gesta Francorum* forms a notable exception.[21] From the Second Crusade onwards, however, we have in addition to such sources a growing corpus of texts written by laymen, usually in the vernacular. Some are narrative accounts, but others are exhortatory, reflective, retrospective or elegiac, poems and songs being prominent among them.[22] The crusade cycles in the *Chansons de geste* represent the most impressive of the literary texts and they have been the subject of close study.[23] In such sources we find the crusading message being interpreted in ways that we can assume fitted closely the values and beliefs of their patrons and audiences, who were largely aristocratic.[24] A few of the sources are famous, notably Joinville's *Vie de saint Louis*. Joinville's account contains a detailed narrative account of the king's Egyptian crusade, but it is much more than that: an account of a friendship, a portrait of ideal Christian kingship, and a window into Joinville's own view of what crusading meant. It is descriptive, explanatory, didactic, apologetic, devotional and much else besides.[25] By the mid-thirteenth century the laity had found its own voice in such literature; their attitudes towards crusading, including their reasons for continuing to take the cross (or not doing so), become clearer, although as always due allowance has to be made for the special character of the evidence.

Secondly, although medieval historians still tend to neglect visual evidence, much recent research has been conducted into celebrations of crusading in sculpture and painting.[26] At the very least, these depictions have a good deal to tell us about attitudes. For example, Nurith Kenaan-Kedar and Benjamin Kedar have plausibly suggested that the moving

---

21 Edgington, 'The First Crusade'. Marcus Bull is engaged on a new edition and study of the *Gesta Francorum*.

22 M. Routledge, 'Songs', in *OIHC*, 91–111; Trotter, *Medieval French Literature*; N. Daniel, *Heroes and Saracens. An Interpretation of the Chansons de geste* (Edinburgh: Edinburgh University Press, 1984); C. T. J. Dijkstra, *La Chanson de croisade. Étude thématique d'un genre hybride* (Amsterdam, 1995); Noble, 'The importance'.

23 J. A. Nelson and E. J. Mickel, eds, *The Old French Crusade Cycle* (11 vols, Tuscaloosa: University of Alabama Press, 1977–2003).

24 For example, W. C. Jordan, 'The representation of the crusades in the songs attributed to Thibaud, count palatine of Champagne', *JMH* 25 (1999), 27–34.

25 Dufournet and Harf, eds, *Le Prince et son historien*.

26 *OIHC* forms a good introduction to this. For bibliography see C. T. Maier, 'The *bible moralisée* and the crusades', in *EC*, 209–22, at p. 210 notes 3–4.

representation of a returning crusader sculpted at the priory of Belval, and now located at Nancy in Lorraine, depicts Count Hugh of Vaudémont and his wife Aigeline. Strikingly, although Hugh is shown *crucesignatus* for the Second Crusade, it is his status as a pilgrim that is emphasized. We know from Joinville's account that he cherished a similar view of his role a century later. It is likely that Joinville was a little old-fashioned in his approach to the issue, but the earlier example accords with much other evidence that the French nobles on the Second Crusade saw themselves primarily as penitential pilgrims.[27] On a much grander scale, the central tympanum of the abbey church of Sainte-Madeleine at Vézelay in Burgundy, created c. 1120/32, is a powerful statement of the eschatological significance of the First Crusade.[28] Christoph Maier has demonstrated that *bibles moralisées* can contain multi-layered didactic references to crusading ideas.[29] Whatever else it has to tell us, the surviving artistic evidence convincingly communicates the point that crusading in its heyday was centrally located in the cultural values of Europe: it was no marginal or esoteric practice, but something that would impact, directly or indirectly, on the lives of many. Individual commitment may not be explained by such artefacts, but the societal context for it is illuminated.[30]

Groups

The leaders

The intentions of crusade commanders and leaders have exercised the minds of historians to an unusually large degree, and as a group they call for special attention. Although recent research has stressed that crusading armies were not easily controlled or diverted, the fact remains that they were large and powerful instruments that in the right circumstances could advance an individual's own interests. For obvious reasons, this applied most clearly at the start. Bohemund of Taranto's life took a radically different course after he joined the First Crusade: the expedition enabled him to become prince of Antioch, though he was ultimately out-manoeuvred by Alexius Comnenus and returned to his

---

27 N. Kenaan-Kedar and B. Kedar, 'The significance of a twelfth-century sculptural group: le retour du croisé', in *DGF*, 29–44.

28 A. Katzenellenbogen, 'The central tympanum at Vézelay, its encyclopaedic meaning and its relation to the First Crusade', *Art Bulletin* (1944), 141–51.

29 Maier, 'The *bible moralisée*'.

30 C. Morris, 'Picturing the crusades: the uses of visual propaganda, c. 1095–1250', in *CTS*, 195–209.

lands in southern Italy.[31] The Norman's ambition was so overt that it is easy to see why hostile commentators like Anna Comnena and Geoffrey Malaterra regarded his crusading zeal as feigned; and it is possible to detach Bohemund from the devotional context of his age altogether, as Rowe does when he dismisses Bohemund's visit to the shrine of St-Léonard-de-Noblat, to thank the saint for engineering his release from Turkish captivity, as 'an ostentatious piece of pious humbug'.[32] Not all modern historians have judged Bohemund so severely. Norman expansion was a prominent feature of the age and a number of scholars have been led to place Bohemund's activities within a broader setting that included southern Italy, Sicily and England; in all these areas the Normans succeeded, at times, in combining their conquests with a cause that was sponsored by the Church. The idea has become entrenched of a Norman 'ruthless piety' that fused with a syncretist approach towards state-building in novel environments.[33] This is something of a stereotype. But there is no doubt that Bohemund's recruitment campaign in France in 1106, and his Durazzo expedition of 1107, did show a remarkable readiness to seize any opportunity that presented itself.[34]

If Bohemund can seem to be the personification of determined ambition, Raymond count of Toulouse can easily appear as the Norman's polar opposite: a pure-hearted, indeed naive, man who stood by his oaths, and in the eyes of some acted as Urban II's undeclared lieutenant.[35] Yet Raymond set his sights on the government of Jerusalem and, when he lost it to Godfrey, resourcefully laid the foundations for a state in the Lebanon instead. With rich lands in the south of France, Raymond's case raises many questions, the key one being whether he only resolved to stay once he had experienced the crusade in its entirety. Jonathan Riley-Smith in particular has probed the question of whether original intentions can be read from outcomes.[36] Debate has also occurred in the case of the other commanders of the First Crusade who stayed in the east. Hans Eberhard Mayer argued that Baldwin of Boulogne, who conquered

---

31   Rowe, 'Paschal II'; Harris, *Byzantium and the Crusades*, pp. 78–80; Lilie, *Byzanz*, pp. 65–8.
32   Rowe, 'Paschal II', p. 182.
33   D. C. Douglas, *The Norman Achievement 1050–1100* (London: Eyre and Spottiswoode, 1969), esp. pp. 91–109.
34   Douglas, *The Norman Achievement*, p. 67, has a balanced judgement.
35   J. H. and L. L. Hill, 'Justification historique du titre de Raymond de St Gilles, "Christiane milicie excellentissimus princeps"', *Annales du Midi* 66 (1954), 101–12; Mayer, *The Crusades*, 2nd edn, pp. 67–8.
36   Riley-Smith, 'The motives'.

Edessa, was planning from the start to establish himself in the east,[37] while Alan Murray and Jonathan Riley-Smith have queried whether Godfrey's understanding of his status as ruler of Jerusalem was as self-effacing as has generally been thought.[38]

After the First Crusade there were fewer pickings to be had in the east. The notorious exception is the Fourth Crusade, and if many of that expedition's problems stemmed from the absence of royal leadership, one argument in the hands of the conspiracy theorists is that the baronial leaders quickly realized the similarity between their situation and that of the crusaders in 1099: they possessed rich lands and competition for rulership over them could only imperil their situation.[39] Granted that these lands lacked the kudos of the Holy Land, they included what was generally regarded as the finest city in the world. Boniface of Montferrat, the prime suspect of setting up a conspiracy among the crusading leaders, came from a family whose strong associations with crusading and the Latin East were gained through the adroit management of dynastic marriage and office-holding. He fully appreciated what was at stake, which was precisely why he was such a good choice as commander of the crusade.[40] But Baldwin of Flanders, who like Raymond of Toulouse a century earlier ruled a thriving principality at home, also set his heart on becoming first Latin emperor of the conquered Constantinople.[41] Overall, a comparison of the First and Fourth Crusades reveals the hazards of any attempt at generalized comment about the intentions of the leaders with regard to staying or returning.

In the case of those crusades that were commanded by crowned rulers we face a different set of issues. Such leaders did not regard it as wrong to conquer while they were engaged on God's work: Richard I seized Cyprus, Louis IX regarded Damietta as his city to do with as he wished, and Frederick II spent most of his crusade enforcing his dynastic rights in both Cyprus and the Holy Land.[42] But there can be little question of their having taken the cross in order to achieve these goals, as might plausibly be argued in the case of leaders of lower status. Rather, the issues shift to a range of other factors that might be regarded as key motivators: political, financial, dynastic or more broadly ideological. It is arguable, for instance, that even if Richard I

---

37   H. E. Mayer, *Mélanges sur l'histoire du royaume latin de Jérusalem* (Paris: Imprimerie nationale, 1984), 10–48.
38   Murray, 'The title'; Riley-Smith, 'The title'.
39   Villehardouin, quoted by Powell, 'Myth', p. 134.
40   Queller and Madden, *The Fourth Crusade*, pp. 26–30.
41   Queller and Madden, *The Fourth Crusade*, pp. 201–2.
42   Hiestand has even questioned whether Frederick's expedition was a crusade at all: Hiestand, 'Friedrich II', p. 143.

shared the visceral sense of loss that the events of 1187 induced in his contemporaries, he saw his participation in the Third Crusade in terms of expectation and status as much as personal remorse; this would help explain his decision twice to abandon the march on Jerusalem.[43] Even Louis IX, whose dedication to Jerusalem was so profound that he was reflecting on the city's fate on his deathbed, was prepared to forego a visit to its shrines while it remained in Muslim hands because it would set a poor example.[44] Men like Richard and Louis could not set aside their status when they took the cross: they might share many of the religious feelings of their nobles and even of the ordinary pilgrims, in the same way that they went out of their way to share their sufferings, but they also carried obligations of rank that made their experience of crusading different from that of others.

Arguably this applied *a fortiori* to Frederick II. Part of the demystification of the *stupor mundi* ('world's marvel') that has characterized recent study has been the argument that the emperor, though unusually curious, sceptical and sophisticated, was not unorthodox in his own religious views.[45] But this is not the same thing as saying that he was a zealous crusader. Even more so than Philip Augustus, Frederick almost certainly regarded his crusade in the light of what he ought to do as emperor and regent of Jerusalem, a political and ideological duty that he took seriously but approached without the personal investment that was so conspicuous in the case of Louis IX. And as Björn Weiler has reiterated, this established a pattern that became ever more apparent in the interplay of European diplomacy as the century went on.[46] Again and again the papal *curia* reacted to the desperate plight of the Latin East by appealing to kings to take action. The latter responded by asserting their zeal and concern, so taxes were levied, vows solemnly made and preparations falteringly begun, only to be interrupted by wars, deaths, dynastic disputes and rebellions. As a result the key issue surrounding such rulers as Henry III and Edward I of England, Alfonso X of Castile, Håkon IV of Norway, James I of Aragon and Philip IV of France, is that of whether they were sincere in their claim to desire 'above all else' to go on crusade.[47]

---

43 Gillingham, *Richard the Lionheart*, p. 112, perceives genuine remorse coupled with an appreciation of the status attached to crusading.
44 Richard, *Saint Louis*, pp. 140, 326.
45 Riley-Smith, *The Crusades*, p. 149; Abulafia, *Frederick II*.
46 Weiler, 'The *Negotium Terrae Sanctae*'.
47 Lloyd, *English Society*, 198–243; A. Forey, 'The crusading vows of the English King Henry III', *Durham University Journal* 65 (1973), 229–47; J. M. R. García, 'Henry III, Alfonso X of Castile and the crusading plans of the thirteenth century', in B. Weiler and I. Rowlands, eds, *England and Europe in the Reign of Henry III (1216–72)* (Aldershot: Ashgate, 2002), 99–120; S. Schein, 'Philip IV and the crusade: a reconsideration', in *CS*, 121–6; Purcell, *Papal Crusading Policy*, pp. 55, 89–90, 110–13.

Clearly, the agenda has shifted: from the question of how far the motivation of rulers who took the cross can be equated with that of the crusaders whom they led, to the question of whether the failure to set out should be interpreted as indicating deficient intentionality from the start.

The nobility

That there would be an army for such commanders to lead hinged on the response of Europe's fighting *élite*. Normally these men would be of noble birth and described as *milites*, which implied that they possessed the military equipment, chargers, support staff and training required to fight as heavily armed cavalry.[48] In 1096 Urban II wrote to the monks at Vallombrosa that in issuing his call to crusade it was the *milites* that he hoped above all to arouse 'to restrain the savagery of the Saracens by their arms', a highly revealing comment that, if hindsight was not already at work, may show that the pope regarded the presence of ordinary pilgrims as, at best, a price that had to be paid to mobilize Christendom in the most comprehensive manner.[49] Some, if not most, of the intentions that have been ascribed to the nobles affected the rest of the population; but there were also certain specific factors, which grew in importance during the later expeditions, and these make it sensible to consider them as a group separately.

Historians have devoted a good deal of attention to analysing the religious feelings that undoubtedly constitute the key motivating force in the sources. Among these it is spiritual anxiety that is dominant. It arose from a chronic sense of sinfulness and an overwhelming desire to escape the literally unending torments that awaited the worst sinners after death. British historians like Bull, Cowdrey and Riley-Smith, who have emphasized the nature of the early expeditions, above all the First Crusade, as armed pilgrimages, have made it clear that crusading belonged to a large family of penitential practices that included pilgrimage in all its varied forms, the monastic vocation, and asceticism generally. The 'breakthrough' of crusading lay in the fact that arms-bearers could achieve salvation not by renouncing their military skills, which was almost as unendurable as the condition of sinfulness itself, but by using those skills to recover Jerusalem.[50] In the case of the First Crusade, narrative accounts, letters and charters alike concur to give the impression of exhil-

---

48   France, *Western Warfare*, pp. 53–63.
49   L. and J. Riley-Smith, *The Crusades*, pp. 39–40.
50   Cowdrey, 'The genesis'; Bull, *Knightly Piety*, esp. pp. 250–81; Riley-Smith, *The First Crusade*, pp. 13–57; Riley-Smith, *The First Crusaders*, pp. 23–52.

arating relief among the *milites* at this turn-around in their spiritual fortunes. Such feelings appear to have recurred during the preaching of the Second Crusade, thanks largely to the success of Bernard of Clairvaux in recreating the post-Clermont euphoria through his message of Jubilee.[51] And after Hattin there are indications that the sense of anxiety was relocated at the communal level in the form of a shared desperation and sense of responsibility triggered by the fall to Saladin of Jerusalem and the loss of the Holy Land's most revered relic, the True Cross; there is general agreement that Pope Gregory VIII's call to arms, *Audita tremendi*, was an exceptionally emotional text.[52]

But Jerusalem, of course, also featured throughout. We may find it helpful to separate out the various strands of crusader devotion, but because of the centrality of the image of a redemptive *imitatio Christi*, to be achieved by carrying his cross, the various elements of anxiety, contemplative piety and triumphalism made up a single, volatile compound in crusading psychology. Some of the 'Jerusalems' that this entailed – the allegorical (representing the Church), anagogical (prefiguring heaven) and tropological (symbolizing the individual's soul) – overlap and defy precise analysis.[53] But the city itself has bequeathed a solid corpus of historical and archeological evidence and this has been much studied. Interesting research has been published on Jerusalem before and during the Frankish occupation, including the ambitious building programme that took place between 1099 and 1187. Historians have also examined the experience of pilgrimage in the same period, the ramifications of devotion towards Jerusalem in medieval Europe, and the place that the city held at the same time in Muslim and Jewish religious ideas.[54] As a result we have a much fuller view not just of what Jerusalem meant to the crusaders but also of the city they visited, than we did a generation ago.[55]

The last remark applies also to the vexed question of what crusaders thought of their Muslim enemies. We shall return to the cumulative effect of the crusades on interfaith relations in chapter 7, but the 'image of the

51   Mayer, *The Crusades*, 2nd edn, pp. 93–7; Riley-Smith, *The Crusades*, pp. 94–6; Cole, *The Preaching*, pp. 37–52.

52   Mayer, *The Crusades*, 2nd edn, p. 139; Riley-Smith, *The Crusades*, pp. 109–10; Cole, *The Preaching*, pp. 63–5.

53   J. Prawer, 'Jerusalem in the Christian and Jewish perspectives of the early Middle Ages', *Settimane di studio del Centro italiano di studi sull'alto medioevo, 26. Gli Ebrei nell'alto medioevo* (Spoleto: Centro italiano di studi sull'alto medioevo, 1980), 739–95.

54   *HLHL*; Bauer, Herbers and Jaspert, eds, *Jerusalem*; B. Hamilton, 'Rebuilding Zion: the holy places of Jerusalem in the twelfth century', *SCH* 14 (1977), 105–16; B. Hamilton, 'The impact of crusader Jerusalem on western Christendom', *CHR* 80 (1994), 695–713.

55   See the forthcoming, posthumous study by S. Schein, *Gateway to the Heavenly City. Crusader Jerusalem and the Catholic West (1099–1187)* (Aldershot: Ashgate, 2005).

enemy' needs to be considered here in terms of what motivated crusaders. Riley-Smith has argued that the emerging ideology of charity, that was to be so forcefully expressed in the religious movements of the twelfth and thirteenth centuries, was also present from the start in crusading. By fighting to regain Christ's lands, Christians displayed their love for their Saviour and their charity towards fellow Christians who were suffering at the hands of Christ's enemies.[56] This love did not extend towards the Muslims; indeed, charity's alter ego was vengeance, another powerful strand in crusading ideology.[57] It has been convincingly shown that one of the strongest rhetorical themes deployed by popes and preachers alike was that Muslim occupation of the holy places constituted pollution.[58] Possibly the revulsion this generated helped to fuel the massacres that took place in 1099 in Palestine.[59] That said, historians of crusading have not encountered protracted bouts of 'sacred violence' of the type that some scholars of the early modern period have detected in the religious wars fought between Europe's different confessions.[60] It has been suggested that with a few notable exceptions, crusading warfare adhered to the laws of war, such as they were. There were no dramatic differences, for example, between the way captured Muslims were treated during the crusading expeditions and during campaigns fought by the forces that were raised by the settlers in the Latin East.[61] Hatred of the enemy was stirred up by crusade preaching and unusual cruelty was shown at times during crusading campaigns. But it was largely a by-product of the veneration that was felt towards the holiest of Christianity's shrines; this is not to excuse it, merely to say that it was not a primary motor.

In the late twelfth and thirteenth centuries a gradual shift seems to have taken place in the way noble crusaders envisaged their task. Increasingly, they perceived crusading as a form of service performed to Christ, which was rewarded, as a *quid pro quo*, with the spiritual gain of the indulgence. In this way it was rendered more akin to the military activity that they were used to, as vassals, paid troops, or subjects of a king who owed him their support. Like all shifts in perception this is very hard to pin down. From the start the Church tailored the crusading message to the ways of thinking of the fighting nobility by couching it in terms of feudal service to

---

56 Riley-Smith, 'Crusading as an act of love'.
57 Riley-Smith, 'The First Crusade and the persecution of the Jews'.
58 Cole, 'O God, the heathen have come into your inheritance'.
59 Elm, 'Die Eroberung Jerusalems', pp. 46–54.
60 D. Crouzet, *Les Guerriers de Dieu. La violence au temps des troubles de religion vers 1525–vers 1610* (2 vols, Seyssel: Champ Vallon, 1990).
61 Y. Friedman, *Encounters between Enemies. Captivity and Ransom in the Latin Kingdom of Jerusalem* (Leiden: Brill, 2002).

a lord whose patrimony, the Holy Land, had been unjustly seized; and there were precedents for such an approach in the activity of the papal reformers.[62] On the other hand, we have seen that in the mid-thirteenth century a pious crusader like Joinville could still view himself first and foremost as a pilgrim. We can say with confidence that there are signs in the vernacular literature that themes of chivalric endeavour and courtly love came to shape the way the nobility thought about crusading, though we have to enter the caveat that no such literature is available for the time of the First Crusade. In the thirteenth century there were more examples than earlier of crusaders behaving in a foolish way because their good sense was overruled by notions of honour or by the desire to demonstrate prowess.[63] Once all the qualifications have been registered, our evidence points towards the crusading of the noble *élite* becoming more distinctively 'aristocratic' or 'knightly' in tone, though this was far from the major trend it became in the fourteenth century.[64]

The evidential terrain is firmer on the many connections between lineage and crusading. The ground-breaking work in this regard was carried out by Jonathan Riley-Smith. With the technical assistance of F. G. Kingston, Riley-Smith built up a relational database of crusaders and settlers in the Latin East and published his findings from it in his *The First Crusaders*. He claimed that 'crusading relied to a peculiar degree on a combination of individual spontaneity and collective collaboration',[65] and proceeded to argue that on the First Crusade family ties formed the dominant societal context within which collaboration operated. These ties were more important than political forces or even (more surprisingly) feudal networks, and they made themselves felt in a multitude of ways. It has become hard to deny that an individual noble's decision to take the cross was conditioned, from the start, by awareness of lineage. For the spiritual anxieties that drove *crucesignati* related not just to themselves but to the deeds of their dead ancestors. In their preparations to embark on crusades they relied to a large degree on their families and/or on the religious houses with which those families had built up close ties of patronage. If possible, they set out on crusade in the company of their own kin. Most strikingly, families built up traditions of taking part in

---

62 I. S. Robinson, 'Gregory VII and the soldiers of Christ', *History* 58 (1973), 161–92; J. Riley-Smith, 'The First Crusade and St Peter', in *OSHCKJ*, 41–63; Flori, *La Guerre sainte*, pp. 161–226; Riley-Smith, 'Crusading as an act of love'.

63 For example, Robert of Artois at Mansurah in 1250: Richard, *Saint Louis*, pp. 123–4.

64 Riley-Smith, 'The state of mind'. This remains a relatively new area of enquiry from which much can be expected.

65 Riley-Smith, *The First Crusaders*, pp. 21–2.

successive crusades, while ties of lineage endured between the settlers in the east and their relatives in Europe.[66]

Any historical argument of worth is based on evidence, and the drawback to emphasizing the support system that was provided by a combination of family and religious houses is that those nobles who did not have access to it left behind far fewer indications of how they coped. It is likely that to get by they had to keep an eye open for the main chance. In this respect John France's First Crusade differs from Riley-Smith's. France has written of the First Crusade as a welcome 'break' for *milites* who were ambitious and restless, but whose opportunities for self-improvement at home were limited. When on crusade such knights operated within networks, *mouvances*, but these were likely to be fluid, based on ties of dependency and patronage rather than kinship. France sees the appeal of the First Crusade as inherently broad based: 'it offered something for everyone – salvation, cash, land, status'. He concluded his essay on the subject by quoting what is probably the most famous passage in any First Crusade source relating to profit, the rallying cry created at the battle of Dorylaeum: 'Stand fast all together, trusting in Christ and in the victory of the Holy Cross. Today, please God, you will all gain much booty.'[67]

This brings us to the issue of material gain, which can best be explored by continuing to juxtapose the views of Riley-Smith and France. In chapter 2 we encountered the strong argument advanced by Riley-Smith that from the point of view of cost-benefit analysis it would have been folly for families to dig as deep as they did into their patrimonial resources in order to equip members who were setting out on crusade. The only way to counter this argument is to strengthen the benefit side of the equation either with optimism (the Holy Land really was 'flowing with milk and honey'),[68] or an additional, non-economic dividend (such as that the entire lineage would gain in religious terms from the enterprise); and neither option is very effective. Riley-Smith has shown that the 'younger son' thesis was always under-sourced as a proposition,[69] and its weakness leaves those who wish to promote the idea that territorial gain was a major incentive with little firm evidence except those individual cases of crusaders who overtly displayed their territorial ambitions – the equivalents at knightly level of Bohemund of Taranto and Baldwin of Boulogne. And of course there were bound to be *milites* who stayed in the east because their lords stayed, rather than because of the attractions of

66   Riley-Smith, *The First Crusaders*.
67   France, 'Patronage'. See also Flori, *La Guerre sainte*, pp. 322–3.
68   L. and J. Riley-Smith, *The Crusades*, pp. 43–4.
69   Riley-Smith, *The First Crusade*, p. 42.

landholding.[70] As things currently stand, linking any of the major *passagia* to a programme of territorial expansion has become a difficult case to argue.

Booty, however, presents different issues. A general obsession with plunder was characteristic of crusaders, and it is likely that this, rather than land, lay behind the wording adopted in the Clermont decree. It reached its apotheosis in the sack of Constantinople; even if some accounts exaggerate the scale of the pillage, this was certainly massive, reaching 800,000 silver marks according to Villehardouin.[71] The relationship between plunder and motivation has been approached in a number of ways. It is possible to argue that pillaging was a matter of keeping crusades 'fuelled', of finding the resources necessary to feed and more generally sustain the armies in the field. From this viewpoint booty simply fed through the system like food through the body; and in the case of the First Crusade Riley-Smith was able to find few crusaders who returned home carrying material riches.[72] Alternatively, or in addition, pillaging can be detached from intention by being categorized not as a motivation but as a behavioural mode of Europe's noble *élite*. To some high-minded clerics it was regrettable, comparable perhaps to playing dice or consorting with camp followers, but it could be tolerated, as long as it remained within acceptable limits. What mattered was that it should not infect intention, because that would imperil the crusader's chance of salvation. And a third approach, which as noted earlier has been expounded by John France, is the pragmatic stance that the prospect of gain from precious goods, slaves and ransoms was one of the varied attractions of crusading; it operated on the minds of individuals to induce them to take the cross.[73]

The notorious course that was taken by the Fourth Crusade is explicable in terms of any of these approaches. The crusade's entire trajectory can be viewed as an extreme example of the unpalatable decisions that had to be made in order to keep the crusading host from breaking up. In essence this was Villehardouin's line. At a stretch it can even be applied to the sack of Constantinople, in so far as this created a resource that might have carried the crusaders through to the Holy Land if the leadership and momentum for such a venture had not simultaneously melted away.[74] The threat that the nobility's behavioural tendency to pillage could pose to right intention was certainly uppermost in the minds of those clerics who took part in the

---

70 France, *Victory in the East*, pp. 14–15.
71 Queller and Madden, *The Fourth Crusade*, pp. 193–200, 294–5 note 60.
72 Riley-Smith, *The First Crusaders*, p. 149.
73 France, 'Patronage', and *Victory in the East*, pp. 11–16.
74 Queller and Madden, *The Fourth Crusade*, p. 202.

various debates that settled the expedition's fate.[75] And one way to interpret the crusade is to argue that the successive waves of desertions for the Holy Land, by groups that refused to accept the diversions proposed, left the army dominated by those people whose interest in gain had formed a large part of their original motivation.[76]

A complicating factor in the discussion of material gain has been the crusaders' other obsession, the acquisition of relics. Nothing better illustrates the unsatisfactory nature of the 'devotion or profit' paradigm than the hunt for relics, because it manifestly fell into both categories; it was the expression of deep piety, coupled with the hope of 'profit' in the non-material sense of enhancing one's prestige (or that of one's family and/or religious house) once back home. Technically, even the seizure of relics by *force majeure* did not come into the same category as pillage since contemporaries believed that the saint involved could make it physically impossible to move them should he or she so wish. In other words the removal of the relics was the saint's wish and constituted *furtum sacrum* (holy theft).[77] Yet nobody reading Gunther of Pairis's astonishing account of Abbot Martin's relic-hunting at Constantinople in 1204 would regard it as substantially different from the behaviour of his fellow crusaders who seized coins, precious metals, horses and expensive cloths.[78] He and they evinced the notorious Latin greed that horrified the Greeks and helped make the sack such a baleful watershed in the relations between the Churches. It may be that the most workable approach to the whole issue of pillage is to accept that crusaders belonged to a society that was intensely acquisitive, from top to bottom and in religious as well as material terms; the best that churchmen like Urban II and Innocent III could do was to try simultaneously to harness and control these tendencies. It was hard to combat the popular belief, theologically dubious though it was, that God would shower his faithful followers with rewards, that 'righteous war invoked rightful reward'.[79] At best it could be rendered less noxious by reinforcing the importance of right intention.

75 Schmandt, 'The Fourth Crusade'.
76 For example, the revealing incident when the fleet rounded Cape Malea: Queller and Madden, *The Fourth Crusade*, pp. 103–4.
77 P. J. Geary, *Furta sacra. Thefts of Relics in the Central Middle Ages* (Princeton, NJ: Princeton University Press, 1988).
78 Queller and Madden, *The Fourth Crusade*, pp. 194–5; Andrea, *The 'Hystoria Constantinopolitana'*, pp. 106–13.
79 France, *Victory in the East*, p. 24. Cf. Matthew 19:29 for one passage that lent itself to misinterpretation.

The pauperes

In medieval society from the eleventh to the thirteenth centuries any able-bodied adult male could fight, albeit often in a lowly capacity.[80] There were non-combatants on crusades – not just clerics, women (for the most part),[81] and young children – but those males who were too old or ill to be of military use.[82] All others, however, were regarded as armed pilgrims. Nobles, because of their fighting skills, and presumably also because of their resources, were especially sought by the Church, but non-noble crusaders took part in all the *passagia*.[83] It is unlikely that they shared the nobility's consciousness of family traditions of crusading. And it is improbable that their attitudes towards crusading were shaped by such essentially aristocratic concepts as feudal loyalty, chivalric service or the cult of courtly love, except in the case of those who were predisposed towards social mobility and aped the aristocracy. In other respects, though, their motivations had much in common with those of their social superiors: in particular, they shared their spiritual anxieties, their devotion towards Jerusalem and their acquisitiveness in terms of booty and relics. In crusading, a hard and fast division between '*élite*' and 'popular' attitudes does not stand up to close inspection.

None the less, in respect of one type of crusading activity the motivation of a group of non-noble crusaders does call for separate treatment. This type constituted the 'popular crusades' or crusades of the poor (*pauperes*), those hosts that strayed beyond the guidelines established by the Church, sometimes even lacking official sponsorship and formal organization. They comprised, most notably, the initial wave of the First Crusade, the 'Children's Crusade' or crusade of the *pueri* of 1212, and the 'Shepherds' Crusade' or *pastoureaux* of 1251. As we saw in chapter 1, such crusades have been viewed by one school of historians as the crusading expeditions *par excellence*, thanks to the conviction that they attributed to the participants that the latter were not just the agents of God's will, but embodied an eschatological momentum of enormous significance; indeed, that Peter the Hermit's followers at least set out in confident expectation of Christ's Second Coming. That is an extreme position and, given the nature of the

---

80   France, *Western Warfare*, pp. 64–76.
81   The issue of female combatants has received some attention: K. Caspi-Reisfeld, 'Women warriors during the crusades, 1095–1254', in S. B. Edgington and S. Lambert, eds, *Gendering the Crusades* (Cardiff: University of Wales Press, 2001), 94–107; H. J. Nicholson, 'Women on the Third Crusade', *JMH* 23 (1997), 335–49; S. Geldsetzer, *Frauen auf Kreuzzügen 1096– 1291* (Darmstadt: Wissenschaftliche Buchgesellschaft, 2003), pp. 122–53.
82   Porges, 'The clergy'.
83   C. Tyerman, 'Who went on crusades to the Holy Land?', in *HH*, 13–26.

evidence, one that is hard to prove, because the failure of the *parousia* to occur distorted all retrospective narratives of events. Moreover, nearly all the eyewitness accounts of these expeditions were written by agitated observers rather than by the participants, and in the cases of 1212 and 1251 the chroniclers were eager to condemn. Given the exceptional difficulty of reconstructing the intentions and ideas of those who joined the movements, it would be hazardous to offer more than tentative generalizations. It does seem to be the case that for most participants taking the cross was a life-changing experience, entailing a break with the past that was intended to be fundamental. They were attracted by charismatic leaders: Peter the Hermit in 1096, Stephen of Cloyes and Nicholas of Cologne in 1212, and the 'Master of Hungary' in 1251. They were perhaps more tempted by the idea of purgative violence than were other crusaders. They were more disposed to engage in attacks on Jews, though this could simply be due to the fact that they were less susceptible to control than others were. And they had great veneration for Jerusalem, though we have seen that this was not unusual among all those who took the cross.[84]

Arguably it was among the *pauperes* that the idea took deepest root that crusaders were the elect of God, on whose shoulders he had placed the task of recovering Christendom's holiest shrines. In the case of the crusaders in 1212 and 1251 there were also certain social connotations. As we saw in chapter 3, there is evidence that in 1212 it was widespread anxiety caused by the military situation in Spain, fused with continuing distress at the loss of Jerusalem, that gave rise to the crusade of the *pueri*. Its members were convinced that because of their innocence they possessed a divine mandate to achieve what their social superiors had failed, over the course of several crusades, to bring about. In 1251 the ideology was more pointed: in reacting to the setbacks that Louis IX had experienced in the east, the *pastoureaux* believed that the Church had been insufficiently solicitous for the well-being of the king and his army. They were more hostile to clerics than to Jews. In both cases there was an association of purity of intent, the precondition for God's favour, with the most wretched in society. Only the *pauperes* could bring about what the greed, vanity and pride of the upper classes had barred them from doing. That much is probably valid: but it would be rash to deduce from it that these movements represented a chasm between the social groups in their basic attitudes towards crusading, let alone in broader terms.[85]

---

84 Riley-Smith, *The First Crusade*, pp. 49–57; Flori, 'Une ou plusieurs "première croisade"?'; Dickson, 'La genèse'; Barber, 'The crusade of the shepherds'.
85 There is no support in the sources for Hilton's comment that the *pastoureaux* of 1251 'seems to bridge the movements of pure enthusiasm for the freeing of Jerusalem with those to come, which aimed to free the unfree and the poor': *Bond Men Made Free*, pp. 99–100.

Much was held in common and the key difference seems to have been organizational. Matthew Paris reported that some of the *pastoureaux* of 1251, 'putting aside the crosses which they had received from the hands of the traitors, [and] reassuming them from the hands of good men, made the pilgrimage in the proper manner'.[86]

The merchants

The Italian naval republics of Genoa, Pisa and Venice make up the last group whose reaction towards crusading demands separate treatment. This is not because the communal organization of public affairs in much of central and northern Italy, and the prominence of commercial activity in economic life there, constituted barriers to people responding to the call of the cross. The time has long passed when crusading was associated with 'feudal society', and viewed as something from which Italy north of Rome was largely excluded. Indeed, scholars like Franco Cardini have conclusively affirmed that the response to the crusade in communal Italy was just as strong as that elsewhere.[87] Rather, it is because in the case of these three sea-powers the issue of material profit as a core motivation arises more forcefully than in any other context.

We shall look at the causal relationship between trade and crusade in chapter 7. Here it is necessary only to note that the Italians' penetration of the markets in the Levant was facilitated by the conquests of the First Crusade, though it is likely that the real surge in east–west trade only occurred in the late twelfth century.[88] The three communes all made vigorous interventions in the eastern Mediterranean during the later stages of the First Crusade and in the vitally important conquest of the seaboard in 1099–1124. Genoa and Pisa were the first to respond; the organization of the Genoese fleet was the stimulus for the formation of a sworn commune in the city, while the Pisan fleet was led by Daimbert, the archbishop of Pisa, who became the first Latin patriarch of Jerusalem.[89] The Venetians were slower to join in, but their expedition of 1122–5 was probably the most formidable of all the fleets despatched, more than 100 vessels in all, and as in the case of the Fourth Crusade it was commanded

---

86 Barber, 'The crusade of the shepherds', p. 12.
87 F. Cardini, 'L'inizio del movimento crociato in Toscana', in *Studi di storia medievale e moderna per Ernesto Sestan, 1* (Florence: Leo S. Olschki, 1980), 135–57; 'La società lucchese e la prima crociata', *Actum Luce. Rivista di studi lucchesi* 8 (1979), 7–29; 'La société italienne et les croisades', *CCM* 28 (1985), 19–33.
88 Riley-Smith, *The Crusades*, p. 188.
89 Mayer, *The Crusades*, 2nd edn, pp. 60–3.

by the doge.[90] All these interventions thus carried substantial implications for domestic affairs in the home cities.

In return for their help the Italians secured important trading privileges, which benefited both the Italian traders and the rulers of the Latin states grouped along the littoral. This was a symbiotic relationship: the idea that the exemptions and rights won by the Italians were so wide-ranging that they must have secured the lion's share of the resulting profits has been challenged.[91] But there is no gainsaying that the situation worked to the benefit of the major communes. Perhaps the Genoese more than their rivals showed that they grasped the connection between an expanding Christendom and commercial profit, displaying active concern not just for the well-being of the states in the Latin East but also for the furtherance of the incipient *Reconquista* along Iberia's eastern coast.[92] In the Third Crusade the French army was transported eastwards on Genoese ships, and it is hard to exaggerate the importance of Italian control of the sea throughout the thirteenth century. The Italians could not help to repel the armies of Saladin or the Mamluk sultans on land, so their assistance could not turn the tide of war; but it is not in dispute that both in the period of initial conquest, and in that of partial recovery in the late twelfth century, they played a crucially significant role.[93]

The question is why. Overall, the debate on Italian crusading motivations has been disappointing and inconclusive.[94] Even though old stereotypes that juxtaposed a 'trading' against a 'crusading' mentality have largely been discarded, a prejudice against the Italian sea-powers subsists; there is much scepticism of the 'well, they would, wouldn't they?' variety, hardly a subtle methodological tool.[95] It is hard to deny that the Italian communes showed the greatest crusading zeal when the prospect of material gain was powerful; in the late thirteenth century,

---

90   Riley-Smith, 'The Venetian crusade'.

91   J. Riley-Smith, 'Government in Latin Syria and the commercial privileges of foreign merchants', in D. Baker, *Relations between East and West in the Middle Ages* (Edinburgh: Edinburgh University Press, 1973), 109–32; M.-L. Favreau-Lilie, *Die Italiener im Heiligen Land vom ersten Kreuzzug bis zum Tode Heinrichs von Champagne (1098–1197)* (Amsterdam: Adolf M. Hakkert, 1989).

92   Williams, 'The making of a crusade'; N. Jaspert, '*Capta est Dertosa, clavis Christianorum*: Tortosa and the crusades', in *SCSC*, 90–110.

93   *CIRCG.*

94   D. Abulafia, 'Trade and crusade, 1050–1250', in *CCCCP*, 1–20; S. Schein, 'From "milites Christi" to "mali Christiani". The Italian communes in western historical literature', in *CIRCG*, 679–89; S. A. Epstein, 'Genoa and the crusades. Piety, credit, and the fiscal-military state', in L. Balletto, ed., *Oriente e occidente tra medioevo ed età moderna. Studi in onore di Geo Pistarino* (Genoa: Glauco Brigati, 1997), 245–59.

95   For example, the dismissive remarks of various historians quoted in Anderson et al., 'An economic interpretation', pp. 354, 360.

when the Mongol disruption of the Near East's commercial routes was at its worst, the Italians failed to respond to repeated calls to save the Holy Land. But in this they were not alone; their lack of enthusiasm formed part of a general trend in a Europe that was wracked by internal conflicts, and of these the Italian naval republics had their full share. There is no sound reason not to view both the populations and the ruling *élites* of the communes as sharing in more general feelings towards the crusade. On the contrary, in a study of the early period of expansion, Christopher Marshall demonstrated that the devotional patterns manifested by crusaders who came from the three sea-powers were virtually identical to those of other crusaders.[96] This is not *naïveté*, but a measured and controlled response to the available evidence. And in a case study of the Genoese attacks on Almería and Tortosa during the Second Crusade, John Bryan Williams argued that the Genoese were far from regarding the venture as a failure even though the economic balance sheet was negative; the prestige that was attached to crusading enabled them to extract political advantage from their defeat. True, this was crusading in Iberia, not the Latin East, but the points that Williams makes apply there too.[97]

One reason for the failure of this debate to catch fire has been the excessively broad terms of reference involved: for why should the inhabitants of these three cities be lumped together, and why should one assume that no shift in motivational impulses occurred in the course of virtually two centuries? By contrast, part of the reason why the debate about the role of the Venetians on the Fourth Crusade has been so lively is that its framework is much more specific. Another, arguably more powerful, reason is that in this instance a diversion took place, and that it turned out to be of enormous benefit to Venice. That said, the Venetians stood to gain much more had the crusaders been successful in their initial objective, which was the conquest of Egypt. It is possible to fall back on the argument that having been disappointed in their hopes of winning Egypt, the Venetians settled instead for Constantinople, but this only works if there is proof of a conspiracy; and as we saw in the previous chapter, there is none. There remains a strong tendency to regard the Venetians as not 'natural' crusaders, less so for example than the Genoese.[98] Yet it is hard to pinpoint any substantive difference between Venetian behaviour while

---

96   C. Marshall, 'The crusading motivation of the Italian city republics in the Latin East, 1096–1104', in *EC*, 60–79.

97   Williams, 'The making of a crusade', p. 45.

98   For example, Angold, *The Fourth Crusade*, p. 50: 'the crusade … did not mean too much to the Venetians'.

on crusade and that of any other crusaders.[99] It is true, for example, that in 1122–3 the Venetian fleet sailing east in response to Calixtus II's crusade summons 'seemed to be in no hurry to get to Palestine';[100] it delayed for a long time to try and seize Corfu from the Byzantines, who were being recalcitrant about confirming Venetian trading privileges. But that was no different from Richard I's adventures at Messina and on Cyprus; and the situation in the east in 1190–1 was at least as grave as it had been in 1122–3.

In his breezily polemical restatement of the case for Venetian responsibility for the diversion of the Fourth Crusade, Donald Nicol deployed *ex silentio* arguments relating to the absence of a Venetian treatment of events; not until Martin da Canal's 'Les Estoires de Venise' in the late thirteenth century was the Fourth Crusade described at any length by a Venetian. Nicol reasoned that this pointed towards a well-concealed conspiracy.[101] As an argument, 'the successful cover-up' is no stronger than its bed-fellow *cui bono?*, but it is undeniable that the comparative weakness of the sources describing responses to the crusade call at Genoa and Pisa, as well as at Venice, forms the most daunting obstacle to any satisfactory evaluation of reactions there. Few of the later sources yield the kind of detail provided by the Genoese Caffaro and the Venetian Monk of the Lido for the years of initial conquest in the Holy Land. If the evidence to convict the Italians in these three cities of being primarily driven by the profit motive falls away on close inspection, it none the less remains difficult to construct an alternative view of their crusading response that is altogether convincing. And this is frustrating because, if any single theme has run through this chapter, it is that a balanced analysis of intention demands not just a reasonable volume but a satisfying variety of surviving evidence.

99 Though it is striking that we know the names of just two residents of Venice who took the cross for the Fourth Crusade: Doge Dandolo and Walframe of Gemona (and he was probably not a native Venetian): Queller and Madden, *The Fourth Crusade*, pp. 67–8.
100 Nicol, *Byzantium and Venice*, p. 78.
101 Nicol, *Byzantium and Venice*, pp. 124–6.

5

Crusading Outside the Latin East in the Twelfth and Thirteenth Centuries

The next two chapters will differ from the three that have preceded them to the extent that they could only be written from a pluralist perspective of what we mean by crusading. In this chapter my intention is to explore the principal theatres of military activity that were affected by the extension of crusading practices during the central Middle Ages. What differentiated these theatres was in part geography and in part the nature of the enemy. Two principal areas of extension were Iberia, where the opponents of the crusaders were Muslims, and the lands adjacent to the Baltic Sea, where their enemies were, for the most part, pagans. In both regions the historical background and the religious beliefs of the opposition were key determinants of the way in which crusading was represented and above all legitimated by the Church; they gave to the Iberian *Reconquista* and the Baltic wars profiles which were highly distinctive, together with a continuity of action that has made possible the writing of narrative accounts of events. The third main extension, crusading against individuals and groups that had been baptized as Christians, was more diffuse, geographically and in terms of the enemy. Crusades against Christians were fought in numerous parts of Europe, though they were particularly frequent in the Italian peninsula. And in terms of canon law they fell into three broad categories: those fought against heretics (above all the cathars of southern France), schismatics (such as the Orthodox Greeks and Russians) and Catholic rulers (such as the Staufen imperial dynasty).[1]

---

1 For other attempts at categorization see Riley-Smith, *What were the Crusades?*, pp. 16–22; Purcell, *Papal Crusading Policy*, pp. 66–98.

This amounts to a considerable range of military activity, and the resulting agenda would be unmanageable within the compass of a single chapter if one set out to consider the entirety of the historical writing that has occurred even just in the recent past. Interpreted at their broadest, the Iberian *Reconquista* and the Baltic crusades encompassed most of the major historical developments in these regions; and in both cases the past few decades have witnessed an efflorescence of research and scholarship, generated largely by political changes.[2] Some focusing is therefore essential, and it will take two forms. In the first place, historians have naturally shown a keen interest in the circumstances that brought about the extension of crusading to these conflicts. Who lobbied for it, sanctioned it and sustained it, and on what grounds? Secondly, once crusading had become associated with a particular zone of combat or type of war, what were the consequences? How did it affect the conduct and outcome of the warfare, both materially and in terms of contemporary perceptions? And, scarcely less important, what was the impact on the fortunes of the crusading cause in the Holy Land?

Spanish Crusading

For a number of reasons it makes sense to consider the *Reconquista* first. With the exception of a crusade that was proclaimed in 1268 against the Muslim colony at Lucera in southern Italy,[3] it was the only significant extension of crusading against Muslims in the twelfth and thirteenth centuries, and without question it was the first area to which crusading was transplanted. The first context in which Spanish crusading features in recent scholarship is the *précroisades*, the series of military combats in eleventh-century Europe that arguably paved the way for the First Crusade. Great successes like Alfonso VI's conquest of Toledo in 1085 were widely reported outside the peninsula, while the same king's defeat at Sagrajas in the following year led to an appeal for outside aid that brought a large French expeditionary force across the Pyrenees. The early *Reconquista* also exercised a substantial impact on the Church. Cluny had strong ties of patronage with the monarchy of Leon-Castile, and the reform papacy showed a great deal of interest in the fighting. Alexander

---

2   Much of this research is published in Spanish, German and other foreign languages and the results are slow to filter through into English-language scholarship, on which this chapter is largely based.

3   C. T. Maier, 'Crusade and rhetoric against the Muslim colony of Lucera: Eudes of Châteauroux's *Sermones de rebellione Sarracenorum in Apulia*', *JMH* 21 (1995), 343–85.

II, Gregory VII and even Urban II considered the military threat posed to Christianity by Islam, and its eschatological context, at least as much in terms of the struggle in Iberia as in that of wars occurring in the Middle East. The conflict in the peninsula forced them to consider the relationship between their project for reforming the Church and the practice of Christian war, and Gregory VII in particular used it as a testing ground for formulating specific ties with the nobility by creating *fideles S. Petri*.

In common with the discussion of *précroisades* generally, this debate has gone through three broad phases. A group of historians led by Erdmann and Defourneaux came close to viewing the eleventh-century *Reconquista* as crusading in all but name.[4] There then ensued a major process of revision. First, H. E. J. Cowdrey undertook a radical reassessment of Cluny's attitude towards holy war that played down instances of direct intervention by its abbots, and recast its significance in more general terms of a concern for the spiritual well-being of its lay donors. 'Cluny had, indeed, done little to sow the seed of the Crusade, but it had done much to prepare the ground for Urban II to sow it.'[5] Secondly, in a detailed analysis of French volunteer service in the *Reconquista* before 1095, Marcus Bull concluded that 'in terms of numbers and motivation, the Spanish theatre could not have been anything more than a very minor factor behind the response of Aquitanians, Gascons and others to the First Crusade'.[6] There was little evidence that volunteers took the opportunity to combine their fighting with a pilgrimage to Compostella, or indeed that religious devotion played any part in their decision to go to Spain. This accorded with Bull's overall argument that it was at the level of a myriad ties with religious houses that the crusading idea germinated. Most recently, Jean Flori has promoted a partial rehabilitation of the role played by the *Reconquista* in terms of the formulation of ideas about holy war and reconquest at the papal *curia*. This has followed the logic of Flori's thesis that the First Crusade (and crusading generally, for those who adopt his definition) was 'a military operation of holy war within the general framework of Christian reconquest'.[7] But this has not entailed a reversion to the idea of crusading as no more than refined *Reconquista*. For Flori, that is unacceptable due to the transformative role that was played by Jerusalem, which manifested itself so clearly in the enthusiasm the Spanish showed to abandon their own conflict against the Muslims in order to go to the east.

---

4 Erdmann, *The Origin*, pp. 136–40, 143, 155–6, 288–90, 314–18; M. Defourneaux, *Les Français en Espagne aux XIe et XIIe siècles* (Paris: Presses universitaires de France, 1949).
5 H. E. J. Cowdrey, 'Cluny and the First Crusade', with quote at pp. 310–11.
6 Bull, *Knightly Piety*, pp. 70–114, with quote at p. 114.
7 Flori, 'Réforme, *reconquista*, croisade', with quote at p. 335. See also his *La Guerre sainte*, pp. 277–91.

For obvious reasons Urban II's attitude towards the war in Spain has attracted particular attention. In letters relating to Spain written both before and during the First Crusade the pope showed his anxiety about the progress of the *Reconquista*, and his concern that the new form of warfare that he initiated in 1095 should not harm it. The former led him in 1089 to assure the Catalans that working for the restoration of the church at Tarragona was as meritorious as embarking on a pilgrimage to Jerusalem,[8] while the latter caused him, in one of the letters that he wrote after the council of Clermont, to urge Catalan knights not to depart for the east, since it would imperil the defence of Tarragona, 'because it is no virtue to rescue Christians from the Saracens in one place, only to expose them to the tyranny and oppression of the Saracens in another'. They should try to fulfil their vows in Spain and should not fear death because anybody who perished 'for the love of God and his brothers' would surely be forgiven his sins.[9] It is a striking letter that can be used by both pluralists and traditionalists in support of their approach. On the one hand, it shows the pope anxious not to allow the extraordinary popularity of his venture in the east to damage the cause of the Church in Spain, and equating them in terms of purpose: the common struggle against Islam. For Erdmann, this was the crucial point: 'Surely no document of the eleventh century more purely and clearly expresses the Christian idea of war upon the heathen.'[10] It could even be said that the text shows that the pope was already willing to transfer crusading as a practice from east to west. On the other hand, it is also possible to argue that the letter was not a profound statement about the crusade, but an *ad hoc* response to a serious problem that had been reported to Urban, and that the wording used by the pope is too selective and cautious to indicate a wholesale equation of the two conflicts. More importantly, and irrespective of what Urban thought, this letter, like another that the pope wrote in May 1098, clearly shows that Spaniards were much more attracted by the war in the east than by operations nearer at hand.[11]

It is important to set out the situation regarding this single letter of Urban II because it encapsulates so many of the key themes in the discussion about the period during which Spanish crusading took root, which lasted from 1095 to 1123. In the latter year the First Lateran Council set out the disciplinary action to be taken against individuals who had taken vows and fixed crosses to their clothing either for the *iter*

---

8   Erdmann, *The Origin*, pp. 314–16.
9   L. and J. Riley-Smith, ed. and trans., *The Crusades. Idea and Reality, 1095–1274* (London: Edward Arnold, 1981), p. 40.
10   Erdmann, *The Origin*, p. 318.
11   Bull, *Knightly Piety*, p. 97.

to Jerusalem or for that to Spain; convicted incendiaries were allowed to serve at either location. In chapters 1 and 3 we saw that early crusading can be hard to pin down institutionally, but this canon makes it clear not just that vow and cross (together with the associated indulgence) were present in Spain, but that they also received the sanction of an ecumenical council of the Church.[12] From that point onwards there can be no real doubt that Spanish crusading existed, as opposed to taking the form of an emergency measure, as it arguably did in Urban II's second Tarragona letter.

Two issues in the period leading up to 1123 have proved more difficult to resolve. One is whether a cluster of military ventures that occurred before 1123 were in fact crusades, notably a joint Catalan-Pisan expedition to the Balearic Islands in 1113–14, and a major campaign led by Alfonso I of Aragon-Navarre against Zaragoza in 1118. Joseph O'Callaghan was in no doubt that these were fully-fledged crusades,[13] and both the present author and Jonathan Riley-Smith have written in similar terms;[14] but it is also possible to see this as a 'formative phase'.[15] The issue hinges on how one interprets a number of practices, notably variously phrased indulgences and signings with the cross, that point in the direction of crusading but are not as coherently expressed as they were to be in 1123. Secondly, did the Spanish view their wars as holy, or solely as wars fought for the rightful recovery of lands that had been seized by the Muslims? Perhaps the former applied to Count Ramon Berenguer III of Catalonia and Alfonso I (Ramon took the cross, though there is no evidence that Alfonso did);[16] but the argument is hard to prove in the case of their subjects. Richard Fletcher has made a strong case for a much slower embrace of crusading ideas by the Spanish in relation to their own struggle against the Muslims. They had to be persuaded, and this job was done in part by their own prelates on their return from councils convened outside the peninsula, and in part by visiting outsiders who were veterans of crusading in the east, or who stopped off in Spain *en route* to that theatre of operations.[17] There are good examples of both dating from the period when the First Lateran Council made its pronouncement, for Archbishop

---

12 O'Callaghan, *Reconquest*, p. 38; Bull, *Knightly Piety*, p. 108.
13 O'Callaghan, *Reconquest*, p. 35.
14 N. Housley, 'Jerusalem and the development of the crusade idea, 1095–1128', in *HH*, 27–40, at pp. 32–5; Riley-Smith, *The Crusades*, p. 89.
15 Bull, *Knightly Piety*, p. 110.
16 O'Callaghan, *Reconquest*, pp. 35–6.
17 R. A. Fletcher, 'Reconquest and crusade in Spain c. 1050–1150', *TRHS* 5th ser. 37 (1987), 31–47; *Saint James's Catapult. The Life and Times of Diego Gelmírez of Santiago de Compostela* (Oxford: Oxford University Press, 1984), pp. 293–300.

Oleguer of Tarragona attended the council among a series of other Church councils in the years 1119–31,[18] while several prominent French veterans of the First Crusade took part in the Zaragoza expedition of 1118 and the fighting in the years that followed.[19] In other words, Spanish crusading zeal was instantaneous and hard to contain in relation to the Holy Land, but had to be nurtured, indeed imported for the most part, in relation to the *Reconquista*. Even O'Callaghan, who saw the *Reconquista* as possessing the attributes of a religious war before it became a fully-fledged crusade, accepted that the arrival of French volunteers 'helped to diffuse knowledge of the Holy Land and of crusading, especially in Catalonia and Aragón'.[20]

There are clear signs that in the early 1120s Pope Calixtus II ambitiously envisaged a crusade that would unfold on two 'fronts', and he offered 'to all those who fight persistently in this expedition [in Spain] the same remission of sins that we gave to the defenders of the eastern church'.[21] In one of the most interesting texts from the 1120s, Archbishop Diego Gelmirez of Compostella wrote of the Spanish fighting their way toward Jerusalem through the Muslim-held south of Spain, a remarkable strategic idea that seems to indicate how hard it remained to persuade the Spanish to embrace holy war outside the framework of the Holy Land.[22] Having said that, the institutional equivalence of the two crusading arenas was now established and the two leading scholars of crusading in the Iberian peninsula, Jose Goñi Gaztambide and Joseph O'Callaghan, have shown that from this point onwards there was virtually no feature of crusading that did not make an appearance in the context of the *Reconquista*.[23] Substantial advances in crusade theology, the preaching and financing of crusades, and the consideration of crusading in canon law, were generally initiated in the context of the Holy Land; but they were applied either piecemeal, or, after the Fourth Lateran Council in 1215, systemically, to Spanish crusading. And the particular conditions in Spain did give rise to some significant institutional innovations. For example, a series of important measures relating to the indulgence, including the stipulation of a year's service as the norm for its granting, the practice of substitution, and the establishment of a specified 'table' of partial indulgences, seem to have first occurred in the context of the remarkable

---

18   Fletcher, 'Reconquest', p. 43.
19   Bull, *Knightly Piety*, p. 107.
20   O'Callaghan, *Reconquest*, pp. 9–10, 35.
21   O'Callaghan, *Reconquest*, p. 38.
22   O'Callaghan, *Reconquest*, p. 39.
23   O'Callaghan, *Reconquest*; J. Goñi Gaztambide, *Historia de la bula de la cruzada en España* (Vitoria: Editorial del Seminario, 1958).

confraternity of Belchite, founded by Alfonso I in 1122.[24] These measures were later applied in the Holy Land, as and when its different circumstances dictated.

Scholarly discussion of the Spanish crusades from 1123 onwards has tended to follow the agenda of ascertaining and explaining the ways in which it developed its own character. One way to consider that character is in terms of a paradox, the possession by the *Reconquista* of both a 'regional' and a 'global' dimension. The paradox was paralleled by the fact that the 'international' military orders, the Hospitallers and Templars, served in the *Reconquista* alongside brethren who belonged to the exclusively Spanish orders, those of Alcántara, Calatrava and Santiago.[25] The most distinctive regional feature of Spanish crusading was the close control that was exerted over it by the Iberian monarchies, especially that of Leon-Castile. As in the Latin East, the ebb and flow of crusading was shaped to a large degree by the Islamic threat, the two intrusions of Muslim power from north Africa (Almoravids and Almohads) that in the eleventh and twelfth centuries compelled the rulers of Leon-Castile and Aragon to look to the papal *curia* for help. But during the interstices between these intrusions, and more radically after the decisive victory over the Almohads at Las Navas de Tolosa in 1212, the initiative lay with the Christians. The southwards push that followed Las Navas de Tolosa, conducted mainly by Castile and Aragon, formed a remarkable contrast with the situation in the east, both in terms of the successes enjoyed and of the mobilization of resources that lay behind these successes.[26]

This was most evident in the sphere of crusade finance. The ideology of sanctified reconquest placed the peninsular monarchs in a position of control over their churches that was unrivalled anywhere in the Catholic world, so Innocent III's innovation of Church taxation for crusading provided them with a milch cow that they exploited ruthlessly. In addition to income taxes on churchmen (*decimas*), the kings established a hold also on the *tercias*, the third of the tithe intended for upkeep of church buildings. Royal envoys to the papal court were normally instructed to ask for a package of measures that included the *tercias* together with crusade preaching and ample grants of the clerical tenths. Attempts made by the *curia* to reserve a share of proceeds for the Latin East (the Holy Land or the Latin empire of Constantinople) rarely succeeded.[27] Such financial

---

24   Housley, 'Jerusalem', pp. 33–4; O'Callaghan, *Reconquest*, pp. 39–40.
25   A. Forey, *The Military Orders from the Twelfth to the Early Fourteenth Centuries* (Basingstoke: Macmillan, 1992).
26   O'Callaghan, *Reconquest*; D. W. Lomax, *The Reconquest of Spain* (London: Longman, 1978).
27   O'Callaghan, *Reconquest*, pp. 152–76; P. Linehan, *The Spanish Church and the Papacy in the Thirteenth Century* (Cambridge: Cambridge University Press, 1971).

measures lay at the heart of the Spanish crusading enterprise: there is evidence for individuals taking the cross to serve, but the substantive gain from the *Reconquista*'s crusading status in manpower terms derived from the service provided by the brethren of the military orders and their hired mercenaries.[28] However, O'Callaghan has shown that this is not the same thing as saying that crusading in Spain lacked any devotional framework. There is abundant evidence of crusade preaching, liturgical preparations before battle, the use of religious banners on campaign, appeals to the saints for help, and the commemoration of those who fell. Not all such activities were explicitly crusading in nature, and Spain lacked the devotional resonances of the Holy Land, but O'Callaghan's work demonstrates that the extension of crusading to Spain had a religious as well as a military and financial character.[29] Others remain sceptical, especially with relation to the outlook of the upper class. Simon Barton, for example, has written of the Castilian nobility that 'the search for wealth, status and power, the chief motors of aristocratic behaviour down the ages, was always likely to take precedence over religious or ideological considerations'.[30] And it is undeniable that the strongly monarchical, and eventually national, profile of Spanish crusading is not helpful to attempts to gauge its popularity, since it brings into play a whole range of political, cultural and financial considerations that simply do not feature in the case of crusading to the Holy Land.

The indigenous quality of much Spanish crusading is well established, but so too is the reverse side of the paradox, its ongoing location within the broader context of Christendom, the persistence of the broader vision that first led popes like Urban II and Calixtus II to extend crusading practices to the *Reconquista*. On a number of occasions, starting with Calixtus II's crusading project in the 1120s, the conflict in Spain was integrated at a theoretical and practical level with plans for crusading in the Latin East. The most important of these occasions was the Second Crusade. In a classic study, Giles Constable showed that contemporaries viewed the successes achieved in the peninsula during the Second Crusade, the capture of Lisbon and Tortosa and the short-lived seizure of Almería, as part of a general Christian offensive against Islam.[31] The breadth and *dirigisme* involved were expressed most succinctly by

---

28   Forey, *The Military Orders*, pp. 44–97.
29   O'Callaghan, *Reconquest*, pp. 177–208.
30   S. Barton, 'Traitors to the faith? Christian mercenaries in al-Andalus and the Maghreb. c. 1100–1300', in R. Collins and A. Goodman, eds, *Medieval Spain. Culture, Conflict and Coexistence. Studies in Honour of Angus MacKay* (Basingstoke: Palgrave Macmillan, 2002), 23–45, at p. 38.
31   Constable, 'The Second Crusade'.

the chronicler Helmold of Bosau: 'The initiators of the expedition deemed it advisable to design one part of the army for the eastern regions, another for Spain, and a third for the Slavs who live hard by us.'[32] One of the most striking features of this broad perspective was the readiness of the Anglo-Flemish-German naval contingent that was *en route* for the east to assist Afonso Henriques of Portugal in besieging Lisbon. In the past their presence at the siege has been regarded as serendipitous, but Jonathan Phillips has argued that the evidence points towards a carefully laid plan in which St Bernard played a part.[33] Whatever the feelings of the native Christian population towards the conflict against the Moors, it is apparent that many who lived outside Iberia could be persuaded to accept the papal and Bernardine equation of the *Reconquista* with the war in the Holy Land. In fact the siege of Lisbon produced two of the most revealing texts for the general development of crusading ideas in the mid-twelfth century, the *De expugnatione Lyxbonensi* and the 'Lisbon Letter'.[34]

Some of those who came to fight in Iberia during the Second Crusade planned to proceed onwards to the Holy Land, while others such as the Genoese at Almería and Tortosa envisaged no combat outside the peninsula.[35] This two-fold pattern persisted through the twelfth and thirteenth centuries. On occasion nobles from northern Europe travelled overland to fight, though the sizeable force from France that was recruited in 1212 had already left for home when the battle of Las Navas de Tolosa took place.[36] But more frequently a spell of service in peninsular fighting proved possible for crusaders sailing to the eastern Mediterranean from north-western Europe. Among the attractions of doing so was the hope of securing booty from which the campaigning in the east could be financed. Crusaders from many of the northern European countries assisted the Portuguese king, Sancho I, in taking Silves in 1189, lured by his promise of the chance to pillage the town. And a large contingent of recruits for the Fifth Crusade also took part in the Portuguese *Reconquista* in 1217, facilitating the capture of Alcácer do Sal.[37]

---

32 Cited by J. Phillips, 'Saint Bernard of Clairvaux, the Low Countries and the Lisbon Letter of the Second Crusade', *JEH* 48 (1997), 485–97, at p. 496.
33 Phillips, 'Saint Bernard of Clairvaux', and see also H. V. Livermore, 'The "conquest of Lisbon" and its author', *Portuguese Studies* 6 (1990), 1–16.
34 Phillips, 'Ideas of crusade'; S. B. Edgington, 'Albert of Aachen, St Bernard and the Second Crusade', in *SCSC*, 54–70, esp. pp. 61–7.
35 Jaspert, '*Capta est Dertosa*'; Williams, 'The making of a crusade'; R. Hiestand, 'Reconquista, Kreuzzug und heiliges Grab: die Eroberung von Tortosa 1148 im Lichte eines neuen Zeugnisses', *Gesammelte Aufsätze zur Kulturgeschichte Spaniens* 31 (1984), 136–57.
36 O'Callaghan, *Reconquest*, pp. 70–1.
37 O'Callaghan, *Reconquest*, pp. 58–9, 79–80.

In 1213, when he proclaimed the Fifth Crusade, Innocent III cancelled preaching for the crusade in Spain. This was the downside of the *dirigisme* that had been remarked on by Helmold of Bosau. Potentially it was a momentous step, which the pope took because of the ongoing crisis in the Latin East and his calculation that because of their great victory at Las Navas de Tolosa, Spaniards could at last be spared for the defence of the Holy Land. In 1217 large numbers of Frisian crusaders cited Innocent's measure when they declined the Portuguese request to attack Alcácer do Sal.[38] But it soon became apparent that the peninsular rulers would not tolerate this downgrading of the *Reconquista*. It damaged their pockets, status and self-esteem, and it made them dangerously dependent on the services of the military orders. The constant pressure that they exerted on the *curia*, conjoined with victories and advances that formed a welcome counter-balance to the gloomy news that constantly arrived from the east, ensured the stream of crusade concessions that characterized the middle decades of the thirteenth century. Few Spaniards fought in the east. The conquests of his father Fernando III enabled Alfonso X of Castile to develop an extra-peninsular policy that involved crusading, but it did not benefit the Latin East in any way.[39] Most of the fleet that King James I of Aragon started to take eastwards in 1269, as part of Louis IX's second crusade, was allegedly compelled to turn back by a storm, though James went on to play a prominent if sceptical part at the council of Lyons a few years later.[40] Even after the disasters of 1291 it proved impossible for the *curia* to reserve the revenues of the Spanish Church for the needs of the Latin East. The kings of Castile continued to regard the income of their Church as ring-fenced for the needs of the *Reconquista*, though for a variety of reasons this was largely stalled for the next two centuries. More striking is the fact that the rulers of the Aragonese federation displayed the same attitude, given that they no longer even shared a frontier with the Moors.[41]

For reasons of space it has been necessary to detach the *Reconquista*, and the crusading that was imported into it, from the overall history of medieval Iberia.[42] In one respect, however, it would be foolish to neglect the broader impact: this is the relationship between crusading and *convivencia* (coexistence). It has undergone dramatic changes in recent years. Until comparatively recently the willingness to tolerate the religious and cultural practices of those Muslims and Jews who were living under

---

38 O'Callaghan, *Reconquest*, pp. 78–9.
39 García, 'Henry III'.
40 Riley-Smith, *The Crusades*, p. 174; Throop, *Criticism*, pp. 222–35.
41 Housley, *The Later Crusades*, pp. 266–321.
42 P. Linehan, *History and the Historians of Medieval Spain* (Oxford: Oxford University Press, 1993).

Christian rule was viewed as one of the most distinctive characteristics of the peninsular kingdoms during the central Middle Ages, and one which was largely unaffected by the ideologies of crusade and *Reconquista* that were promoted by Church and court. Spain was not viewed as a paradise for non-Christians, but the emphasis was certainly on the many signs of positive interaction.[43] The underlying message was that the Iberian peninsula, rather like Venice, was a special case in medieval Europe, in that it was much less susceptible than other regions to the crusading message. At the same time, reacting against the older school of Spanish history which had adopted a pietistic and triumphalist view of its medieval centuries as a sort of 'continual crusade', Spanish historians largely ignored crusading. Indeed, as recently as 2000 one Spanish historian of the crusades lamented a continuing tendency among his colleagues not to integrate their country's history with the European mainstream.[44]

But on *convivencia* the historiographical ground has shifted to a remarkable extent in recent years. It is increasingly accepted that the worldview of medieval Christian communities, in Spain as elsewhere, was both complex and volatile. David Nirenberg in particular has shown that *convivencia* and interfaith violence alternated as responses to situations that altered with bewildering rapidity; this was not dissimulation or hypocrisy, but the response of ordinary people to a conflicting range of interests and impulses. '*Convivencia* was predicated upon violence; it was not its peaceful antithesis.'[45] Arguably this was true above all of life at the frontier, where for different reasons one might expect to find either peaceful coexistence or antagonism to be the dominant mode of conduct, but where both can be seen functioning, depending on the circumstances.[46] At the same time more Spanish historians are becoming interested in crusading as a phenomenon that neither dominated nor by-passed the peninsula, but was one force among many that shaped its development. This can only be for the good, enabling the study of crusading in Spain to be placed within the variety of local and regional contexts that it demands, and moving on from the institutional analysis that has to date constituted the bulk of the scholarly agenda.

---

43 For example, J. N. Hillgarth, *The Spanish Kingdoms 1250–1516* (2 vols, Oxford: Oxford University Press, 1976–8), 1: 155–214. See also the numerous studies of R. I. Burns on Valencia under Christian rule, e.g. *Muslims, Christians, and Jews in the Crusader Kingdom of Valencia. Societies in Symbiosis* (Cambridge: Cambridge University Press, 1984).
44 J. M. R. García, 'Historiografía de las Cruzadas', *Espacio, Tiempo y Forma*, serie 3, *Historia Medieval* 13 (2000), 341–95, at p. 369.
45 Nirenberg, *Communities of Violence*, with quote at p. 245.
46 A. MacKay, 'Religion, culture, and ideology on the late medieval Castilian-Granadan frontier', in *MFS*, 217–43.

Crusading along the Baltic[47]

The extension of crusading to northern Europe can be dated with precision to the spring of 1147, when Pope Eugenius III issued the encyclical *Divina dispensatione*.[48] The pope proclaimed that individuals could take the cross for the Second Crusade to fight not just in the expeditions to the east but also in Iberia and against the Wends, the pagan Slavs who adjoined Saxony east of the Elbe. It is apparent that Eugenius and Bernard of Clairvaux, who prompted the move in response to urgent lobbying from the Saxons, were reacting to the surge of enthusiasm generated by the preaching of the crusade in 1146–7. It seems clear that both men were carried away by the excitement of the moment. They must have been aware that this new crusading front was different in several respects from the theatre of operations in Iberia. This was not part of the Church's eschatological struggle against Islam, which could readily be envisaged as taking place in a number of geographical locations, but a war of conquest, colonization and conversion. As early as 1108 a Flemish clerk in the circle of the archbishop of Magdeburg had argued as powerfully as he could that the war in the north should be incorporated into the crusading movement, referring to the region as 'our Jerusalem', but there were strong practical arguments against it.[49] Preaching crusades in this area brought with it the danger of diverting German manpower from the eastern crusades, a danger that was concealed in 1147 by the sheer size of the response to the preaching of the Second Crusade. It also associated the process of conversion with conquest, which ran contrary to the traditional approach of a Church that prided itself on its ability to convert peacefully, in contrast to Islamic practice.[50]

There were a number of answers to this latter conundrum, and they were all applied in the course of the preaching of the Baltic crusades. The argument that was used most frequently was that the peaceful extension of the faith in northern Europe through missionary preaching was imperilled by the violent response of pagan rulers, who killed Catholic preachers and harassed their converts into apostasy. A more radical approach was to press into service the parable of the wedding feast in Matthew 22 and

---

47   A. V. Murray, comp., 'Crusade and conversion on the Baltic frontier 1150–1550: a bibliography of publications in English', in *CCBF*, 277–85.
48   Constable, 'Second Crusade' is currently the fullest account. See *SCSC*, pp. 215–16 for recent publications in German.
49   Housley, 'Jerusalem', pp. 37–8; P. Knoch, 'Kreuzzug und Siedlung: Studien zum Aufruf der Magdeburger Kirche vom 1108', *Jahrbuch für die Geschichte Mittel- und Ostdeutschlands* 23 (1974), 1–33.
50   J. V. Tolan, *Saracens. Islam in the Medieval European Imagination* (New York: Columbia University Press, 2002), p. 261.

argue that Christ had sanctioned coercive conversion (*compelle intrare*). The thirteenth-century canonist Hostiensis asserted that pagans in any case had no rights of lordship, which had to be founded on God's grace; thus they possessed no right in natural law to defend their lands against the attacks of Catholic crusaders. This was highly contentious on several grounds and it did not answer the question of what the crusaders were doing there in the first place.[51] The text of 1108 that called for crusading in the north ingenuously celebrated the material gains to be won in what its author depicted as a new Canaan. 'These gentiles are most wicked, but their land is the best, rich in meat, honey, corn and birds; and if it were well cultivated none could be compared to it for the wealth of its produce.' He went on to appeal to his audience 'to save your souls and . . . acquire the best land in which to live'.[52] We have seen that from the First Crusade onwards churchmen were sensitive to the need to establish 'right intention' (*intentio recta*) in the case of crusading to the Holy Land, and they were even more aware of the danger involved in clothing wars of conquest in religious garb.

The ideology that underpinned the Wendish Crusade of 1147 has been disputed. It is clear enough that in the minds of Bernard and Eugenius the platform was a two-fold programme of redemption for the crusaders and conversion for the Slavs. Hans-Dietrich Kahl has argued that Bernard's activity was driven by eschatological convictions, including the belief that the second coming was imminent.[53] Friedrich Lotter was not convinced.[54] But the most debated contribution that Bernard made consisted of an extraordinary phrase used in one of his letters, that 'either the [pagan] rite or the people is to be extinguished' ('aut ritus ipse aut natio deleatur'). It is possible to read this comment as proof that one of the most influential of twelfth-century churchmen subscribed to the old-fashioned *topos* that pagans should be offered the choice between baptism and death. But Lotter has argued convincingly that the language used, especially the word *natio*, indicates that Bernard was referring to the break-up of the Wends' communities, in order to facilitate missionary activity. If the Wends embraced Christianity freely, as the Poles and Bohemians had done, they need not be conquered; but if not, they must be subjected to

---

51   J. Muldoon, *Popes, Lawyers, and Infidels. The Church and the Non-Christian World 1250–1550* (Liverpool: Liverpool University Press, 1979), surveys the whole debate.

52   L. and J. Riley-Smith, *The Crusades*, pp. 74–7, for the full text of the document.

53   H.-D. Kahl, 'Crusade eschatology as seen by St Bernard in the years 1146 to 1148', in *SCC*, 35–47 – too condensed but containing references to Kahl's many other works.

54   F. Lotter, 'The crusading idea and the conquest of the region east of the Elbe', in *MFS*, 267–306, at pp. 289–90. See also his *Die Konzeption des Wendenkreuzzugs: ideengeschichtliche, kirchenrechtliche und historisch-politische Voraussetzungen der Missionierung von Elb- und Ostseeslawen um die Mitte des 12. Jahrhunderts* (Sigmaringen: Thorbecke, 1977).

German lordship so that their souls could be saved.[55] As it transpired, the issue was academic, since this first northern crusade shattered on the rocks of political opportunism and self-interest.[56]

Until recently it was believed that the extension of crusading status to the northern wars by Eugenius III was definitive, and that irrespective of any qualms they may have had, the pope's successors accepted what had occurred as a *fait accompli*. Iben Schmidt, however, has now shown that Eugenius's actions were followed by what look like protracted second thoughts on the part of the papal *curia*.[57] Pope Alexander III demoted the Baltic crusade to the lower level of 'penitential warfare', akin to crusading but not sharing the status, in terms of spiritual reward, of expeditions that were directed to the Holy Land. In the past Innocent III has sometimes been viewed as an enthusiast for Baltic crusading, but he took much the same line that Alexander had, and it was Honorius III (1216–27) who made the decisive shift to acknowledging the full 'crusade-worthiness' of the northern wars. Schmidt's discovery is surprising, since Honorius is still seen by most scholars as essentially unoriginal in his policies. Gregory IX and Innocent IV refined Honorius's approach, co-ordinating it skilfully with their shared preoccupation with conversion. Others have concurred with Schmidt's emphasis on the importance of Honorius III,[58] and it is beginning to look as if the definitive emergence of the Baltic crusade should be placed within the context of the wave of optimism that was experienced at the papal *curia* in the early decades of the thirteenth century about the possibility of mass conversions, not least because of prophecies that the Last Days were at hand. It appears that this was enough to overcome concerns about opening up another major crusading front at a time of ongoing crisis in the Latin East, concerns which were certainly strongly felt by Honorius III, most of whose pontificate was taken up with the troubled progress and ultimate failure of the Fifth Crusade.[59]

But as Schmidt also showed, papal policy towards the north was always largely reactive. It used to be believed that the popes 'made a determined bid for power in the Baltic world between 1198 and 1268',[60] even to

55 Lotter, 'The crusading idea', pp. 288–92. Riley-Smith, *The Crusades*, p. 96, believed that 'it has never been satisfactorily explained'.
56 For Danish involvement see K. V. Jensen, 'Denmark and the Second Crusade: the formation of a crusader state?' in *SCSC*, 164–79.
57 I. M. F. Schmidt, 'The popes and the Baltic crusades 1147–1254', Cambridge PhD thesis 2004; it is to be hoped that Dr Schmidt's findings will be published in whole or in part in the near future.
58 Powell, *Anatomy*, pp. 110–111; Rist, 'Papal policy'.
59 Powell, *Anatomy*.
60 E. Christiansen, *The Northern Crusades. The Baltic and the Catholic Frontier 1100–1525* (London: Macmillan, 1980), pp. 118–31 with quote at p. 122.

create something akin to a papal state along the shores of the Baltic. But this was based on a misreading of the evidence. In the late twelfth and early thirteenth centuries it was the dominant Catholic powers in the region, the kings of Denmark and the missionary see of Riga, that shaped the pace of crusading through their policies of conquest and conversion, and the flow of envoys that they despatched to Rome to secure crusading privileges for them. Such policies were underpinned and fuelled by the region's wealth of natural resources, which attracted German settlers and traders. And in the thirteenth century the Teutonic Order, working from its military bases in the upper reaches of the Vistula valley, embarked on the most successful phase of the Baltic crusades, the conquest of Prussia. Without the regular preaching of crusades in its support, especially in the German lands, it is doubtful whether the order could have subjugated the pagans, since it still had heavy commitments in the Latin East. Like the Iberian kings at this point, the order made excellent use of the full validation of Baltic crusading to generate resources for its war, but whereas in Iberia the emphasis was on access to indigenous resources, especially Church finance, in Prussia it was recruits that the order wanted above all. And whereas in Iberia the confrontation with Granada marked the close of the *Reconquista*'s golden age, the conquest of Prussia brought the Teutonic Knights into almost immediate conflict with another ethnic group of pagans, the Lithuanians, which caused crusading warfare to continue for another century.[61]

The processes of conquest and colonization in the Baltic region bequeathed a vast amount of evidence in the shape of narrative and documentary sources originating in the area itself; many of them were published in excellent editions by German scholars working in the late nineteenth and early twentieth centuries. Similarly, the Teutonic Order has always attracted research in the German-speaking lands, and in recent years its study has benefited, albeit to a lesser extent than the Hospitallers and Templars, from the revival of interest in the military orders.[62] The role played by crusaders, and by funds raised through crusading mechanisms such as redeemed vows and legacies, has generated less interest, but since the 1970s the Baltic front has begun to catch up with other areas where crusades were waged. In 1975 a chapter on the subject appeared in the third volume of the collaborative *History of the Crusades*.[63] Five years later Eric Christiansen published what was

---

61 Christiansen, *The Northern Crusades*, pp. 70–131.
62 Forey, *The Military Orders*; H. Boockmann, *Der Deutsche Orden. Zwölf Kapitel aus seiner Geschichte* (3rd edn, Munich: C. H. Beck, 1989).
63 E. N. Johnson, 'The German crusade on the Baltic', *HC* 3: 545–85.

remarkably the first full-length scholarly treatment of the subject. Christiansen's book covered the full range of crusading through to the secularization of the Teutonic Order's state in Prussia in 1525. Christiansen established the shifting political, economic and military context but maintained his focus on the theme of crusading.[64] In a sequence of four volumes published between 1975 and 1989 William Urban surveyed all the crusading that occurred in the region.[65]

Since Christiansen and Urban the most important development has been the growing interest of Scandinavian historians, especially Danish ones, in the crusades. Between 1998 and 2001 Kurt Villads Jensen, John Lind, Carsten Selch Jensen and Ane Lise Bysted participated in a research project entitled 'Denmark and the crusading movement'. They view crusading as one of the most important channels through which the Baltic region became integrated into Catholic Europe. Once published, their results are sure to add to our understanding of a whole range of subjects, including the dynamic behind Danish overseas expansion, the contribution that the crusades made to the region's economic activity, and their impact on the non-Catholic indigenous, Russian schismatics as well as pagan Slavs and Balts. It is too soon to state with any confidence what overall picture of the Baltic crusades will emerge as a result of this fresh research, but enough has already been published to give a reasonable idea.[66] Thus Carsten Selch Jensen has highlighted the role that crusading played in the towns that bordered the Baltic, in the religious lives of not just their warrior class but also their commercial elites. Vera Matuzova described the hostile image of the pagan Prussians created by Peter of Dusburg, while Thomas Lindkvist assessed the contribution that crusading made to political life in Sweden.[67] In such instances we can see lines of investigation being pursued that closely resemble what is being done for other crusading theatres, in part because the themes (such as the construction of identities and images of the enemy) form items on an agenda that is common to many practising historians today.

---

64   Christiansen, *The Northern Crusades*.
65   W. Urban, *The Baltic Crusade* (2nd edn, Chicago: Lithuanian Research and Studies Center, 1994); *The Prussian Crusade* (Lanham, MD: University Press of America, 1980); *The Livonian Crusade* (Washington, DC: University Press of America, 1981); *The Samogitian Crusade* (Chicago: Lithuanian Research and Studies Center, 1989).
66   Notably in *CCBF*, which contains a number of essays by members of the 'new Scandinavian school', as well as historians from the Russian Federation and the Baltic states.
67   C. S. Jensen, 'Urban life and the crusades in northern Germany and the Baltic lands in the early thirteenth century', in *CCBF*, 75–94; V. I. Matuzova, 'Mental frontiers: Prussians as seen by Peter von Dusburg', ibid., 253–9; T. Lindkvist, 'Crusades and crusading ideology in the political history of Sweden, 1140–1500', ibid., 119–30.

A welcome feature of recent research into Baltic crusading has been the openness of its practitioners to a diversity of motivations, including devotion. To some extent this is a reaction against older trends. A number of Danish historians of crusading have remarked on the fact that one reason why Scandinavian historians used to neglect the Baltic crusades was their preoccupation with socio-economic explanations.[68] This led them to dismiss crusading language and rituals as little more than rhetoric. As Kurt Villads Jensen put it, 'within this framework of explanation, there was no difference between the Viking expeditions of the tenth and eleventh centuries and the Christian expeditions from the twelfth century onwards.'[69] It is interesting that this was the exact reverse of the quasi-reverential treatment accorded the *Reconquista* in Iberia, the contrasting approaches being due to the influence of confessional beliefs and national feelings. In both areas historians seem now to be sensitized to the need to take into account the full range of factors that shaped events, and as in Iberia, so in the north, interpretations are becoming more balanced. Nobody would deny that the Baltic crusades were wars of conquest fought with the goals of control and exploitation, but what is striking is the fact that intermingled with these themes was that of the religious salvation of the crusaders and their opponents. This began in 1147 and never ceased to register. This did not have to happen, so it is important to probe how it came about and what differences it made.[70] As for individual motivations, they were probably as diverse as the spectrum of groups that promoted and fought the crusades. Self-interest jostled with altruism, politics with the hope of personal redemption; and kings, princes, prelates, papal legates, military orders and trading towns alternately co-operated and fought each other, in a region where the competition was as brutal as the climate.

Crusading against Christians

The wars against Moors in Iberia and pagans in the north were Catholic Europe's principal frontier conflicts in the central Middle Ages; and looking at such evidence as Urban II's Tarragona letters, and the Magdeburg

---

68   K. V. Jensen, 'Introduction', in *CCBF*, xvii–xxv, at p. xx; T. K. Nielsen, 'The missionary man: Archbishop Anders Sunesen and the Baltic crusade, 1206–21', ibid., 95–117, at p. 99; J. M. Jensen, '*Sclavorum expugnator*: conquest, crusade, and Danish royal ideology in the twelfth century', *Crusades* 2 (2003), 55–81, at p. 55.
69   Jensen, 'Introduction', p. xx.
70   A point made by Christiansen, *The Northern Crusades*, pp. 250–1.

appeal of 1108, it is not hard to see how the crusade came to be extended there. The third extension, 'internal crusading', was inherently more problematic, involving the use of the crusade against those who, through baptism, themselves bore the cross of Christ. Although, as stated at the outset, the whole of this chapter reflects and springs from a pluralist view of what crusading entailed, it is crusading against Christians, which some contemporaries termed *crux cismarina*, that has encountered the strongest resistance from historians of the crusades who take issue with pluralism. They continue to regard it as in essence a distortion of crusading ideals rather than an extension of the practice.[71]

Probably the one thing that historians are agreed on is the series of dates at which crusading against Christians began. In 1199 Innocent III proclaimed a crusade against Markward of Anweiler, a lieutenant of the former emperor Henry VI who was opposing the pope's claim to rule the south as regent for the minor Frederick II. The *casus belli* was a political one and Markward was not accused of holding heretical beliefs, so this was the first example of what some historians have termed 'political crusades'.[72] Five years later the diversion of the Fourth Crusade led to the creation of the Latin empire of Constantinople and to the almost immediate use of the crusade for its defence against counter-attack from the exiled Byzantines and Bulgaria.[73] Crusades followed against other Orthodox communities, including the Russian principalities.[74] And in 1208 Innocent III proclaimed the Albigensian Crusade in an attempt to suppress southern French catharism by force.[75] What is striking about this series of events is first that they occurred in the short space of a decade, and secondly that they were all associated with Innocent III. From one point of view this convergence was fortuitous, the result of crises that Innocent simultaneously confronted in southern Italy and Languedoc, coupled with the fate that overtook the Fourth Crusade. But it would be foolish to deny that the vigour of the pope's response derived from personal attributes, and from his strongly held views about the office he occupied and the relationship between the Church and the practice of crusading. Undoubtedly, the institutional clarification that occurred

---

71 Some of what follows is derived from my paper, 'The non-Islamic crusades: a historiographical perspective of the last half a century', given at the Third International Crusades Conference held at Teruel, Spain, in 2001, and from the discussion that followed its delivery.

72 J. R. Strayer, 'The political crusades of the thirteenth century', in *HC* 2: 343–75, at p. 346; E. Kennan, 'Innocent III and the first political crusade: a comment on the limitations of papal power', *Traditio* 27 (1971), 231–49; Housley, *The Italian Crusades*, pp. 1–2.

73 P. Lock, *The Franks in the Aegean , 1204–1500* (London: Longman, 1995).

74 Christiansen, *The Northern Crusades*, pp. 126–31.

75 A. P. Evans, 'The Albigensian crusade', in *HC* 2: 277–324.

around 1200 made it seem to the *curia* that it would be easier to direct crusading, but this alone does not explain Innocent's actions. There are signs that previous churchmen had been tempted to use crusading against Christian enemies but had not taken that step.[76] Innocent's forthright decision to do so is the more impressive given his clear awareness of what it could well entail for the embattled Holy Land, an awareness which, it is now clear, made him draw back from sanctioning the Baltic crusade.

Rebecca Rist has recently shown that while Innocent III's successors accepted his innovation, they had different ideas about the direction in which it should be taken. They were subjected to a range of different pressures, and they learnt from experience that crusading was not always the appropriate response.[77] Once the inquisition had been organized crusading against heretics largely disappeared, the major exception being the crusades against the Hussites in the 1420s, when political and religious factors became so entangled that the use of military force on a large scale seemed to be the only way to resolve matters.[78] Similarly, once the Latin empire of Constantinople had finally collapsed in 1261, and conflict between the Teutonic Knights and the Russians subsided, crusading against Orthodox schismatics became rarer. But the 'political' crusades persisted, becoming by far the most frequent manifestation of 'internal' crusading for several generations to come. In the thirteenth and fourteenth centuries they were associated above all with the pursuit of papal territorial goals in Italy, principally the endless task of controlling the lands that were legally subject to the Church in the centre of the peninsula. In the crusades that they proclaimed against the Emperor Frederick II and his sons, the people of Sicily who rebelled against their French overlords in 1282, and the Aragonese rulers who accepted the Sicilians' invitation to rule them, the popes and their allies deployed resources on just as large a scale as those that were engaged at the time in the Latin East, in Iberia and in Prussia.[79]

Until the late 1970s the judgement of historians on 'internal' crusading was overwhelmingly negative. Good examples are Palmer Throop's *Criticism of the Crusade* (1940) and Steven Runciman's third volume in his *A History of the Crusades* (1954). Both viewed the *crux cismarina* as a diversion, an abuse of power on the part of the papal *curia*, one that was recognized as such and roundly condemned by contemporaries. The result

---

76 N. Housley, 'Crusades against Christians: their origins and early development, c. 1000–1216', in *CS*, 17–36.

77 R. Rist, 'The Development of the Idea of "Internal" Crusade, 1198–1245', Cambridge PhD thesis 2004.

78 Housley, *The Later Crusades*, pp. 249–59.

79 Housley, *The Italian Crusades*.

was not just a waning of respect for the papal office, but the decline of enthusiasm for crusading generally, due to suspicion that the authority that was directing Christendom's efforts could no longer be trusted. Throop characterized the response to crusading against Christians with such phrases as 'the severest indictments of the Church', 'a storm of denunciation', and 'disgust with papal crusade policy'.[80] Runciman wrote: 'The Crusade commanded respect only when it was directed against the infidel. The Fourth Crusade, directed, if not preached, against the Christians of the East, was followed by a Crusade against the heretics of southern France and the nobles that showed them sympathy; and this was succeeded by Crusades preached against the Hohenstaufen; till at last the Crusade came to mean any war against the enemies of Papal policy, and all the spiritual paraphernalia of indulgences and heavenly rewards was used to support the lay ambitions of the Papal See... The Holy War was warped to become a tragic farce.'[81] Pierre Toubert in 1963, and Elizabeth Kennan in 1971 and 1981, published articles about 'political' crusades whose titles alone revealed that they subscribed to the same viewpoint;[82] and in her 1975 book on papal crusading policy Maureen Purcell headed the section in which she studied the extension of crusading 'Diversion of crusading indulgences'.[83] Some historians had begun to question this view, especially those who had examined in detail the arguments deployed by the popes in their crusading bulls. Their response, however, could only be a defensive one as long as a traditional definition of crusade reigned supreme, because from such a perspective crusading against Christians was by its very nature a diversion.

It was the new methodology proposed by Jonathan Riley-Smith in *What were the Crusades?* (1977) that made it possible to examine these crusades without the presupposition that they constituted a misuse of papal authority. We have seen that his definition of crusade did not associate it with any particular location or enemy. It followed that crusading against Christians, whether they were heretics, schismatics or political enemies of the papacy, was not inherently a deviation of the practice, and Riley-Smith included all three in his brief survey of the main crusading fronts. Ten years later the radical difference that this pluralist approach could

---

80 Throop, *Criticism*, pp. 26, 28, 44.
81 Runciman, *A History*, 3: 471–2.
82 P. Toubert, 'Les Déviations de la croisade au milieu du xiiie siècle: Alexandre IV contre Manfred', *Le Moyen Age* 69 (1963), 391–9; Kennan, 'Innocent III'; 'Innocent III, Gregory IX and political crusades: a study in the disintegration of papal power', in G. F. Lytle, ed., *Reform and Authority in the Medieval and Reformation Church* (Washington, DC: Catholic University of America, 1981), 15–35.
83 Purcell, *Papal Crusading Policy*, pp. 66–98.

make became fully apparent in Riley-Smith's *The Crusades. A Short History*, in which crusades waged against Christians were described alongside those fought against non-Christians without any sign of the usual cargo of condemnation. One thing that immediately became clear was that from a pluralist perspective the thirteenth century produced the greatest volume of crusading, with as many as three or four crusades in progress at certain points. On the one hand, this established the continuing popularity of crusading. On the other, it was apparent that the multiplication of fronts siphoned resources away from the Holy Land at its time of greatest need.[84]

Riley-Smith's research pupils at the universities of Cambridge and London have conducted most of the detailed examination that has since occurred into 'internal crusading'. My early publications focused on the 'political' crusades. In *The Italian Crusades* (1982) I addressed two tasks. The first was that of analysing the ways in which crusades against Christian lay rulers were justified, preached, recruited and financed, comparing these with the procedures followed in the case of crusades to the eastern Mediterranean; and the second task was to test the claim that these crusades encountered the 'storm of denunciation' described by Throop and others. On the first issue, the broad equivalence of approach that I encountered has been accepted as showing that in many respects those crusaders who fought in Italy went through the same processes, legal, financial and liturgical, as those who took the cross to wage war elsewhere. This has since been confirmed by the studies of Simon Lloyd, Christoph Maier and Christopher Tyerman.[85] On the second issue I concluded that there was a broad acceptance of 'political' crusading, with the exception of those recruits and funds that had been raised for the needs of the Latin East and were redirected by the papal *curia* towards crusading in Italy. Contemporaries acknowledged the right of the popes to defend the Church and faith from 'the enemy within', but they resented the fraud that was often perpetrated on its behalf. A research question of this kind was bound to be more difficult to address comprehensively than that of the procedures followed, and my stance on this issue has come in for a fair amount of criticism, for example from Jean Flori, Sylvia Schein and Christopher Tyerman.[86]

---

84 Riley-Smith, *The Crusades*, pp. 152–78.

85 Lloyd, *English Society*, esp. pp. 113–53; Maier, *Preaching*; Tyerman, *England and the Crusades*, pp. 152–86.

86 Flori, 'Pour une redéfinition', p. 340; S. Schein, *Fideles Crucis. The Papacy, the West, and the Recovery of the Holy Land 1274–1314* (Oxford: Oxford University Press, 1991), pp. 5–7; C. J. Tyerman, 'The Holy Land and the crusades of the thirteenth and fourteenth centuries', in *CS*, 105–12.

Three years after *The Italian Crusades* was published, the question of contemporary criticism was addressed in a broader context by Elizabeth Siberry. She showed that many of the authors whose views had been taken as representative by Throop in reality had personal or political axes to grind. It was clear that much greater methodological care was needed in examining attacks on papal policy.[87] More recently, Michael Lower studied the reactions of the French barons in 1239–41 toward papal attempts to direct human and financial resources for crusading. He concluded that the French were far from willing to act as mere executors of the *curia*'s policy and were prepared to defy Gregory IX on the issue. This interpretation of the outlook of lay people was in harmony with what Marcus Bull and Caroline Smith have discovered for other periods: that contemporaries could be pious without being submissive, and that they formed their own views about the way crusading should be conducted.[88] Rebecca Rist has examined the full range of argumentation, theological and legal, that was deployed by the *curia* when it preached crusades against Christians, and she has brought into the equation the ways in which the Jews were affected by shifting papal policies towards non-Catholic individuals and groups.[89]

Although internal crusading has now attracted a reasonable amount of attention, there is much that remains to be done. Little has been written on the papacy's attitude towards the Russian principalities in the context of crusading. More curiously, given its momentous role in French history, less research has been devoted to the Albigensian Crusade than to other forms of 'internal' crusade.[90] Narrative histories of the war abound, but we still have in print no 'institutional' study of the crusade, though we know enough to be fairly confident that there were no big differences of approach.[91] As things stand, it is hard to see how there will be any major input from students of crusading at the conferences that will inevitably be organized to mark the anniversary of the crusade's initiation in 2008; and this means that the view presented of the crusaders will probably be both hostile and outdated.

Contemporary reactions to the Albigensian Crusade appear to have varied considerably. Some contemporaries viewed coercion as the wrong

---

87   Siberry, *Criticism*.

88   Studies by Lower and Smith are forthcoming. For Bull, see *Knightly Piety*; 'The roots'.

89   Rist, 'The Development'.

90   M. Barber, *The Cathars. Dualist Heretics in Languedoc in the High Middle Ages* (Harlow: Longman, 2000), pp. 235–6, surveys the current reading, noting that 'there is still space for a modern narrative in English'.

91   Woehl, *Volo vincere*, is a detailed analysis of Simon de Montfort's armies in the south, but because its author adopts the traditionalist definition of crusade, she completely ignores crusading practices.

response, or believed that the crusaders from northern France were driven by greed rather than zeal for the faith: once again, the question of *intentio recta* played a central role.[92] A similar range of reactions had followed the capture of Constantinople by the Fourth Crusade a few years previously.[93] In this respect, as in that of the 'political' crusades, gauging response presents problems that appear insuperable. It is far from easy to evaluate the importance of the strident views expressed by someone like Matthew Paris. We are on firmer and more promising ground in assessing the perceptions of the enemy that characterized the different types of 'internal' crusade; for example, it would be interesting to examine how anti-cathar rhetoric paved the way for papal invective against the Staufen. Clearly, the research situation has moved forward in the course of thirty years. While no consensus has emerged, or seems likely to do so, about the reception of the crusades that were directed against Christians, we know much more about their origins, nature and impact than we once did.

---

92 Siberry, *Criticism*, pp. 158–68.
93 Angold, *The Fourth Crusade*, pp. 111–28.

6

Crusading after 1291

1291–1400

It would seem obvious that once we pass 1291 we enter a landscape dominated by the pluralist approach towards crusading.[1] There no longer existed any Latin states in Palestine and Syria to be defended, so there were no more *passagia* launched to assist them. Crusading therefore moved on into other regions where expeditions took place that met the broad set of criteria viewed by pluralists as comprising the definition of crusade. As a summary this is valid, but it should not obscure the striking fact that for nearly half a century after the fall of Acre most of the enthusiasm and energy that went into crusading in the east remained focused on the Holy Land, in terms not of defence but of recovery. The subject of what has come to be called 'recovery planning' has long attracted some interest,[2] but in the last third of the twentieth century a number of research historians addressed it in depth. They were far from agreeing on certain issues, but the substantial body of published work that resulted did make it clear that the period stretching from the Mamluk conquest through to the outbreak of the Anglo-French war in 1337 was much more than just an epilogue to the age of the great crusades.

One feature of these decades was the proliferation of written treatises setting out the essential requirements of a 'recovery crusade' and suggest-

---

1 For bibliography up to 1991 see my *The Later Crusades*, pp. 462–500. For detail on events see my 'The crusading movement, 1274–1700', in *OIHC*, 260–93.

2 For example, A. S. Atiya, *The Crusade in the Later Middle Ages* (2nd edn, New York: Kraus, 1970), pp. 29–127.

ing how they could be met. Some of these treatises pre-dated 1291 by some years, and in terms of strategic thinking about recovery it is arguable that 1291 is less meaningful as a date than it might appear to be. Though the loss of the final settlements robbed the western Europeans of valuable bridgeheads, it also freed up the overall scenario. And since at least the early 1270s the situation of the settlers in the Latin East had been so precarious that in practice a crusade that aimed to achieve anything major was actually one of 'recovery' rather than defence. Some historians have come to think of the whole period from c. 1270 to c. 1340 as possessing a unity that was characterized on the one hand by the difficulty of securing peace in Europe and on the other by an awareness of the intractable strategic situation that was posed by the military power of the Mamluks and Mongols.[3] It was natural that westerners who became familiar with this two-fold dilemma, and who were painfully aware of the recent past of crusading failure and its corrosive effect on Christian morale, should proscribe the simple launching of another crusade. In its place they espoused a process of information-gathering, consultation and careful planning, building on precedents established by Pope Innocent III. This is another illustration of the danger which we encountered in chapter 3 of treating the final decades of the Latin settlements in the east in stereotypical 'decline and fall' terms.

The several dozen treatises 'De recuperatione terrae sanctae' that survive from these decades vary greatly in terms of their provenance, the knowledge, objectivity and insight of their authors, and not least the accessibility of the texts themselves. It was only in the late nineteenth century that the genre received full recognition, from the French historian of the crusades Joseph Delaville le Roulx.[4] Editions of the texts vary considerably in quality and the treatise that most scholars would regard as the finest, the 'Liber secretorum fidelium crucis' (1306–21) by the Venetian patrician and merchant Marino Sanudo Torsello, has to be consulted in an edition that will soon be 400 years old.[5] Despite the weakness of the overall editorial tradition, scholars have studied these treatises and the lives of their more prominent authors with a good deal of enthusiasm.[6] Provided we bear in mind that they represented no more

---

3 For example, Housley, *The Later Crusades*, pp. 7–39; Tyerman, *England and the Crusades*, pp. 229–58.

4 J. Delaville le Roulx, *La France en orient au XIVe siècle: expéditions du maréchal Boucicaut* (2 vols, Paris: Ernest Thorin, 1886).

5 J. Bongars, ed., *Gesta Dei per Francos, sive orientalium expeditionum et regni Francorum Hierosolymitani historia* (2 vols, Hanover, 1611), vol. 2.

6 A. Leopold, *How to Recover the Holy Land. The Crusade Proposals of the Late Thirteenth and Early Fourteenth Centuries* (Aldershot: Ashgate, 2000).

than the views of those authors, we can learn a great deal from them about the extent of contemporary knowledge of the east, including the strengths and weaknesses of the Muslims and Mongols.[7] Often they afford us a view of why contemporaries thought past crusades had failed, and what overall perspective they held of the way crusading had developed since 1095. And they naturally give us an insight to what reasonably well-informed people considered to be the key problems that faced anybody setting out to organize a recovery crusade. In Marino Sanudo's case the financial detail alone is invaluable.[8]

Further than that it would be rash to go. But if the treatises can tell us nothing conclusive about the state of public opinion, they are a strong indicator of the seriousness with which the mounting of a recovery crusade was taken by the leading rulers of the times, because so many texts were written during bouts of intensive planning and negotiation.[9] These began in the immediate aftermath of the fall of Acre, when Edward I of England was still looked to as the most suitable leader of a *passagium*.[10] When Edward died the baton passed to Philip the Fair of France, who seemed to warm to the idea following an earlier antipathy towards crusading.[11] Philip's sons Philip V and Charles IV in turn engaged in detailed talks with the papal court and with their own subjects and advisors, and Philip VI of France, the first ruler from the Valois dynasty, perhaps got further than anybody had since 1291 towards actually raising the men, money, shipping and allies that were the *sine qua non* for an attempt to recover the Holy Land. The crusading plans of all these rulers have now been exhaustively examined.[12] In terms of action the results were limited, the most substantial campaigning that occurred being the Order of St John's conquest of Rhodes, completed in 1309. But the papal *curia* helped to sustain an air of anticipation by its

---

7   E. Edson, 'Reviving the crusade: Sanudo's schemes and Vesconte's maps', in R. Allen, ed., *Eastward Bound. Travel and Travellers, 1050–1550* (Manchester: Manchester University Press, 2004), 131–55.

8   F. Cardini, 'I costi della crociata. L'aspetto economico del progetto di Marin Sanudo il Vecchio (1312–1321)', in *Studi in memoria di Federigo Melis* (5 vols, Naples: Giannini, 1978), 2: 179–210; N. Housley, 'Costing the crusade: budgeting for crusading activity in the fourteenth century', in *EC*, 45–59.

9   For example, J. N. Hillgarth, *Ramon Lull and Lullism in Fourteenth-Century France* (Oxford: Oxford University Press, 1971); C. J. Tyerman, 'Marino Sanudo Torsello and the lost crusade: lobbying in the fourteenth century', *TRHS* 32 (1982), 57–73.

10   Lloyd, *English Society*, pp. 198–243; Tyerman, *England and the Crusades*, pp. 111–32.

11   Schein, 'Philip IV'; J. Riley-Smith, 'The crown of France and Acre, 1254–1291', in D. H. Weiss and L. Mahoney, eds, *France and the Holy Land. Frankish Culture at the End of the Crusades* (Baltimore, MD: Johns Hopkins University Press, 2004), 45–62.

12   C. J. Tyerman, 'Sed nihil fecit? The last Capetians and the recovery of the Holy Land', in *WGMA*, 170–81; 'Philip V of France, the assemblies of 1319–20 and the crusade', *BIHR* 57 (1984), 15–34; 'Philip VI and the recovery of the Holy Land', *EHR* 100 (1985), 25–51.

ongoing attempt to impose an embargo on all western trade with the Mamluk lands, which was widely regarded by advocates of a recovery crusade as the essential preliminary to a military assault.[13]

What we can learn from these processes of planning, consultation and high-level diplomatic haggling remains a matter for debate. Take, for example, what might well be regarded as the most revealing barometer for Catholic feelings in the aftermath of the disaster of 1291: the trial and suppression of the Knights Templar in 1307–12. Until about 1970 historians saw the downfall of the order in terms of Philip the Fair's unscrupulous manipulation of public hostility towards the Templars as a means of securing their rich assets so that he could rescue his own finances from collapse.[14] More broadly, it was viewed as evidence for the rise of the secular state and its exertion of control over the resources and loyalties of both Church and laity.[15] From this viewpoint crusading too was reduced to a propaganda tool to be deployed against fellow rulers, a mechanism to exert pressure on the papal *curia*, and a rhetorical device for rallying domestic opinion behind unpopular policies. Although not totally erroneous, this interpretation of the fall of the Templars now seems too straightforward.[16] That the trial's origins and outcome were connected with the expulsion of the Christians from the Holy Land seems certain, but it reflects a public response to 1291 that was diverse and complex, extremely hard for us to read. It was no longer possible for most rulers, churchmen or laity to experience an unqualified surge of enthusiasm for the recovery of Palestine, but that is far from saying that Catholic Europe could turn its back on the Holy Land. Instead, zeal for crusading and the demands of practical politics constantly clashed and interwove in bouts of frenetic and often ill-tempered negotiations that persisted for years, until the outbreak of hostilities between England and France in 1337 brought this period to a close. With hindsight it is not hard to pinpoint the range of

---

13 Housley, *The Avignon Papacy*, pp. 199–213; Leopold, *How to Recover the Holy Land*, pp. 119–36; J. Trenchs Odena, '"De Alexandrinis" (El comercio prohibido con los musulmanes y el papado de Aviñón durante la primera mitad de siglo XIV)', *Anuario de estudios medievales* 10 (1980), 237–320.

14 For example, Runciman, *A History*, 3: 434–6.

15 See above all the work of J. Strayer, e.g. *The Reign of Philip the Fair* (Princeton, NJ: Princeton University Press, 1980).

16 For example, Barber, *The New Knighthood*, pp. 295–301; A. Forey, 'The military orders, 1120–1312', in *OIHC*, 184–216, at pp. 215–16: 'it is difficult to reach definitive conclusions'. It is likely that the anniversary of the trial in 2007 will revive the debate. In the mean time, J. Riley-Smith has reopened the question of Templar guilt: 'Were the Templars guilty?' and 'The structure of the orders of the Temple and the Hospital in c. 1291', in *MC*, 107–24, 125–43.

problems – military, financial, political and ideological – that impeded the translation of will into action; but it is much more difficult to be confident about the strength of the underlying convictions, and hence about the possibility of an alternative outcome.

Even after 1337 it would be wrong to say that the Holy Land ceased to play a role in the crusading activity that occurred. There is general agreement, however, that increasingly that role was indirect, and lay more in the realm of ideas, emotions and images than in the sphere of practical planning.[17] The best example is the crusade that Peter I, king of Cyprus, led to capture Alexandria in 1365. Peter promoted his expedition, during a tour of the courts of western and central Europe in 1362–4, as a 'recovery crusade', and the assault on Alexandria that followed was depicted as a renewed attempt to execute the Egyptian strategy that had failed in the Fifth Crusade and the first crusade of Louis IX of France. At the time he sailed, however, Europe had been buffeted for many years by plague, economic reversals and warfare. Such conditions were the reverse of propitious for an agenda that had been challenging enough in much more favourable circumstances. Historians have tended to view the whole enterprise as at best a quixotic adventure by a man who took too seriously his notional title as king of Jerusalem: 'Peter indeed was born a century too late' was the verdict of Sir George Hill.[18] At worst it was an act of culpable recklessness that plunged his island kingdom into war with the most powerful Islamic state in the Middle East. It is not impossible that the king's quirky personality was to blame – he would become seriously unbalanced just a few years later, provoking assassination in 1369. But Peter Edbury has put forward an alternative explanation that interprets the king's attack on Alexandria as an attempt to control the chief rival to Cyprus's principal port, Famagusta. This *entrepôt* had enjoyed great prosperity following the fall of Latin Syria, but it was now in decline thanks to Alexandria's vastly superior location and facilities. The situation was aggravated during the 1340s by the papacy's abandonment of its policy of maintaining a commercial embargo on the sultanate. The best outcome would be Cypriot tenure of Alexandria, which the Arab chronicler an-Nuwairī considered viable; but even if this proved impossible, the port

---

17   A. Demurger, 'Le Religieux de Saint-Denis et la croisade', in F. Autrand, C. Gauvard and J.-M. Moeglin, eds, *Saint Denis et la royauté: études offertes à Bernard Guenée* (Paris: Publications de la Sorbonne, 1999), 181–96, at p. 188.
18   G. Hill, *A History of Cyprus* (4 vols, Cambridge: Cambridge University Press, 1940–52), 2: 319. Cf. Runciman, *A History*, 3: 441: 'the first monarch since Saint Louis of France to have a burning and overwhelming desire to fight the Holy War'.

could be returned to the sultan in exchange for the granting to Cypriot merchants of more favourable trading terms there.[19]

There exists evidence that Peter was swayed primarily by such economic considerations, but it is indirect and far from overwhelming, and it is possible to construct an alternative view of his actions that emphasizes his love of war and his awareness of his crusading ancestry. Either way, Peter's attacks on his Muslim neighbours, which spanned his whole ten-year reign, do bring together a group of major themes that recur throughout the recent writing concerned with the survival of crusading in the middle decades of the fourteenth century. The Holy Land continued to feature, but as a combination of inspiration and reference point, both historical and religious, rather than as a hard and fast military objective. Before 1337 it was possible for an enthusiast like Marino Sanudo Torsello to set out in a remarkably objective way the detailed political, military and financial prerequisites for the recovery of Palestine; by 1365 it had become necessary to rely instead on a good deal of optimism coupled with a belief in the workings of providence. As Edbury put it, 'it is hard to believe that [Peter I] could really have believed that his army could take Jerusalem from the Mamluks and then defend it against the might of the Muslim world.'[20] In practice the continuation of crusading practices and activities in the eastern Mediterranean was driven by three other forces. One was the substantial Catholic presence in the region, in the shape of Cyprus, Venice's colonies, naval bases and commercial interests, the order-state of the Knights Hospitallers in the Rhodian archipelago, and the numerous minor Latin rulers and states which had sprung up among the Greek islands and in the Peloponnese in the wake of the Fourth Crusade.[21] The second was the willingness of the papal court, temporarily situated at Avignon, to respond to lobbying from these powers by treating their cause as a crusade. And the third was the fact that the resulting combats were integrated into contemporary perceptions of chivalrous behaviour as a field of particular esteem and honour. Each has attracted scholarly attention.

Given the diversity of interests and the mutual antagonisms that characterized the range of Catholic powers in the east, no focused strategic

---

19   P. W. Edbury, *The Kingdom of Cyprus and the Crusades, 1191–1374* (Cambridge: Cambridge University Press, 1991), pp. 141–79. Edbury has restated the argument in 'Christians and Muslims in the eastern Mediterranean', in M. Jones, ed., *NCMH, VI, c. 1300–c. 1415* (Cambridge: Cambridge University Press, 2000), 864–84, at pp. 879–81.
20   Edbury, *The Kingdom*, p. 162.
21   Lock, *The Franks*; M. Balard, 'Latins in the Aegean and the Balkans in the fourteenth century', in M. Jones, ed., *NCMH, VI, c. 1300–c. 1415* (Cambridge: Cambridge University Press, 2000), 825–38.

goals could be expected to emerge: their calls for crusade were bound to be largely responsive and sometimes contradictory. They were responding, moreover, to an enemy, the cluster of Turkish emirates in Anatolia, who themselves had little more in common than religion and ethnicity.[22] The result was fragmentation and, to a large extent, waste of effort. There was the major problem that although the fourteenth century witnessed a gradual *rapprochement* between the Catholic and Orthodox Churches, cooperation with the restored Byzantine empire continued to be hindered by mutual suspicion.[23] Even enthusiasts for crusading like the legate Pierre de Thomas found it impossible to sew the various scattered conflicts of the region together into a meaningful whole. Given their naval expertise and resources, the Latins could usually defeat the Turks at sea, but on land they could achieve little more than to capture and hold onto part of the port of Smyrna.[24] This disappointing track record was well reflected in the activities of the Hospitallers, who took part in most of the crusading against the Turks but dedicated much more energy to the government and settlement of Rhodes and to fruitless plans for their own expansion. The acrimonious letters of rebuke that the master and convent received from the popes form perhaps the most telling commentary on the frustration that informed contemporaries felt at the desultory and tangled fighting that took place in the 1340s and 1350s.[25]

The pope usually credited with extending the crusade to this zone of conflict was Clement VI. Alain Demurger has questioned this: basing his argument mainly on the vocabulary used in the papal letters, he argued that Clement drew back from acknowledging the struggle to be a fully-fledged crusade.[26] Others, including the present writer, have argued that the papal *curia* transplanted the crusade in the fullest sense to the Aegean world.[27] In doing so it was responding to some skilled lobbying from the Catholic powers there: they showed a canny awareness of the broad-based interpretation of crusading that had become characteristic of the papal

---

22   I. M. Kunt, 'The rise of the Ottomans', ibid., 839–63.

23   Housley, *The Avignon Papacy*, pp. 213–22; N. Bisaha, 'Petrarch's vision of the Muslim and Byzantine east', *Speculum* 76 (2001), 284–314.

24   Housley, *The Later Crusades*, pp. 49–70; K. M. Setton, *The Papacy and the Levant (1204–1571)* (4 vols, Philadelphia: American Philosophical Society, 1978–84), 1: 163–326.

25   A. Luttrell, 'The Hospitallers at Rhodes, 1306–1421', in *HC* 3: 278–313. For context see A. Luttrell, 'The crusade in the fourteenth century', in J. Hale, R. Highfield and B. Smalley, eds, *Europe in the Late Middle Ages* (London: Faber and Faber, 1965), 122–54, which gives a clear impression of the scholarly state of play forty years ago.

26   A. Demurger, 'Le pape Clément VI et l'Orient: ligue ou croisade?', in J. Paviot and J. Verger, eds, *Guerre, pouvoir et noblesse au Moyen Âge. Mélanges en l'honneur de Philippe Contamine* (Paris: Presses de l'Université de Paris-Sorbonne, 2000), 207–14.

27   Housley, *The Avignon Papacy*, pp. 31–6, 117–22.

curia's approach. But there is general agreement that issues of prestige and advantage also played a role.[28] At this time the papal *curia* was on the back foot, exiled from its see at Rome and caught between the scissors of unrelenting demands from secular rulers for a greater share of Church wealth, and a growing tide of anti-clerical feeling in society at large. Involvement in the combats against the Anatolian Turks bestowed less prestige than sponsoring attempts to recover the holy places, but it did raise and enhance the public profile of the *curia*. Moreover, in the naval leagues (*societates*) that comprised the organizational format adopted for most of the fighting against the Turks, the *curia* could be more interventionist than was possible in the case of large-scale *passagia*. The war against the Turks was a useful mirror to show the powers of the west what they ought to be doing instead of constantly fighting against each other. In addition, from the 1360s, when the Ottoman Turks crossed into Thrace, there was novelty: an Islamic power was penetrating space that hitherto had been exclusively Christian. After the diversion of efforts southwards that was engineered (without much difficulty, it has to be said) by Peter I of Cyprus, Pope Gregory XI (1370–8) showed a good deal of resolve to drive the Turks back beyond the Straits.[29] But any development of his approach was then wrecked by the outbreak of the Great Schism in 1378.

The fact that the schism did not put an end to the persistence of crusading in the east is clear proof that the latter owed relatively little of its impetus to papal initiative. Indeed, perhaps the most striking feature of crusading in this period is its full integration into chivalric culture. We possess only scattered clues as to what the population at large thought about the war against the Turks before 1400, but we are well informed on the views of the noble *élite*. Nearly all historians agree that the narrative sources, buttressed by chivalric treatises, biographies, romances and poems, are unanimous in portraying a world in which combat against the 'pagans', 'Saracens' or 'unbelievers' was a thoroughly praiseworthy activity.[30] Terry Jones argued that there was a good deal of contemporary criticism of this volunteer service, which is reflected in Chaucer's (allegedly) ironic depiction of his 'verray parfit gentil knight' in *The Canterbury Tales*, but this iconoclastic thesis has won few supporters.[31] Most of

---

28 Wood, *Clement VI*.

29 A. Luttrell, 'Gregory XI and the Turks: 1370–1378', *Orientalia Christiana periodica* 46 (1980), 391–417.

30 Housley, *The Later Crusades*, pp. 394–403; Tyerman, *England and the Crusades*, pp. 259–301; M. Keen, *Chivalry* (New Haven, CT: Yale University Press, 1984).

31 T. Jones, *Chaucer's Knight. The Portrait of a Medieval Mercenary* (revd edn, London: Methuen, 1994).

the evidence shows that those who went out to fight with the naval leagues, the Hospitallers at Rhodes, or Peter of Cyprus at Alexandria, were well regarded by their contemporaries. The conflict in the Mediterranean was one of the 'fronts' most eagerly sought out by individuals or groups to display their prowess, win their spurs and advance their careers. There are examples scattered throughout the middle and last decades of the century, but arguably the clearest is that of Jean le Maingre, Marshal Boucicaut, who at different times fought against the Ottomans, the Mamluks and the Moors.[32] At the end of the day both the survival of the crusade in the east beyond 1337, and its diffusion to areas of Christian–Muslim combat beyond the Holy Land, hinged upon the readiness of such men to place body, expertise and resources in the service of the faith.

The clearest evidence for the ongoing appeal of combat against non-believers to the fighting classes of the fourteenth century derives not from the eastern Mediterranean but from the Baltic region. Here military conflict continued in the form of a gruelling war between the Teutonic Order and pagan Lithuania.[33] The order tried to compensate for its shortage of trained fighters by promoting its war as a field of chivalric and crusading endeavour. A number of scholars, above all Werner Paravicini, have demonstrated just how widespread and successful its efforts were. Thousands of nobles from western and central Europe made their way eastwards to take part in the *Reisen* ('journeys') that were organized by the Knights each summer and winter, weather conditions permitting, into the pagan lands lying to the east. A wide range of sources testify to the way these volunteers set about preparing, funding and conducting their journeys, and it is apparent that much of the infrastructure of pre-1291 crusading survived in this area of conflict, including the importance of kinship ties and commercial links. Given the limited opportunities for advertising the war, its popularity must have been largely due to the eager receptivity of the noble *élite* to the message that was reaching them; though it is likely that the hospitality offered by the order played some role in sustaining enthusiasm, especially among the many who went to Prussia more than once.[34]

One of the clearest messages to emerge from studies of the *Reisen* is that the 'chivalric crusading' that they epitomized was largely couched in terms of individual aspiration, adventure and reputation. The sense of a

32   N. Housley, 'One man and his wars: the depiction of warfare by Marshal Boucicaut's biographer', *JMH* 29 (2003), 27–40.
33   S. C. Rowell, *Lithuania Ascending. A Pagan Empire within East-Central Europe, 1295–1345* (Cambridge: Cambridge University Press, 1994).
34   W. Paravicini, *Die Preussenreisen des europäischen Adels* (2 vols, Sigmaringen: Jan Thorbecke, 1989–95); Christiansen, *The Northern Crusades*, pp. 149–70.

Catholic community that was united in the pursuit of a common cause, the pull of an eschatological reading of military events, and the formation of a demonic 'image of the enemy', features that had all been important in crusading during the twelfth and thirteenth centuries, were either absent or very muted. To a large degree this was true also of those noble volunteers who headed not for Königsberg, the favourite jumping-off point for the *Reisen*, but for Rhodes, Cyprus or Smyrna. Although the word *peregrini* ('pilgrims') continued to be used to describe such volunteers, the massive devotional commitment that had been characteristic of earlier crusading had vanished. This is an important point in considering the transition from the fourteenth to the fifteenth century. As we shall see, a consensus attributes much of the reason for the partial revival of crusading that occurred in the latter period to the threat that was clearly posed to Christendom by the advance of the Ottoman Turks. It is tempting to assume that the same must have applied during the first period of Ottoman westwards conquest, the years between the Turkish victory over the Serbs at Kosovo in 1389 and their own defeat by Tamerlane at Ankara in 1402. From this perspective the crusade of Nicopolis (1396) in particular is characterized as the first major encounter between Catholic Europe and the enemy that would dominate its field of vision in the east for the next two centuries.

Alongside Peter I's attack on Alexandria, Nicopolis was the most significant clash of arms between Christians and Muslims in the fourteenth century, and like the Alexandria raid it has provided material for much debate.[35] The crusade's origins in particular have been much examined. In 1972 J. J. N. Palmer advanced the thesis that the expedition was remarkably broad based in its conception. The most prolific and dedicated crusading enthusiast active in the second half of the century was the Picard Philippe de Mézières, and Palmer argued that his idealistic viewpoint shaped the thinking of the planners. Not only was the crusade a level-headed and forward-thinking response to the successes of the Turks in the southern Balkans, it was also seen as a way to heal the wounds caused by the Anglo-French conflict, and as a mechanism to bring the Great Schism to a close. The Wilton Diptych, a masterpiece of High Gothic that was painted for King Richard II in the years immediately before the crusade, was construed as full of references to this great programme.[36] So although the campaign itself was marred by a series of follies and blunders

---

35 See *Annales de Bourgogne* 68 (1996), a special issue for the 600th anniversary of the campaign.
36 J. J. N. Palmer, *England, France and Christendom, 1377–99* (London: Routledge and Kegan Paul, 1972), pp. 180–210.

that culminated in a shocking defeat south of the fortress town of Nicopolis in September 1396, in initiation and planning at least it bore a strong resemblance to such ambitious ventures as the First, Second and Fifth Crusades.

Much of this interpretation has dissolved away under closer examination. During restoration work on the Wilton Diptych a discovery was made that renders its crusading iconography rather less plausible.[37] There was certainly a background of elevated and resonant idealism, on which Mézières placed his personal stamp, but the principal motor for the force that set out from Dijon in the spring of 1396 was the political ambition of Philip the Bold of Burgundy; and the context within which the volunteers offered their services was that of chivalric honour.[38] Nor do our sources reveal a strong sense of alarm about what the Turks might do if they were not driven back; indeed, at one point Philip was considering sending the Burgundian contingent to fight in Prussia, and in general views of what the crusaders were aiming to achieve were distinctly muddled. There are still unresolved issues about Nicopolis, and due to the weakness of the Turkish sources and the tendentious character of the western ones they are likely to remain.[39] But in the light of its unsettled agenda and inchoate command structure, which were aggravated by the highly individualistic ethos of its participants, it is not surprising that the crusaders were defeated.

The Fifteenth Century

What is surprising is that crusading survived Nicopolis, given the way circumstances around 1400 were conspiring against it. Six years after the battle the Ottoman Turks suffered a defeat at Ankara at the hands of the Tatars that was so severe that it put them out of the picture for a generation. In 1386 the conversion of the Lithuanians to Christianity

---

37 D. Gordon, *Making and Meaning: The Wilton Diptych* (London: National Gallery Publications, 1993).

38 In his treatment of Nicopolis, R. Vaughan, *Philip the Bold. The Formation of the Burgundian State* (London: Longman, 1962), pp. 59–78, argued this case, but it was developed more fully by J. Paviot, *Les Ducs de Bourgogne, la croisade et l'orient (fin xive siècle – xve siècle)* (Paris: Presses de l'Université de Paris-Sorbonne, 2003), pp. 17–57. Jim Magee reached similar conclusions in 'Politics, society and the crusade in England and France, 1378–1400', unpublished PhD thesis, University of Leicester, 1997, ch. 4; see his 'Crusading at the court of Charles VI, 1388–1396', *French History* 12 (1998), 367–83.

39 N. Housley, 'Le maréchal Boucicaut à Nicopolis', *Annales de Bourgogne* 68 (1996), 85–99; Demurger, 'Le Religieux'.

began when the Poles achieved the diplomatic *coup* of a dynastic marriage between their monarch Jadwiga and Grand Prince Jogailo, thereby subverting the rationale of the Teutonic Order's *Reisen*. It took several years for the message of Lithuanian conversion to filter through to the European aristocracy, but once it was incontrovertible the practice of treating the war as a crusade could no longer continue. At Tannenberg (Grünwald) in 1410 the Teutonic Knights suffered a heavy defeat at the hands of the Poles and Lithuanians and their order entered a period of decline.[40] 'Chivalric crusading' declined with it, which indicates how strongly it had always depended on the promotion of the *Reisen*: the war against Islamic Granada in southern Spain was sporadic in nature and never exerted an equivalent appeal. The Portuguese aristocracy were soon afterwards provided with a new outlet for their crusading zeal in combat in north Africa, but they were unusual.[41] Nor could the papacy be proactive in promoting crusades, for the Church remained in schism until union was achieved at the Council of Constance in 1417. As for the broad mass of the population, so far as we can see it had shown little interest in crusading for over a century. So it would be understandable if the rich crop of work that has recently been published about the century from the fall of Acre to the battle of Nicopolis were to represent the last phase in crusading's impact on the European world.

But it did not, and there are clear signs that the scholarly interest aroused by the fourteenth century is starting to be replicated in the case of the fifteenth.[42] Much of that interest is naturally focused on the impact of the Turks, but before addressing that aspect, it is important to signal the importance of the series of five crusades launched against the Hussite heretics in Bohemia, which began in 1420 and ended in 1431.[43] The Hussite crusades remain one of the biggest lacunae in the study of crusading.[44] Very little has been written about these campaigns despite the fact that, militarily and politically, they were just as significant as the Albigensian Crusades two centuries previously. To some extent the reason is the subject's linguistic demands, though the bulk of the evidence relating to the promotion and organization of the expeditions is in Latin and German. It is possible that the problem is more general in nature: a failure, outside the frontiers of Germany and the Czech Republic, to

---

40 Christiansen, *The Northern Crusades*, pp. 219–49.

41 P. Russell, *Prince Henry 'the Navigator'. A Life* (New Haven, CT: Yale University Press, 2000).

42 *CFCMI*, esp. editor's introduction.

43 F. G. Heymann, 'The crusades against the Hussites', in *HC* 3: 586–646.

44 T. A. Fudge, ed. and trans., *The Crusade against Heretics in Bohemia, 1418–1437. Sources and Documents for the Hussite Crusades* (Aldershot: Ashgate, 2002), shows what can be done.

engage closely with the history of central Europe. In the United Kingdom at least, for a variety of reasons, there is an ongoing neglect of continental European history throughout the late Middle Ages, with a few exceptions such as the Hundred Years War.[45] Whatever the reasons for it, the lack of research into the crusades against the Hussites is all the more regrettable given the impressive volume of published work on the Hussite revolution itself, above all the *magnum opus* by František Šmahel.[46]

Though the paucity of published work makes it very difficult to comment on the Hussite crusades in detail, some points can be made about their broader significance in terms of fifteenth-century crusading. The ability of the Church to launch five large-scale crusades so soon after the healing of the schism shows that in purely institutional terms the practice of crusading retained viability. It is true that King Sigismund of Hungary, under whose aegis as emperor-elect the expeditions were promoted, was particularly well placed to deploy the crusading format to generate military activity, and it also true that the German princes who played the key role in mobilizing the troops needed were alarmed as much by the political (and even the social) implications of the Hussite revolution as by its religious threat. The circumstances behind the Hussite crusades were exceptional from a number of viewpoints, and nobody has argued that they demonstrated either a dramatic revival of papal authority over the crusades or a readiness on the part of the laity to respond as willingly as it once had done to the call to take the cross. But they were not regarded as anachronistic. Indeed, from the effort that the Hussites put into publicly denouncing the use of the crusade against them we may infer that crusading, as a means of creating military capacity, was still something to be feared.[47]

Hussitism was far from being just a regional problem. The threat that the Hussites were perceived to pose to the unity of a Church that had just been painfully reunited after nearly four decades of division was feared beyond the borders of the empire; there were interesting episodes of English and Burgundian involvement.[48] That said, the launching of the Hussite crusades did not answer the question of whether crusading could still function as a means of mobilizing the common efforts of all Christen-

---

45 The neglect was already 'notorious' forty years ago: 'Introductory Note' to Hale, Highfield and Smalley, eds, *Europe in the Late Middle Ages*, p. 13.

46 F. Šmahel, *Die Hussitische Revolution* (3 vols, Hannover: Hahnsche Buchhandlung, 2002).

47 Housley, *Religious Warfare*, pp. 58–9.

48 Y. Lacaze, 'Philippe le Bon et le problème hussite: Un projet de croisade bourguignon en 1428–1429', *RH* 241 (1969), 69–98; G. Holmes, 'Cardinal Beaufort and the crusade against the Hussites', *EHR* 88 (1973), 721–50.

dom against a non-Christian, external threat. The test here was clearly the Ottoman Turks. The reunified Church that emerged from the council of Constance was soon faced with a resurgent Ottoman sultanate. One thing is crystal clear: through to the outbreak of the Reformation the papal *curia* recognized the threat posed by the Turks, and responded to it first and foremost with attempts to promote crusades. No pope after Martin V (1417–31) was able to ignore the Turks, and there were some who distinguished themselves. Eugenius IV launched the crusade that met with disaster in November 1444 at Varna. Nicholas V responded to the fall of Constantinople in 1453 by attempting to organize a crusade, while Calixtus III devoted most of his energies during his short reign (1455–8) to combating the Turks. Calixtus's successor, Pius II, made the most significant contribution towards papal crusading efforts. His crusading programme was ambitious and he vowed to lead the crusade in person, dying at Ancona in August 1464 while awaiting the Venetian galleys that were supposed to transport the pope and his troops across the Adriatic. Undoubtedly Pius's commitment to crusading has an element of the heroic about it. Paul II, Sixtus IV, Innocent VIII and Alexander VI lacked his lustre, but each in turn responded as best he could to a series of devastating blows, including the loss of most of the Venetian bases in the eastern Mediterranean and a Turkish landing at Otranto in 1480.[49]

The Vatican Archives contain a vast amount of evidence relating to these initiatives and it has been thoroughly explored, above all by Kenneth M. Setton.[50] No more than in the fourteenth century could these recurrent surges of organizational activity be detached from the broader concerns of the papal *curia*. One of Eugenius IV's successes was to wrest control over the crusade from the conciliar fathers at Basel, and both Eugenius and Pius II viewed it within the context of restoring papal authority in full. After 1453 there was a growing fear that the Ottomans would invade Italy, thereby threatening the Papal State and Rome itself. But if it was in the interests of the papal *curia* to promote crusading, it was also expensive and time consuming. Moreover, it proved to be a Sisyphean task, for the response to papal efforts was cumulatively more disappointing than at any previous time. Calixtus III experienced a measure of success, in the two-fold shape of the relief of Belgrade in 1456 by an army of crusaders enlisted by Giovanni da Capistrano, and of a series of

49 Housley, *The Later Crusades*, pp. 80–117; Setton, *The Papacy*, vol. 2. For recent work on Pius II see N. Bisaha, 'Pope Pius II's letter to Sultan Mehmed II: A reexamination', *Crusades* 1 (2002), 183–200; N. Bisaha, 'Pope Pius II and the crusade', in *CFCMI*, 39–52, 188–91.
50 Setton, *The Papacy*, vol. 2.

naval victories in the Levant.[51] From his reign onwards, however, pope after pope found it impossible to stir Europe's rulers and population into action. The fifteenth century, like the thirteenth and fourteenth, produced a cluster of rulers, such as Alfonso V of Aragon/Naples, Philip the Good of Burgundy, Matthias Corvinus of Hungary, the Emperor Maximilian and Charles VIII of France, who all pronounced themselves eager to lead crusades but failed to take action. There is no consensus among historians as to their underlying sincerity, but the general pattern of unfulfilled promises is strongly reminiscent of earlier periods.[52]

Such sources as Pius II's *Commentaries* show that nobody was more aware than the popes themselves of their inability to rekindle the 'Clermont spirit' among their contemporaries. But research has shown that it would be wrong on that basis to dismiss the crusading response to the Ottoman Turks as a sterile topic for investigation. In the first place, it is clear that the fall of Constantinople made a deep impact on much of the Catholic west, probably more so than the fall of Acre had done; the threat posed by the Turks as a result of their seemingly relentless conquests in Asia Minor and the Balkans was strongly registered. An 'image of the Turk' (*imago Turci*) was created that came to play a significant role in the religious, political, and cultural discourse of Renaissance and Reformation Europe. The anxieties, self-doubts and internal antagonisms of the Catholic world contributed as much to its shaping as what the sultan and his armies were doing, but it included a process of demonization, in which the Turks' hatred of learning and culture, derived from their inescapable ethnicity as Scythian barbarians, featured almost as much as their resolve to replace Christianity with Islam.[53] It was a complex and multi-faceted image and its reception in the various parts of Europe was moulded by each region's political and religious identity.[54]

Nor was it only at Rome that attempts continued to be made to set in motion a crusade. In some areas actively threatened by the Turks, notably Hungary, the political *élites* proved capable of displaying remarkable indifference towards the danger that they faced; as yet nobody has satis-

---

51 Ibid., pp. 161–95; Housley, 'Giovanni da Capistrano'.

52 For studies on these rulers see Housley, *The Later Crusades*, pp. 470–4. On Matthias Corvinus see J. Bak, 'Hungary and crusading in the fifteenth century', in *CFCMI*, 116–27, 224–7.

53 Housley, *Religious Warfare*, pp. 131–59.

54 For example, C. Sieber-Lehmann, 'An obscure but powerful pattern: crusading, nationalism and the Swiss confederation in the late Middle Ages', in *CFCMI*, 81–93, 208–15; N. Nowakowska, 'Poland and the crusade in the reign of King Jan Olbracht, 1492–1501', ibid., 128–47, 227–31.

factorily explained this.[55] On the other hand the Valois court of Burgundy, under Philip the Good and to some extent his son Charles the Bold, continued to nourish the association of crusading with chivalric aspiration that had been so prominent during the lead-up to Nicopolis. This used to be seen partly as a revenge syndrome, but Jacques Paviot has shown that the evidence for such an interpretation is weak. It is much more likely that, as in the case of the Nicopolis expedition, it was the political ambitions of the dukes that primarily stimulated Burgundian interest over the course of several decades. These were coupled with an awareness of the glittering crusading past shared by both constituent parts of the Burgundian lands, Burgundy and the Low Countries, and the sense of an opportunity to be seized, given the absence of initiatives from the royal court during Charles VII's reign. There was a good deal of small-scale activity in the form of information-gathering missions, naval expeditions and financial outlays in the east, and the failure of the Burgundian court to produce action on a more significant scale was probably caused not by a lack of commitment *per se* but by its over-ambitious agenda.[56]

In both inspiration and expression, Burgundian crusading aspirations were mainly backward looking; the famous Feast of the Pheasant held at Lille in 1454, one of the chief platforms for Philip the Good's crusade programme, reminds one strongly of the chivalric paraphernalia created by the Teutonic Knights to entertain volunteers for their *Reisen*.[57] But recent research has shown that in one major respect the crusading response to the Turks after 1453 was more up to date. Italian humanism was in the first flush of self-confident creativity when Constantinople fell. Some humanists had already associated themselves with the call for a new crusade, and the events of 1453 accentuated both their fears of what might happen to the 'New Learning' if the Turks were not driven back, and their perception that their own careers might be advanced by throwing their abilities behind a cause that commanded respect and attracted funding at most of the European courts. In recent years the fertilization of crusading ideas and rhetoric that resulted has attracted a good deal of interest, much of it focusing on the role of Aeneas Silvius Piccolomini, who became pope as Pius II. Before his election Piccolomini advocated the crusading cause in his capacity as Frederick III's secretary (i.e. advisor); he fascinated participants at the series of imperial diets that met in 1454–5

---

55 Bak, 'Hungary'.
56 Paviot, *Les Ducs de Bourgogne*.
57 M.-T. Caron and D. Clauzel, eds, *Le Banquet du faisan* (Arras: Artois Presses Université, 1997).

with his rhetoric, thanks in large part to the novelty of the oratorical techniques that he used. After his election as pope in 1458, his humanistic approach towards crusading was overlaid by religious themes, but these did not entirely drive out the new ideas and language that he had introduced earlier in his career. A group of humanists of exceptional talent dedicated themselves to advancing the crusade, and their treatises, orations and letters were often sophisticated, brilliant and highly learned. Too often the fact that they ultimately proved futile has caused them to be dismissed as insincere exercises in composition. Increasingly, they are being seen as well intentioned, and strikingly innovative in both structure and content.[58]

Not all humanists approved of crusading. On the very eve of the Reformation Leo X made a major attempt to rally Christendom's rulers in a great crusade.[59] Erasmus regarded Leo's planned crusade against the Turks as fatally flawed both in conception and in intended organization.[60] It is probably fair to say that nobody expected Leo to succeed where so many others had failed. By this point it had become clear that an international expedition (*passagium*) against the Turks, composed of forces derived from a range of nations that marched in response to a papal summons and under the banner of a shared Christianity, was at heart anachronistic. On the other hand, the Granada war of 1482–92 had shown not just that the crusading mechanism could still work, thereby confirming the lesson of the Hussite crusades, but that it could generate military success. The difference surely was that the war against Granada, which brought the *Reconquista* to a close, was conducted by the authorities of a single power, Castile. Isabel of Castile and her consort Fernando of Aragon made full use of the crusade, especially its fundraising capabilities, to advance an extremely arduous military undertaking, but they maintained tight control over all aspects of the war itself. This was a war initiated and managed by an embryonic state, though relying to some extent on crusading mechanisms.[61]

This makes it sound as if the Catholic monarchs were making almost Machiavellian use of crusading (as Machiavelli himself came close to

---

58   N. Bisaha, *Creating East and West. Renaissance Humanists and the Ottoman Turks* (Philadelphia: University of Pennsylvania Press, 2004); M. Meserve, 'Italian humanists and the problem of the crusade', in *CFCMI*, 13–38, 183–8; J. Helmrath, 'The German *Reichstage* and the crusade', ibid., 53–69, 191–203.

59   Setton, *The Papacy*, 3: 142–97.

60   N. Housley, 'A necessary evil? Erasmus, the crusade, and war against the Turks', in *CTS*, 259–80.

61   J. Edwards, '*Reconquista* and crusade in fifteenth-century Spain', in *CFCMI*, 163–81, 235–7.

asserting in *The Prince*). A significant feature of recent research on the Granada war, however, has been the demonstration that the campaigns were advanced with the help of a cluster of ideas and emotions that had strong links with past crusading. The association of the war against the Moors with the practice of chivalry remained strong in Castile and underwent a revival in the course of the 1480s. The conflict generated powerful surges of eschatological expectation, focused around Joachite programmes, which had found a warm welcome in Iberia and assumed unusual forms there. And national feeling, which in the late medieval and early modern periods often found its fullest expression in messianic terms, was stimulated by the burdensome demands that the war imposed on Castilian society. Alain Milhou and others have shown that these were distinctive contours in Castilian thought at the time, and Peter Russell has traced similar themes in the Portugal of Prince Henry 'the Navigator' and his circle.[62] The result was that the Granada war marked as much a beginning as an end, for the programmes of Castilian and Portuguese expansion that followed hard on its completion fed off the same group of values and expectations. The version of Iberian history that used to link *Reconquista* and *conquistadores* has thus been given a new lease of life, though without its former nationalistic trappings and with much greater sensitivity towards the methodological problems involved in tracing the formation, flow and influence of such systems of ideas.

Research has indicated, however, that around 1500 crusading was changing rapidly, and that it had become characterized by two polarities. One polarity was basically geographical, in so far as military success and expansion in the west was balanced by defeat and retreat in the east. This is not to deny an interaction between the two areas, for as Hankins and Bisaha demonstrated, the triumphalism and self-awareness that were strong features of the humanistic response to the Turks helped to shape European reactions to the inhabitants of the New World. As Bisaha put it: 'In many ways the Turkish advance provided compelling conditions under which humanists constructed a coherent vision of Western culture and its inherent superiority to other societies.'[63] The second polarity was structural. In practical terms crusading was largely moribund, having come to consist almost solely of fundraising techniques. A link with the traditions of pilgrimage that went all the way back to 1095, and had continued to

---

62 A. Milhou, *Colón y su mentalidad mesiánica en el ambiente franciscanista español* (Valladolid: Casa-Museo de Colón Seminario Americanista de la Universidad de Valladolid, 1983); Russell, *Prince Henry*.

63 Bisaha, *Creating East and West*, with quote at p. 183; J. Hankins, 'Renaissance crusaders: humanist crusade literature in the age of Mehmed II', *Dumbarton Oaks Papers* 49 (1995), 111–207.

enjoy a form of life after 1291 in the shape of 'chivalric crusading', had all but come to an end. Non-Iberians who took part in the Granada war on an unpaid basis, for example, probably numbered no more than some dozens.[64] It is possible that the preaching of indulgences generated its own brand of penitential devotion, but this involved neither travel nor combat. It was in the realm of ideas and images that crusading could still excite and inspire, as it clearly did, for example, in the case of Christopher Columbus.[65] In terms of inspiration, indeed, it is even possible that veneration for Jerusalem enjoyed something of a revival around 1500. It has certainly become hard to argue that Colombus's generation had 'turned its back' on the core crusading values, in the sense of rejecting holy war, shunning indulgences or favouring a peaceful accommodation with Islam.[66] The problem was that there was no longer much opportunity for them to take the cross, nor indeed much point in their doing so.

The Early Modern Period

Study of crusading in the sixteenth and seventeenth centuries has largely been shaped by these twin polarities, which if anything became more pronounced as time went by. The confrontation with the Ottoman sultanate reached its climax in the middle decades of the sixteenth century, when the Christian resistance to the Turkish advance became militarily more effective. This came about not because papal calls to arms were finally heeded but because the defence both of the western Balkan lands and of the Mediterranean sea-ways was handled by branches of the far-flung Habsburg family. Its members had established mechanisms at their disposal for the mobilization of the men, money, ships and war material that were required. The fundraising that had underpinned the Granada war comprised an indispensable feature of this process, while the messianism that had flourished in fifteenth-century Iberia shaped Habsburg *Hauspolitik* under both Charles V and Philip II. It is sometimes possible to detect the ethos of crusading in the Spanish armies, for example among the combatants at Lepanto in 1571 and the troops who manned the forts in north Africa. These survivals and permutations have received some attention, and the continuing commitment of the papal court to promoting resistance to the Turks is not in question.[67] But the practice of

---

64 Edwards, '*Reconquista*', p. 178.
65 F. Fernández-Armesto, *Columbus* (Oxford: Oxford University Press, 1991).
66 Housley, *Religious Warfare*, pp. 160–89.
67 Housley, *The Later Crusades*, pp. 118–50; Setton, *The Papacy*, vols 3–4.

crusading had been marginalized. More than that, Géraud Poumarède has recently emphasized that the Turkish war was 'desacralized', rendered commonplace. For while some groups of men still made their way to the frontiers or served in the Christian fleets as volunteers, trained and paid armies were now the order of the day. These, Poumarède has argued, did not see the war against the sultan's forces as different from any other conflict in which they might be hired to serve.[68]

At the same time, the Reformation dealt a decisive blow to crusading by destroying the framework of Christendom with which it had always been associated. Politically and ideologically, crusading had functioned as the reverse and alternative to conflict between Christians; paradoxically, it was an instrument of Christian peace and unity.[69] During the early phase of the reform movement it was possible to argue, in broadly traditional terms, that the Protestants were heretics and schismatics, and that their armed suppression was akin to that of the cathars and Hussites. At Toulouse in 1567 the Catholics responded to the Huguenot siege by forming a sodality of cross-bearers, whose members were granted plenary indulgences by the pope. They were making explicit reference to their region's past, framing their struggle against the Huguenots in terms that inevitably recalled the confraternities formed during the Albigensian Crusade. But this was a measure of desperation by an embattled community in a country plagued by civil war and lacking a lead from the royal court.[70] In practice a crusading response to Protestantism was rarely adopted for sound political reasons, and in the second half of the century the argument that had been used to underpin it looked threadbare, given that most Protestants had not been baptized as Catholics in the first place. The use of the crusade against Protestants therefore failed to become entrenched; there has even been some dispute about the extent to which the Spanish Armada was constituted as a crusade.[71] That being so, it could be asked why the loss of northern Europe, which had been steadily losing its interest in crusading since around 1400, actually mattered in terms of the interfaith conflict that was raging in the Balkans and Mediterranean. The simple answer is that diplomatically it mattered because of the perennial fear of Protestant alliances with the Turks. In broader terms

---

68   G. Poumarède, *Pour en finir avec la croisade. Mythes et réalités de la lutte contre les Turcs aux xvie et xviie siècles* (Paris: Presses universitaires de France, 2004), pp. 530–617.
69   T. Mastnak, *Crusading Peace. Christendom, the Muslim World, and Western Political Order* (Berkeley: University of California Press, 2002).
70   Housley, *Religious Warfare*, pp. 194–8. See also L. Racaut, 'The polemical use of the Albigensian Crusade during the French Wars of Religion', *French History* 13 (1999), 261–79.
71   Tyerman, *England and the Crusades*, p. 362; F. Fernández-Armesto, *The Spanish Armada. The Experience of War in 1588* (Oxford: Oxford University Press, 1989), pp. 36–40.

it mattered too because the contraction of crusading to the Catholic lands compounded the narrow association of the anti-Ottoman struggle with the Habsburgs and their allies. From all points of view, between 1500 and 1600 crusading shrank to become a shadow of its former self.

Historians working in a variety of fields have, however, questioned whether its decline was so precipitate. In the first place, there has been a volume of work on what has sometimes been called 'the Protestant crusade', a term endowed with a variety of meanings ranging from a providential view of warfare, through the celebration of a nation's crusading past, to a continuing premium placed on the chivalric value of combat against 'infidels'.[72] Secondly, some historians have emphasized that outside the inner circles of papal ideology and Habsburg power, armed resistance to the Ottomans was at times clothed in language and ritual which resonated with crusading ideas: in other words, the survival of a crusading worldview was broad based and, much as in the past, quite compatible with the pragmatic contacts dictated by day-to-day life in frontier zones.[73] And historians of the Order of St John during its Malta period (1525–1798) have discovered that the Knights were less isolated than had been supposed. Their links with the major Mediterranean powers were strong and their stated mission of hostility towards the Muslim states aroused sympathy and at times even created programmes for action, although none of them reached the battlefield.[74]

This last area of research extends into the seventeenth century.[75] As will now be obvious, the answer to the question 'When was the last crusade?' will depend very largely on the definition that is held to. But clearly things changed drastically with the Reformation. In the light of recent research, it is hard to deny now that crusading remained a significant force in late medieval Europe. It would be rash to make the same claim for the early modern period, even though a whole system of ideas, images, practices, and ideological formulations whose roots can be traced back to crusading continued to impinge on so many aspects of European life.[76] Elements of that system persisted even into the period when Enlightenment ideas were making their greatest impact, so that the

---

72   On the last theme see J. R. Goodman, *Chivalry and Exploration 1298–1630* (Woodbridge: Boydell, 1998).

73   C. W. Bracewell, *The Uskoks of Senj. Piracy, Banditry, and Holy War in the Sixteenth-Century Adriatic* (Ithaca, NY: Cornell University Press, 1992).

74   For example, D. F. Allen, 'Upholding tradition: Benedict XIV and the Hospitaller order of St John of Jerusalem at Malta, 1740–1758', *CHR* 80 (1994), 18–35.

75   K. M. Setton, *Venice, Austria, and the Turks in the Seventeenth Century* (Philadelphia: American Philosophical Society, 1991).

76   Poumarède, *Pour en finir*, pp. 5–196.

upsurge of curiosity about crusading that occurred in the nineteenth century came just a few generations after genuine expressions of commitment, albeit by a few. Two things can be said with confidence. The discoveries of the last thirty years about the period after 1291 have been remarkably diverse and far-reaching; and it would be foolish to claim that this large terrain of enquiry has now been so thoroughly mapped out that no further revelations will come to light.

7

Consequences: The Effect of the Crusades on the Development of Europe and Interfaith Relations

Although there is much that is contested in the history of crusading, one advance that has been made in the course of the last half century would probably be disputed by nobody: that the crusades played a central rather than a peripheral role in the development of medieval Europe. Directly or indirectly, they affected the lives of most people who lived in the twelfth and thirteenth centuries, and of many during the late Middle Ages.[1] This is an important discovery, but paradoxically it brings with it problems, because the nature and extent of changes generated by an activity that is mainstream are often less easy to identify than those caused by the marginal. In the field of medical advances, for example, Piers Mitchell has concluded that 'it can never be known how medicine in the medieval period would have evolved without the effects of the crusades', a sentence in which the word 'medicine' could be replaced by many others.[2] So the issues considered in the first part of this chapter involve a disconcerting number of uncertainties and intangibles. The second part of the chapter presents a contrasting vista. It has always been apparent that crusading exercised a big impact on relations between Catholic Christianity and other faiths, and it is hard to counter the argument that the impact was entirely destructive.

---

1 C. Tyerman, 'What the crusades meant to Europe', in P. Linehan and J. L. Nelson, eds, *The Medieval World* (London: Routledge, 2001), 131–45.
2 P. D. Mitchell, *Medicine in the Crusades. Warfare, Wounds and the Medieval Surgeon* (Cambridge: Cambridge University Press, 2004), p. 218.

Crusading and Medieval Europe

Our uncertainties begin with the effect of crusading on the medieval Church, particularly its attitude towards warfare. Given the pacifist thrust of much of Christ's teaching and the condemnation of war to be found in many Church Fathers, the Church's readiness to promote a wide range of military conflicts is striking.[3] Pure pacifism found virtually no expression within Catholic Christianity in the Middle Ages; it was driven underground into an association with heretical groups, above all the Waldensians. An attempt was made to contain warfare within acceptable channels and limits, through the formation of doctrines of just war (*ius ad bellum*), and legitimate ways of waging war (*ius in bello*). But these doctrines were slow to develop; and when they did take shape they were framed so loosely, and offered the ingenious so many escape routes, that the exponents of virtually any war found ways of justifying both its initiation and its mode of conduct. And churchmen did not only legitimate; in their own ways they participated. During what was probably the most protracted conflict fought in the Middle Ages, the Anglo-French war in the fourteenth and fifteenth centuries, churchmen on both sides were vigorous in their promotion of the national cause. As a matter of course they offered up prayers, blessed banners and accompanied armies and fleets on campaign. The mobilization of the saints followed the same pattern. Theologically, legally and sacramentally, warfare was firmly accommodated within the Church's world.[4]

Scholars such as David Bachrach, Ernst-Dieter Hehl and Frederick Russell, who have studied the militarism of the medieval Church, have been conscious of the fact that the time when legal thinking was at its most creative, between c. 1050 and c. 1300, was also the heyday of the Jerusalem crusade.[5] They have explored the links between crusading and the wider issues that churchmen had to face, but it has proved difficult to come to definitive conclusions. It is hard to argue that if the crusades had not occurred the Church would have been more circumspect about issues relating to war. The lobbying from rulers for their wars to be validated had been incessant from the time of Constantine and it had been particularly

---

3   W. J. Sheils, ed., *The Church and War*, SCH 20 (Oxford: Blackwell, 1983) has a number of relevant essays.

4   P. Contamine, *War in the Middle Ages*, trans. M. Jones (Oxford: Blackwell, 1984), pp. 260–302; Beaune, *The Birth*, pp. 152–71.

5   D. S. Bachrach, *Religion and the Conduct of War c. 300–1215* (Woodbridge: Boydell, 2003); Hehl, 'War, peace and the Christian order'; Russell, *The Just War*.

strong in the eighth and ninth centuries.[6] Once the early medieval practice of lay advocacy had been condemned by the reformers of the eleventh century, 'hands-on' clerical involvement in warfare also became unavoidable. This was epitomized by Pope Gregory VII, whose most recent biographer, H. E. J. Cowdrey, confirmed Erdmann's judgement that 'Gregory was the most warlike pope who had ever sat in St Peter's chair'.[7] Gregory did not initiate clerical involvement in warfare, but by associating it overtly with the goals of Church reform he gave it moral underpinning. By the mid-twelfth century the consequences were clearly visible to outsiders: Anna Comnena, in the *Alexiad*, viewed the casual association of western European churchmen with combat as scandalous.[8]

Of course, Gregory VII was also important in the formation of crusading ideas, and this is typical of the way crusading forms one thread in a larger pattern of activities, confounding our attempts to isolate it and so pinpoint its influence. It would be foolish to deny that the frequent preaching of crusades, which among other things were holy wars, accentuated the clergy's association with violence, particularly given the virulent tone of some sermons.[9] Moreover, both clerics and their secular rulers muddied the waters by conflating dynastic or national warfare within Europe with the cause of the Holy Land.[10] In medieval society the dividing line between wars that were just and holy was always indistinct: we saw in chapter 1 that one school of thought about the crusades regards all legitimated warfare as crusading. So a case can be made for blaming crusading for the quasi-veneration with which war was so often regarded in the Middle Ages. On the other hand, it could also be argued that the constant probing of intention and conscience that was generated by this explicit identification of violence with God's will played a significant role in sustaining an ethical dimension in European warfare. There were sceptics, including a patriarch of Jerusalem and some of the early Templars, who questioned the justice and validity of the Christian presence in Palestine.[11] And the legal issue of whether pagans could be dispossessed solely on religious

6   Bachrach, *Religion*, pp. 7–63.

7   Cowdrey, *Pope Gregory VII*, pp. 650–8, with quote at p. 652.

8   Anna Comnena, *Alexiad*, trans. E. R. A. Sewter (Harmondsworth: Penguin, 1969), pp. 317–18.

9   Cole, 'O God, the heathen have come into your inheritance'.

10   E. H. Kantorowicz, 'Pro patria mori in mediaeval political thought', *AHR* 56 (1950–1), 472–92; J. Strayer, 'France: the Holy Land, the Chosen People, and the Most Christian King', in J. F. Benton and T. N. Bisson, eds, *Medieval Statecraft and the Perspectives of History. Essays by Joseph R. Strayer* (Princeton, NJ: Princeton University Press, 1971), 300–14.

11   Leclercq, 'Un document'; Leclercq, 'Gratien'.

grounds created debate not just in the mid-thirteenth century but again in the early fifteenth, in the context of Portuguese expansion.[12]

It seems likely that these two viewpoints are equally valid and that crusading helped both to militarize the medieval Church and to sustain an ongoing critique of what warfare was for in a world that was supposedly Christian. One of its distinctive contributions was to set up alternatives and ideal constructs, the most famous being St Bernard's dichotomy between *militia* (the practice of knighthood) and *malitia* (the practice of evil), while a constant refrain in papal peace-making was that warring Christian princes should join forces to fight against the Saracens and Turks. Defeat on crusade caused more consternation than defeat in ordinary warfare, and in certain circumstances a migration of response could take place. Would the great *crise de conscience* that afflicted France after Agincourt, the belief evident on both sides of the Channel that the French had forfeited God's support through their sinfulness, have occurred without the history of similar responses to defeats on crusade? Similarly, would the Hussites have projected their armed struggle in the same period as a holy war, had they not been reacting to the preaching of a crusade against them? Both ideological responses could of course be located in scripture, but the impact of crusading ideas on national messianism, which was arguably at stake in France and Bohemia, has also received some attention in recent years.[13]

We might expect the terrain to become more secure when we move from ideas to institutions and devotional behaviour, but in fact it rarely is. Because crusading was for so long a ubiquitous feature of the Church's activities, disentangling its impact from that of other practices is sometimes impossible. The most obvious example is the influence of crusading on the papacy's spiritual authority and political power. It used to be a commonplace that crusading reinforced both of these, and there is a kernel of truth in the view that the popularity of crusading to Jerusalem and the 'reach' of the medieval papacy rose and fell together. But given the emphasis that is currently being placed on the limitations of papal influence, even in the central Middle Ages, and our realization that the laity formed its own views about crusading, this should not be exaggerated.[14] Certainly, the argument that crusading brought a massive dividend to the papacy is all too easily turned on its head, making it a

---

12 Muldoon, *Popes*; Housley, *Religious Warfare*, pp. 182–6.
13 N. Housley, 'Pro deo et patria mori: sanctified patriotism in Europe, 1400–1600', in P. Contamine, ed., *War and Competition between States* (Oxford: Oxford University Press, 2000), 221–48.
14 Morris, *The Papal Monarchy*, pp. 579–82; Riley-Smith, 'The state of mind'.

huge burden that had to be supported, eating up time and resources that could have been directed to greater advantage elsewhere. This applied even to Pope Innocent III, whose view of his crusading duties was thoroughly integrated with his overall conception of his office. Using the needs of the Latin East as leverage to secure peace within Christendom could just as easily be directed against the papacy as by it. Crusading was nobody's property.

The one area in which the development of the medieval papacy was indubitably shaped by crusading was that of the *curia*'s control over the Church at large. The overall centralization of the Church would surely have occurred anyway: its origins can be detected in the mid-eleventh century, several decades before the council of Clermont, when advocates of Church reform started looking towards Rome for support.[15] But the financial needs created by crusading accelerated this trend and helped give it its raw fiscal edge. The system of papal taxation, notably through tenths, but also through other benefice taxes like annates, intercalary fruits and (in Spain) *tercias*, was created for crusading purposes and, initially at least, derived its moral justification from it. It is now becoming apparent that the whole system worked less to the benefit of the papacy than that of the range of secular leaders to whom the financial proceeds were normally channelled. The picture that has emerged is of the papacy taking it upon its shoulders to levy and assemble the bulk of the funding required, in the process incurring most of the unpopularity that such taxation caused at all levels of the clergy.[16] In this respect too, crusading proved to be a very mixed blessing for the papacy.

These points about the centralized taxation of the Church also apply, *mutatis mutandis*, to the multiplication of indulgences in late medieval Europe. The extraordinary popularity of indulgences was not stimulated solely by the shift that occurred in crusade preaching towards the raising of cash alongside or instead of volunteers; but this was certainly a major constituent of the trend which conflated the devotional emphasis on works with the substantial volume of specie that could be released in an increasingly commercial society. The 'marketing' of indulgences was central to all preaching campaigns against the Turks in the fifteenth and early sixteenth centuries, and powerful crusade commissars like Raymond Perault (Peraudi) were instrumental in bringing up-to-date technologies and methods into the process. It is true that Luther's outburst against indulgences in 1517 was sparked off by a campaign which had as its goal not a crusade but the rebuilding of St Peter's in Rome, but critical attacks

---

15 Robinson, *The Papacy*, Part 1.
16 For example, Linehan, *The Spanish Church*; Lunt, *Financial Relations*.

by Erasmus at much the same time were aimed at Pope Leo X's crusading plans, while Jan Hus's polemical assault a century earlier was a response to papal fundraising for a crusade against King Ladislas of Naples.[17]

It might be supposed that secular governments must have benefited from crusading. The challenge of mounting the great *passagia* in the late twelfth and thirteenth centuries was met to a large degree by monarchs, who could deploy this sacred cause to validate organizational advances that would otherwise have taken much longer to implement, given that they usually entailed the extension of central authority. Recent studies of the armies raised by Richard I and Frederick Barbarossa for the Third Crusade,[18] and by Louis IX for his first crusade,[19] have certainly emphasized the levels of control, supply and financing that they aimed at and to some extent achieved. As in the case of the papacy, however, this argument can easily be turned on its head: that leading a crusade was not an opportunity but an exceptionally arduous task to undertake. The Second Crusade, which Barbarossa had experienced, had shown the price that would be paid for organizational deficiencies. And the reason why these three rulers achieved so much was that they worked with systems of government that they, and/or their predecessors on the throne, had already brought to a sound level of achievement. Arguably this applies more to Richard than to Barbarossa and St Louis; in the latter instances the personal contribution, stemming from a markedly individual response to crusade, marked radical advances in the way German and French government worked. This is true above all of St Louis: the establishment of *enquêteurs*, nearly all of them mendicants, in 1247, and the far-reaching reforming measures of the 1250s, can be confidently described as crusade-driven measures. They were 'developed largely in response to the failure of the king's first crusade and his hopes for success in a future one'.[20]

The administrative challenges and tight timetables imposed by crusading did not encourage the adoption of radically new methods of military organization. Theorists like Marino Sanudo Torsello and Ramon Lull could indulge in blueprints for reform, but those engaged with the realities of assembling armies bypassed such ideas: it was taxing enough having to cope with the unpredictable in the shape of crusading volunteers, and it is

---

17 R. N. Swanson, *Religion and Devotion in Europe, c. 1215–c. 1515* (Cambridge: Cambridge University Press, 1995), pp. 217–25; Housley, 'A necessary evil?' A forthcoming collection of essays on indulgences edited by R. N. Swanson will include an essay by myself on crusade indulgences, 1417–1517.
18 Tyerman, *England and the Crusades*, pp. 57–85; Hiestand, 'Precipua tocius christianismi columpna'.
19 Jordan, *Louis IX*.
20 Jordan, *Louis IX*, pp. 182–3.

not surprising that leaders worked with the methods they knew. The slow changes that occurred in the recruitment of western European armies were therefore to a large degree reflected in, rather than caused by, the structuring of the armies that set out on crusades: from the fluid mixture of lordship, cash and kinship on the First Crusade, through the widespread adoption of contractual service in the thirteenth century, to the supplemented standing armies that fought for Fernando and Isabella in Granada.[21] It has become clear that the financing of crusading activity shadowed this slow process of change.[22] To quote Giles Constable, 'most crusades and pilgrimages to the Holy Land in the twelfth century were financed privately'.[23] Following attempts at public levies that proved only partially successful in the late twelfth century, the innovation of clerical taxation under Innocent III provided a dependable though never sufficient funding 'staple'. This remained in place throughout the late Middle Ages and was bolstered principally by the gains reaped from indulgences.[24]

While administrative debts to crusading are hard to prove, there is evidence of its influence on ideologies of secular power. This is clearest in France and Castile. The lustre of the royal crusading tradition in France was emphatically enhanced when St Louis was canonized in 1297, admittedly not on the grounds of his two crusades. Thereafter the expectation of French leadership in the case of any major *passagium* to the east was bound up with the essence of royal authority in France throughout the late Middle Ages; it still exerted some impact at the court of Francis I. Admittedly, it is not easy to disentangle the precise role played by crusading from similar attributes, such as the defence of the papacy and Church, and purity of religious belief; together, these made up the altruistic profile suitable for the *rex christianissimus*.[25] The equivalent in Castile was the king's obligation to pursue the *Reconquista*; in chapter 5 we saw that this image justified a heavy burden of taxation for the Church. Because of Castile's turbulent dynastic politics, the image featured prominently as a charge levelled against rulers who were allegedly proving negligent in their fulfilment of this sacred duty.[26] It is probable that France and Castile were not the only countries affected. Janus Møller Jensen has argued that

---

21 Contamine, *War*.
22 Cazel, 'Financing'.
23 G. Constable, 'The financing of the crusades in the twelfth century', in *OSHCKJ*, 64–88, at p. 70.
24 Housley, *The Later Crusades*, pp. 439–44.
25 Beaune, *The Birth*, pp. 172–93; Strayer, 'France'.
26 T. F. Ruiz, 'Unsacred monarchy: the kings of Castile in the late Middle Ages', in S. Wilentz, ed., *Rites of Power. Symbolism, Ritual, and Politics since the Middle Ages* (Philadelphia: University of Pennsylvania Press, 1985), 109–44.

participation in the Wendish crusade played a key part in the way Valdemar I of Denmark projected his royal authority.[27] And another candidate for ideological influence is ducal Burgundy, where crusading became embedded in the self-image of the Valois dukes from John the Fearless onwards. But the extinction of the Burgundian state after the death of Charles the Bold at Nancy in 1477 cut short the development of the image, for as Jacques Paviot noted, Charles's Habsburg successors had more impressive crusading pedigrees at their disposal.[28]

Whether we are considering ecclesiastical or secular authorities, the impact of crusading on medieval institutions of government was strong because of the organizational and financial demands that it posed; increasingly, however, it looks as if it forced the pace rather than generating innovation in its own right. Great figures like Innocent III or Louis IX, instituting dramatic changes to cope with the challenges of crusading, were less typical than others who muddled through mainly by demanding more out of existing structures. The changes that resulted were incremental, and it makes sense to consider the overall relationship not in terms of cost-benefit but of progressive interaction. Recent research has suggested that much the same approach works best for the economic effects of the crusades. Sweeping claims used to be made about crusading 'opening up' Europe's economic life.[29] These have largely been replaced by a more synergistic view, micro- rather than macro-economic, one made up of countless instances of the two areas of activity feeding off each other. This confuses the causal process, but it creates a picture much more in line with our own experience of the way things happen.

The funding of the early crusades to the east through the land market illustrates this well. It has always been clear that raising cash was a preoccupation of crusaders because some of the earliest papal privileges granted to people who took the cross related to the easing of their credit burdens. But the extensive quarrying of monastic charters has now illuminated the process. This has revealed a lively interaction between aristocratic lineages and religious houses, in which arable and pasture, fish ponds and vineyards, rents and tolls, were sold, pledged, or incorporated into legal settlements with the goal of raising specie, equipment, pack animals and not least spiritual support to meet the demands made by crusading. The effects on local politics of the land transfers that took place could be substantial. Study of the early crusades has therefore confirmed

---

27 Jensen, *Sclavorum expugnator*.
28 Paviot, *Les Ducs*, p. 293.
29 For example, H. C. Krueger, 'The crusades and European expansion', in J. A. Brundage, ed., *The Crusades. Motives and Achievements* (Boston, MA: D. C. Heath, 1964), 59–62.

the findings of economic historians that western Europe already possessed a commercialized economy in the late eleventh century, one whose further progress was constrained mainly by inadequate supplies of silver. Crusading almost certainly pushed this exchange market to its limits, in the process benefiting largely religious landowners, many fewer of whom went on crusade.[30]

These pulsing networks of local activity have in the past attracted less attention than the Mediterranean carrying trade, especially that conducted by the fleets operated by the Italian sea-powers. Any view that depicts the Italians 'breaking into' the Muslim or Byzantine markets of the eastern Mediterranean as a result of the First Crusade encounters big obstacles. First, the Italians were already trading with Alexandria and, in the case of Venice, with Constantinople, well before 1095; and secondly, while reliable estimates of volume are largely lacking for the twelfth century, those that we possess indicate that the Syrian market failed to attract major investment until the century's last quarter. With the exception of a short period in the early thirteenth century, even the Levant's most prominent ports, Acre and Tyre, could not challenge the hegemony of Constantinople and Alexandria.[31] This is not to deny the significance of the range of services that these ports and the western fleets that frequented them were able to provide to crusaders: not just passage and naval protection but food supplies, replacement mounts, war materials and credit facilities. But it remains the case that the clearest convergence between trade and crusade came about during the Fourth and Fifth Crusades, when attention was focused on the conquest of the Bosphorus and the Nile delta.

The easiest causal link that has been established was Venice's acquisition of a substantial group of territories and bases, which the republic cherry-picked in the immediate aftermath of the conquest of Constantinople in 1204; this unquestionably lay behind Venetian prosperity in the first half of the thirteenth century.[32] In turn, much of the crusading that occurred in the middle decades of the fourteenth century flowed from Venetian lobbying at the papal *curia* to protect their lands and trade in the Aegean area against Turkish attack. In the fifteenth century too the viability of a crusade against the Ottomans depended to some extent on Venice's reluctant acceptance that the use of force was necessary to defend its trading interests in the east.[33] It should be noted that there also existed

30 Riley-Smith, *The First Crusaders*, pp. 109–39; Constable, 'The financing'; Tyerman, *England*, pp. 195–208.
31 Abulafia, 'Trade and crusade'.
32 L. B. Robbert, 'Venice and the crusades', in *HC* 5: 379–451.
33 Housley, *The Later Crusades*, pp. 56–64, 80–117.

a 'negative' correlation between trade and crusade in the form of the papacy's attempts to impose trading embargoes on Muslim powers in preparation for a crusade. These did have some effect, most notably after 1291, when the embargo on direct trade with Mamluk Egypt and Syria diverted western traders to Lusignan Cyprus, acting as a major factor behind Famagusta's commercial boom.[34]

Similar issues have arisen in associating the Baltic carrying trade with the crusading that was directed against the pagans of northern Germany and the east Baltic lands. During two phases of the Baltic crusades in particular the interests of traders and crusaders were closely aligned and their relationship proved mutually beneficial. The first was during the crusades against the Livs during the thirteenth century. The town of Riga from the start served the twin purposes of promoting conversion and trade along the reaches of the Dvina valley; it is highly unlikely that the missionary ambitions of men like Albert of Riga could have been fulfilled had his neophytes not lived in areas yielding vast stores of natural commodities that were much sought-after in the Catholic heartlands. In much the same way that Italian galleys plying the Syrian routes carried pilgrims and crusaders alongside their cargoes, the cogs that sailed to and from Riga when the Baltic was ice-free shipped both crusaders and merchandise.[35] Secondly, there was the rather more sophisticated relationship that Werner Paravicini discovered when he examined the *Reisen*. Some of the Teutonic Order's guests came to Prussia by sea, but more importantly, their credit needs were met by merchants who were based at Königsberg on account of their trading business. The impressive number of stone buildings that were erected in Königsberg during the *Reisen* can be attributed in large measure to the money that entered the local economy as a result of the spending that this credit made possible. Bruges similarly benefited from its status as the most important centre for loan repayments.[36]

Quantification is impossible, but it may be the case that the credit infrastructures that were created both in the Mediterranean and in the Baltic were just as important an offshoot of the interaction between trade and crusade as the more conspicuous carrying trade. Crusaders always needed specie, and nobody was better placed to provide it than the merchants on whose vessels they travelled and with whom they socialized and worshipped in the ports that formed their disembarkation points. Cazel argued that 'in essence the crusades redistributed some of Europe's wealth

34 E. Ashtor, *Levant Trade in the Later Middle Ages* (Princeton, NJ: Princeton University Press, 1983), pp. 3–63.
35 Jensen, 'Urban life'.
36 Paravicini, *Die Preussenreisen*, 2: 163–318.

out of the hands of the clergy and nobles into those of the bourgeoisie and peasantry'.[37] Given the breadth of crusading's appeal this verdict is questionable; indeed, it is probably misguided to talk of a net transfer of wealth from any one social or national group to another; but given that aristocratic crusaders had the greatest needs as well as the largest resources to draw on, it does seem likely that the overall effect was to free up for trading purposes wealth that otherwise may have remained tied up in land.

The area where the link between crusading and commercial activity is at its clearest is that of papal taxation. From the time of Pope Gregory X (1271–6) the entire Catholic world was divided into collectorates for this purpose. This organized system of collection could not have operated without the ability and willingness of the Italian mercantile and banking companies (*societates*) to co-operate, primarily by transferring specie in bullion or on account from the most distant corners of the Catholic community. The French economic historian Yves Renouard analysed in comprehensive detail the intermeshing of the *curia*'s collectorates with the infrastructure of the principal banking firms, which were mainly Tuscan. When some of these companies came under pressure and collapsed at the turn of the thirteenth century, the damage done to the transfer of resources, on which large-scale crusading had come to depend, was considerable. Nonetheless, the popes during the early Avignonese period were driven by necessity to recreate the relationship, until it crashed for a second time in the economic storms of the 1340s.[38] Anthony Luttrell and Nicholas Coureas have explored the ramifications of these financial networks for the Order of St John and the Cypriot Church, which had to step in as alternative financial channels and providers for crusading in the east.[39]

However much imprecision remains, the twin discoveries of how broad based and extensive the practice of crusading was, and of how much effort and preparation were invested in it, have had the overall effect of emphasizing its impact on economic life. This is an inevitable consequence of the discovery of the 'home front' by historians of crusading over the course of the last thirty years. There can be no doubt that crusading was one of the features of medieval life that gave Catholic Europe its remarkable rate of

---

37   Cazel, 'Financing', p. 149.

38   Y. Renouard, *Les Relations des papes d'Avignon et des compagnies commerciales et bancaires de 1316 à 1378* (Paris, 1941); *Recherches sur les compagnies commerciales et bancaires utilisées par les papes d'Avignon avant le Grand Schisme* (Paris, 1942).

39   A. T. Luttrell, 'Interessi fiorentini nell'economia e nella politica dei Cavalieri Ospedalieri di Rodi nel trecento', *Annali della Scuola normale superiore di Pisa*, 2nd ser: *Lettere, storia e filosofia* 28 (1959), 317–26; N. Coureas, 'Cyprus and the naval leagues, 1333–1358', in N. Coureas and J. Riley-Smith, eds, *Cyprus and the Crusades* (Nicosia: Society for the Study of the Crusades and the Latin East and Cyprus Research Centre, 1995), 107–24.

growth. This established an inherent dynamism that characterized the central Middle Ages;[40] just as importantly, it survived the demographic body-blows of the fourteenth century to make possible the overseas expansion of the fifteenth.[41] The reverse process has occurred in scholarship on military techniques and tactics. It used to be thought that the crusaders learned a good deal from their experience of warfare in the Middle East, particularly in terms of castle design. But the demolition work carried out by revisionists has been thoroughgoing and little now remains of this argument. Certainly, the crusaders had to adapt their tactics to handle the unfamiliar combat techniques that they encountered. Their success rate in adaptation was high, though there were certainly many blunders. More importantly, there were few lessons that the crusaders could usefully take back with them to the west, simply because modes of combat there were different; for instance, the integration of infantry into battle formations appears to have been more advanced in the Latin East than in the west.[42] It is likely that the most useful lesson was which of his companions a lord could most rely on *in extremis*. As for the debate on castle building, 'experiment and experience, rather than architectural influences from the other end of the Mediterranean, were the deciding factors'.[43]

In fact the impact of crusading as a military experience seems to have occurred not in such technical areas as recruitment and fighting practices, but in the more intangible field of social values. Chivalry has been subject to a massive amount of re-evaluation in recent years, but its relationship with crusading has been confirmed as a highly important one. Parallel though clearly overlapping avenues of research have established that in large measure the core values of both crusading and chivalry were the products of the laity, which created them in accordance with its own agendas, modes of thought and behaviour.[44] Although the influence of the Church was always felt, and was particularly strong in the case of crusading, its teachings were never accepted without a certain amount of reshaping. It was probably inevitable that an interaction would occur between crusading and chivalry, especially after the reforms of Pope Innocent III laid an increasing emphasis on military effectiveness. We saw in the previous chapter that this interaction was at its richest in the late Middle Ages. Much of the continuing attractiveness of crusading to

---

40   R. Bartlett, *The Making of Europe. Conquest, Colonization and Cultural Change 950–1350* (London: Allen Lane, 1993).
41   F. Fernández-Armesto, *Before Columbus: Exploration and Colonisation from the Mediterranean to the Atlantic, 1229–1492* (Basingstoke: Macmillan, 1987).
42   France, *Western Warfare*, pp. 204–29.
43   H. Kennedy, *Crusader Castles* (Cambridge: Cambridge University Press, 1994), p. 189.
44   Keen, *Chivalry*; Riley-Smith, 'The state of mind'; Bull, *Knightly Piety*.

the aristocracy after 1291 lay in its assimilation into a scheme of mainly military activities, each of which was graded in accordance with its perceived merit: fighting for Christ against unbelievers scored highly because it brought together an unrivalled group of associations, religious, historical, military and in many cases familial. The military orders, especially the Teutonic Knights and the Knights of St John, derived some benefit from being associated with this process, but more prominent as a show-case were a cluster of secular orders of chivalry that had powerful crusading affiliations.[45] One result was that by c. 1500 an extraordinary divergence of opinion had taken root about the moral validity of fighting against non-believers solely on the grounds of differences of faith. Many commentators, especially the north European humanists, including some important clerics, questioned whether it was acceptable; while in aristocratic and courtly circles its worth continued to be taken for granted.[46]

Investigation of this and related themes springs from a recognition that the crusading tradition enjoyed a continuing, if muted, existence in various guises well into the early modern period. Some scholars have gone still further, conducting research into the enthusiasm for crusading history and values that manifested itself after the tradition had finally expired in the Enlightenment. During the nineteenth and early twentieth century, poets, novelists, painters, sculptors, composers and others found in the crusades to the east a subject that was at once exotic, dramatic and inspirational. Elizabeth Siberry in particular has pioneered research into the wide range of works that form the legacy of this revival; some were eccentric and mediocre, others however were not just impressive creations in their own right, but also yield significant insights into the politics, religion and culture of their times. It is a subject that from one point of view shades into the historiography of the crusades, but from another testifies to the continuing appeal of some of crusading's essential elements, among them the call to arms on behalf of the faith, the idea of service to the Saviour, and the devotional focus of the Holy Land.[47]

Crusading and Other Faiths

A case can be made for the argument that one of the last products of this wave of interest in the crusades was John Buchan's novel *Greenmantle*

---

45   D'A. J. D. Boulton, *The Knights of the Crown. The Monarchical Orders of Knighthood in Later Medieval Europe, 1325–1520* (Woodbridge: Boydell, 1987).
46   Housley, *Religious Warfare*, pp. 180–8.
47   E. Siberry, 'Images of the crusades in the nineteenth and twentieth centuries', in *OIHC*, 365–85; 'Nineteenth-century perspectives of the First Crusade', in *EC*, 281–93; *The New*

(1916). Buchan set his narrative in the same year that he wrote it, offering as relief to the greyness, anonymity and stagnation of the Western Front an adventure story full of colour, individualism and lightning activity set in the Turkish empire. His subject was a German attempt to galvanize the languishing Ottoman war effort through the preaching of a *jihad* against the Allies. The subject of *jihad*, to which the Scots novelist gave a dashing and romantic rendering in his trademark style, was highly topical. The Ottoman government had declared the war to be a *jihad* in 1914; more significantly though, the idea of a holy war against colonial powers had by this time acquired some popularity among insurgent Muslims in such regions as Algeria, the Sudan and Libya. From about 1900 the occupying Europeans began to be explicitly depicted as heirs to the crusaders; in this the Muslims, who had largely forgotten about the crusades, took their cue from 'the rhetoric that had washed round western Europe for more than half a century'.[48] In this strange manner the European crusading 'revival' brushed shoulders with its Islamic counterpart; the one largely nostalgic and artistic, the other fuelled by bitter resentment and acting as the vehicle for concrete political aspirations. Given the events of 11 September 2001, it is not surprising that the Islamic view of the crusades has received a good deal of attention of late; but this news-driven focus has behind it a deep hinterland of scholarship, because it has long been clear that the crusades were a watershed in Catholic Christianity's relations with all the faiths that were contiguous to it.[49]

The possibility of alternative outcomes naturally arises. In a remarkable letter to an-Nasir, the Muslim emir of Mauretania, in 1076, Pope Gregory VII wrote of Christianity and Islam as faiths that had a common heritage, referring in particular to their shared reverence for Abraham.[50] Just months earlier Gregory had anticipated the First Crusade with a plan for an expedition to the east to assist the Byzantine empire and even to recover Jerusalem.[51] That being the case, it might be argued that too much should not be read into the 1076 letter; perhaps it proves only that the papal *curia* was happy to play down differences when its objectives in

---

Crusaders. Images of the Crusades in the Nineteenth and Early-Twentieth Centuries (Basingstoke: Ashgate, 2000).

48   J. Riley-Smith, 'Islam and the crusades in history and imagination, 8 November 1898 – 11 September 2001', *Crusades*, 2 (2003), 151–67, with quote at p. 160.

49   Hillenbrand, *The Crusades*; Riley-Smith, 'Islam and the crusades'. On the *jihad*, see R. Bonney, *Jihād. From Qur'ān to bin Lāden* (Basingstoke: Palgrave Macmillan, 2004).

50   Cowdrey, *Pope Gregory VII*, pp. 493–4, recognizing the highly unusual nature of the letter; N. Daniel, *The Arabs and Medieval Europe* (2nd edn, London: Longman, 1979), pp. 254–5.

51   Cowdrey, 'Pope Gregory VII's "crusading" plans of 1074'.

Islamic lands could be attained the more easily by so doing. But, it could also be said, that is the whole point: the need to launch further crusades to defend the lands that had been conquered by the first crusaders effectively trapped the *curia*, forcing it to place its relations with the Islamic authorities of the entire Middle East, from Anatolia to the Nile delta, within a framework of normative hostility. Because of the clever way in which the resident Latin powers in the Aegean lobbied the *curia* to assist them in their conflict with the Turks by promoting it as a crusade, during the years that followed the fall of the crusader states, a more or less seamless transition occurred; for first the coastal emirates of Anatolia, and then the Ottomans, became subject to a crusading response just like the Mamluk sultanate further south.[52] Moreover, thanks to the ability of crusading to acclimatize itself to the western Mediterranean, Christian relations with Islam there, above all in Iberia, were also placed on a footing that was more hostile than it had been. This is particularly the case if we accept the argument advanced by some historians of Iberia that the Spanish were initially unreceptive to the 'importing' of crusade ideas.[53]

The Ottoman sultanate was a bellicose and expansionist state, and it is unlikely that it could ever have been contained by non-military means. In other respects, however, there is much to be said for this summary of the negative impact that the crusades had on Christian–Islamic relations. Crusade tended to lead to *jihad*. It is clear that the intrusion of the armies of the First Crusade into the heart of the *Dar al-Islam* was instrumental in generating both an impetus towards Islamic unity and a revival of *jihad* in the region. After a slow start under Zengi, this two-fold process gathered momentum and enabled Nur ad-Din and Saladin to achieve their victories over the Frankish settlers and their crusading co-religionists from the west. *Jihad* was no more easily sustained than its counterpart and after a notable and much-criticized lapse of zeal under Saladin's successors, the Ayyubids, the task of finally clearing the region of the pollution of Latin rule was left to the military oligarchy of the Mamluks.[54] It is apparent too that the radicalization of the conflict between the faiths in Spain was attributable in part to the import of crusading ideas, though in this area the links between crusade and *jihad* are less clear due to the periodic irruption of zealous Islamic armies from north Africa. Most importantly, the dominant image of Islam within Catholic Christendom, from 1095

---

52   E. Zachariadou, 'Holy war in the Aegean during the fourteenth century', in B. Arbel and others, eds, *Latins and Greeks in the Eastern Mediterranean after 1204* (London: Frank Cass, 1989), 212–25.
53   Fletcher, 'Reconquest'; Barton, 'Traitors'.
54   Hillenbrand, *The Crusades*, pp. 89–255.

until the Reformation, was the negative one that was created and sustained in the course of crusade preaching and Church liturgy.[55] This found expression in a host of crusading narratives, songs and poems, as well as in a substantial body of visual representations. The 'Saracen', a term that at times was used to describe anybody who was neither a Christian nor a Jew, but in practice was applied overwhelmingly to Muslims, was depicted as the enemy of Christ's cross and Church, polytheistic, idolatrous, the agent of the devil, irrational, lacking any positive human attributes and addicted to carnality. Muhammad above all aroused the loathing of crusade preachers and apologists, so much so that even a man of learning and insight like Humbert of Romans was unable to rise above the scatological when dealing with him.[56]

That said, two points immediately have to be made. The first we have already encountered: while the caricature of Islamic beliefs and the accompanying denigration of Muhammad were polemical responses that proved to be remarkably persistent, the demonization of the 'Saracens' was 'softened' in the course of fighting the Muslim armies. Crusading against Muslims did not normally generate 'total war' of the type experienced in the racial or ethnic conflicts of the European twentieth century. It is possible that crusading in the Latin East, like warfare between Franks and Muslims generally, was subject to more constraints than the fighting in the Baltic and Albigensian crusades.[57] The Muslims became human. Both on the Christian and on the Muslim side an appreciation of the enemies' ability as combatants and their merits as human beings took shape and certain enemy leaders, notably Richard I and Saladin, acquired reputations for laudable behaviour that persisted for generations. This paralleled and reflected the multi-faceted representation of the 'Saracen' in western literary texts, in which a more rounded, sympathetic and exotic image was gradually created.[58]

Secondly, the practice of crusading was not by definition anti-Islamic. It was a profoundly Eurocentric movement and it has been noted that the vices attributed to 'Saracens' were all construed as the counterparts to the virtues of faithful Christians. One reason why it was so difficult for Christians to accept Islamic monotheism was that it would have infringed this

---

55   Cole, 'O God, the heathen have come into your inheritance'; A. Linder, *Raising Arms. Liturgy in the Struggle to Liberate Jerusalem in the Late Middle Ages* (Turnhout: Brepols, 2003).
56   J. V. Tolan, *Saracens: Islam in the Medieval European Imagination* (New York: Columbia University Press, 2002), esp. pp. 105–69; Cole, 'Humbert of Romans'.
57   Friedman, *Encounters*; France, *Western Warfare*, pp. 187–203; M. Barber, 'The Albigensian Crusades: wars like any other?', in *DGF*, 45–55. The question calls for further research.
58   The essays in M. Frassetto and D. R. Blanks, eds, *Western Views of Islam in Medieval and Early Modern Europe* (Basingstoke: Palgrave, 2000) present a balanced view.

pattern of opposites.[59] In chapter 2 we observed that amid all the contention that continues to surround the origins of the First Crusade, there is agreement that its roots lay in the way western European society and religious ideas had developed, particularly in terms of a *Christianitas* whose eschatological goals and religious purity were equally threatened by the occupation and pollution of the Holy Land's shrines. Granted that all 'Saracens' were normatively *inimici Christi*, the reason for waging war on them was the specific threat to the faith caused by their tenure of, or threat to, Jerusalem. Most crusaders showed astonishingly little interest in Islam; for the most part they accepted stereotypical views of the enemy because their attention was focused on their own penitential practices and on the military dictates of the campaign they found themselves waging. This is not to say that Muslims living outside the Holy Land and Iberia were 'safe': the Islamic colony at Lucera discovered this in 1300 when Charles II of Naples conducted an 'ersatz-crusade' against them, dissolving a community that had existed for about seventy years and presenting its destruction as a gift to Boniface VIII in the pope's year of jubilee.[60]

Since the Muslims had souls their conversion was regarded as desirable, a complementary objective to the military defeat of Islam. But even those commentators who were most optimistic about the chance of converting the 'Saracens' did not regard crusade and conversion as alternatives.[61] In the same way that Italians could carry on trade with Muslim ports which at other times they crusaded against, so Franciscan and Dominican friars could at different points in their lives preach the crusade and embark on missions to convert Muslims. In addition, some prominent churchmen, such as Ramon Lull, could change their minds about priorities as well as about ways and means.[62] There were many reasons why missionary activity bore the meagre fruits that it did.[63] It is possible to blame the crusades for too much. On the one hand, a negative image of the Muslims had come into being before 1095, largely as a result of the fighting in Spain;[64] and on the other, every generation in the central Middle Ages produced individuals who were fascinated rather than repelled by Islam, who admired and absorbed its learning and sought active dialogue with

59   For example, S. Loutchitskaja, 'L'Image des musulmans dans les chroniques des croisades', *Le Moyen Age* 105 (1999), 717–35.
60   J. Taylor, *Muslims in Medieval Italy: The Colony at Lucera* (Lanham, MD: Lexington Books, 2003), pp. 173–209.
61   B. Z. Kedar, *Crusade and Mission. European Approaches toward the Muslims* (Princeton, NJ: Princeton University Press, 1984).
62   Kedar, *Crusade and Mission*, pp. 189–99.
63   Tolan, *Saracens*, pp. 214–74.
64   Bull, 'Views of Muslims'; Flori, *La Guerre sainte*, pp. 227–60.

Muslims.[65] But it is hard to deny that the images of Muhammad and Islam that most people encountered were the crude depictions that were broadcast in crusade sermons, even if they did not originate there, and which were echoed throughout the vernacular crusading sources. If we are tempted to question how far such depictions penetrated into popular sensibilities, we might reflect on how persistent British wartime propaganda against the Germans has proved to be, so much so that many people hold a negative view of Germans half a century after the Second World War ended.

The situation of the Jews was of course more complicated, both because the relationship between Judaism and Christianity was axiomatic to the way Christians identified themselves, and also because there had always been large communities of Jews within the Catholic world. Within the massive corpus of scholarship that has been published over the last fifty years on Judaeo-Christian relations in the Middle Ages, the consensus remains that the preaching of the crusades was an important though far from unique factor in making the overall position of the Jews less favourable.[66] The most dramatic way in which crusading impacted on the Jews was the series of massacres and pillaging that accompanied the preaching of the first three crusades and the march eastwards of the armies. There were particularly violent attacks in Germany in 1096 and 1146, and pogroms in a number of English towns in 1190, the worst occurring at York. Assaults on Jews also occurred during the two *pastoureaux* in France in 1251 and 1320, and there were later incidents: about 30 Jews were killed at Kraców in 1463 and 20 at Kazimierz in 1500.[67] Recent research has done much to clarify the sequence of events on all these occasions, while at the same time exploring the causes of the attacks and the responses of the Jewish communities and Christian authorities. The latter uniformly disapproved of the attacks but differed widely in the speed and effectiveness of their measures to suppress disorder.

The picture that has emerged of the causality behind the attacks on the Jews is a mixed one. Some pogroms seem to have been largely opportunistic, carried out by groups in pressing need of ready cash against people who could conveniently be singled out for persecution because they were unpopular, and who were rumoured to have stashes of specie. Most, however, were motivated by, or at least justified in terms of, a crude

---

65   R. W. Southern, *Western Views of Islam in the Middle Ages* (Cambridge, MA: Harvard University Press, 1962).

66   *JCZK*; J. A. Watt, 'The crusades and the persecution of the Jews', in Linehan and Nelson, eds., *The Medieval World*, 146–62, incl. bibliography at pp. 161–2.

67   G. Mentgen, 'Kreuzzugsmentalität bei antijüdischen Aktionen nach 1190', in *JCZK*, 287–326, at p. 326; Nowakowska, 'Poland', p. 138.

ideology, thanks to the early infection of crusading ideas with the theme of vendetta, the crusader's personal identification with Christ's suffering on the cross, and the labelling of the Jews as Christ-killers. The Latin and Hebrew sources for the Rhineland massacres of 1096 are unanimous that the vendetta played a key role on that occasion.[68] But Kedar has also drawn attention to the implications of the coercive baptisms that occurred in 1096: 'One may propose the hypothesis that the forcible baptisms of 1096 did not arise *ex nihilo*, but that in the preceding decade, or even earlier, there came into being a streak of popular spirituality that led some Christians of the Rhineland to believe that it was their duty to baptize the offspring of the Jews even against their will.'[69] Much of the reason behind the disturbances in 1146 seems to lie with the virulent anti-Jewish sentiments voiced by the Cistercian monk Rudolf when he preached the crusade; St Bernard stepped in to curtail his preaching, though it has been pointed out that Rudolf was probably only extrapolating from religious themes that had been expounded by Bernard and Peter the Venerable.[70] In relation both to the attacks that took place in England in 1190 and to the French *pastoureaux* of 1320, it has been suggested that the assailants were giving voice to anti-government sentiments.[71]

For all the trauma involved, Jewish communities recovered relatively quickly in demographic and economic terms from these attacks. Chazan has argued strongly that the dynamism of Ashkenazic Jewry was scarcely affected by the losses in 1096; and although the Jews of York were obliterated in 1190, three decades later the community had been reconstituted. In fact a central argument to emerge from Chazan's extensive research into the Hebrew narratives of the First Crusade has been that the Ashkenazic Jews were very well-integrated into north European life, and that their religious behaviour, above all their embrace of martyrdom when threatened with baptism, paralleled the new forms of devotion that we encounter in the crusader sources. Recently, Chazan has argued that both Christian and Jewish sources reveal a key shift in the perceived relationship between divine and human activity: 'differences notwithstanding, they share a common view, first, of God's limited role in what

---

68   Chazan, *European Jewry*, esp. pp. 50–84; Riley-Smith, 'The First Crusade and the persecution of the Jews'; Flori, 'Une ou plusieurs "première croisade"?'

69   B. Z. Kedar, 'The forcible baptisms of 1096: history and historiography', in K. Borchardt and E. Bünz, eds, *Forschungen zur Reichs-, Papst- und Landesgeschichte. Peter Herde zum 65. Geburtstag* (2 vols, Stuttgart: Hiersemann, 1998), 1: 187–200, with quote at p. 199.

70   R. Hiestand, 'Juden und Christen in der Kreuzzugspropaganda und bei den Kreuzzugspredigern', in *JCZK*, 153–208, at pp. 178–92.

71   R. C. Stacey, 'Crusades, martyrdoms, and the Jews of Norman England', in *JCZK*, 233–51; Nirenberg, *Communities*, pp. 46–51.

they both perceive as the remarkable developments of the late 1090s and, second, of the centrality of human will, commitment, and action in the drama of the First Crusade.'[72]

A third area in which crusading inflicted damage was that of the Catholic and Orthodox Churches. Recent scholarship has not substantially altered an overall picture of miscomprehension, disastrous blunders and stalled attempts at *rapprochement*. One goal of Urban II in 1095 was to heal relations with the eastern Church by assisting the Byzantine empire, though the recent emphasis on the recovery of Jerusalem has had the inevitable consequence of pushing this aspiration into the background. Those relations were if anything damaged by the events of the First Crusade. The weight that has been placed on the accident theory as an explanation of the Fourth Crusade, together with an awareness of the continuing attempts at a *démarche* at the highest levels, have made it very difficult to argue that there was a schism in the twelfth century. But the disastrous impact of the Latin conquest of 1204 has not been challenged as a watershed, which brought relations to a new low; 'the sack of Constantinople ensured the alienation of the Orthodox world from the West.'[73] It has however been suggested that the sack itself was less catastrophic than many have believed, and that the key development was the hostility that characterized contacts between Catholic and Orthodox at Constantinople in the years that followed. This was aggravated by a propagandistic depiction of the Latins as barbarians by the Nicaean court in exile, a response that curiously foreshadowed the humanists' reaction to the Turkish sack of the city in 1453.[74]

It cannot be said that the overall picture of the slow recovery of relations, once a severely modified version of the Byzantine political system had been installed at Constantinople in 1261, has been much altered. Genuine altruism, combined with shared fears of the Turks, brought Rome and Constantinople together, but political and military weaknesses on both sides, and a potent legacy of suspicion, held up the process of reunion until the council of Florence at 1439; and by that point the Byzantine state, which always pushed harder for an end to the schism than the patriarch of Constantinople, was on the edge of extinction.[75] The

72 R. Chazan, *God, Humanity, and History. The Hebrew First Crusade Narratives* (Berkeley: University of California Press, 2000), p. 210. See also J. Cohen, *Sanctifying the Name of God. Jewish Martyrs and Jewish Memories of the First Crusade* (Philadelphia: University of Pennsylvania Press, 2004).

73 Angold, *The Fourth Crusade*, p. 262.

74 Angold, *The Fourth Crusade*, pp. 193–262.

75 D. M. Nicol, *The Last Centuries of Byzantium 1261–1453* (London: Rupert Hart-Davis, 1972).

picture that has emerged of late about western attitudes towards the Greeks in the period 1300–1453 is a highly diverse one, in which hostility, sympathy and indifference commingled; the key point being that they no longer featured in the worldview of Catholics as a group of any major significance.[76] Whether relations would have proceeded differently without the events of 1095–9, and more importantly of 1204, can only be a matter for conjecture. Given the powerful attraction of Constantinople, and Byzantium's structural weaknesses, there were bound to be attempts at conquest, and not just western ones. The issue is not whether one of these attempts would have succeeded, but whether one that did not assume the form of an enterprise conceived by the papal *curia* would have damaged the Church to anywhere near the same extent.

The impact of crusading on the Church's treatment of heretics should also be considered. From one point of view this was chiefly an organizational matter: in the absence of a willing secular arm, the most efficient and economical way to mobilize an army was through crusade preaching. But there were also broader ramifications. There can be no doubt that the availability of such a weapon made it easier to move from a non-violent response towards organized dissent, to one that was coercive. To that extent it assisted in giving the final touches to the creation of the 'persecuting society' that was described by R. I. Moore.[77] But such a generalization does not take us very far. In the absence of the crusade there were other mechanisms at the Church's disposal to raise an armed force, and given the long lead-in to the Albigensian Crusade it seems likely that other considerations were more important than instrumentality. The ground is firmer when we come to the Hussite crusades, especially their start, when the deployment of the crusade probably appealed to King Sigismund as a way of cutting the Gordian knot that confronted him in the Czech Crown lands. It is clear that the consequences of doing so were disastrous: not only did the crusade in Bohemia and Moravia prove to be ineffective, but it also gave common military cause to a group of opponents who previously had been internally disunited. It can be argued that the use of crusade crystallized the Hussite self-image, welding together religious, political and national loyalties that otherwise might well have remained separate.[78]

---

76 For example, Bisaha, 'Petrarch's vision'; K. Petkov, 'The rotten apple and the good apples: Orthodox, Catholics, and Turks in Philippe de Mézières' crusading propaganda', *JMH* 23 (1997), 255–70.

77 R. I. Moore, *The Formation of a Persecuting Society: Power and Deviance in Western Europe, 950–1250* (Oxford: Blackwell, 1987).

78 T. A. Fudge, *The Magnificent Ride. The First Reformation in Hussite Bohemia* (Aldershot: Ashgate, 1998); Housley, *Religious Warfare*, pp. 33–61.

The question of identities, and the clusters of ideas, beliefs and images that represent them, has been a very popular topic of historical investigation in recent years;[79] it would be odd if crusading studies had not been affected by it. On the one hand, the 'image of the enemy' (*Feindbild*), whether he was a 'Saracen', Jew or heretic, has received much fruitful attention, particularly from historians of crusading who adopt a pluralist approach to their subject. There has been investigation not just of the common features and differences, but also of the links, theological or political, that contemporaries established between these different groups.[80] On the other hand, as we saw in chapter 5, investigation of the role that crusading played in forging a shared identity among the members of Catholic Christendom has in recent years been pursued by a number of historians working on the crusades in Scandinavia. Crusading has long been associated with the process of European expansion in the central Middle Ages, but the emphasis has lain mainly on resources and techniques; this new research into the beliefs and values that prevailed inside the societies that generated the expansion should provide a much more rounded picture.

Any analysis of the impact that crusading had on interfaith relations will produce a negative balance sheet. There can be no disguising that fact, though the tendency among previous generations of historians was to ignore it or even to celebrate it. Benjamin Kedar has recently pointed out the importance of undertaking in-depth historiographical research as a means of making sure that we maintain a balanced approach: 'having observed the damaging impact of prejudice and passion on some of our predecessors' works, we may sensitize ourselves to notice it more readily in the products of our contemporaries.'[81] That is incontestable, but historians of crusading also owe it to their subject to get as close as they can to the way crusaders and their apologists pictured what they were doing. This is not an attempt to balance the negative with the positive, let alone to explain away what was done; rather, it is a search for a full and measured perspective. One of the greatest advances in recent research has been the thorough exploration of the impact of crusading on European medieval society, even though, as we saw in the first half of this chapter, it is an exploration that remains fraught with uncertainties. This investigation needs to continue in social, economic and religious terms, but it needs

---

79 For example, Part One in Linehan and Nelson, eds, *The Medieval World*.
80 For example, Moore, *The Formation*; A. Patschovsky, 'Feindbilder der Kirche: Juden und Ketzer im Vergleich (11.–13. Jahrhundert)', in *JCZK*, 327–587.
81 Kedar, 'The Jerusalem massacre', p. 75.

to acquire a cultural dimension that hitherto has largely been absent. The issue of what contemporaries understood by crusading, and above all the sense they made of their crusading past, has as yet received little attention. It is astonishing that there exists no book-length treatment in any language of the medieval view of the crusades. More generally, historians have tended to focus on activities rather than patterns of thought. This is understandable given that the latter area has more methodological challenges, but it is also extremely stimulating and would repay careful attention. The fact that the crusades were, very largely, a tragic episode in interfaith relations reinforces the need to grasp as fully as possible the thought world of the protagonists, avoiding the stereotyping that they all too often imposed on their enemies.

Bibliography

This is a list of the secondary works cited in the notes of the book, and is not intended to be a comprehensive bibliography for the crusades. For such a bibliography, complete to 1982, see H. E. Mayer and J. McLellan, 'Select bibliography of the crusades', in HC 6: 511–658. For the period since 1982 there exists no comprehensive listing.

Abulafia, D., *Frederick II. A Medieval Emperor* (London: Allen Lane, 1988).

Abulafia, D., 'Trade and crusade, 1050–1250', in *CCCCP*, 1–20.

Allen, D. F., 'Upholding tradition: Benedict XIV and the Hospitaller order of St John of Jerusalem at Malta, 1740–1758', *CHR* 80 (1994), 18–35.

Alphandéry, P., *La Chrétienté et l'idée de croisade*, ed. A. Dupront (2 vols, Paris: A. Michel, 1954–9, new edn 1995 with postscript by M. Balard).

Anderson, G. M., et al., 'An economic interpretation of the medieval crusades', *Journal of European Economic History* 21 (1992), 339–63.

Anderson, P., *Passages from Antiquity to Feudalism* (London: NLB, 1974).

Andrea, A. J., ed., *The Capture of Constantinople. The 'Hystoria Constantinopolitana' of Gunther of Pairis* (Philadelphia: University of Pennsylvania Press, 1997).

Andrea, A. J., ed., *Contemporary Sources for the Fourth Crusade* (Leiden: Brill, 2000).

Angold, M., 'The Byzantine empire, 1025–1118', in D. Luscombe and J. Riley-Smith, eds, *NCMH*, IV, *c.1024–c.1198, Part Two*, 217–53.

Angold, M., *The Fourth Crusade. Event and Context* (Harlow: Pearson Longman, 2003).

Angold, M., 'The road to 1204: the Byzantine background to the Fourth Crusade', *JMH* 25 (1999), 257–78.

Ashtor, E., *Levant Trade in the Later Middle Ages* (Princeton, NJ: Princeton University Press, 1983).

Atiya, A. S., *The Crusade in the Later Middle Ages* (2nd edn, New York: Kraus, 1970).

Aubé, P., *Godefroy de Bouillon* (Paris: Fayard, 1985).

Auffarth, C., '"Ritter" und "Arme" auf dem Ersten Kreuzzug. Zum Problem Herrschaft und Religion, ausgehend von Raymond von Aguilers', *Saeculum* 40 (1989), 39–55.

Bachrach, B., 'The siege of Antioch: a study in military demography', *War in History* 6 (1999), 127–46.

Bachrach, D. S., *Religion and the Conduct of War c. 300–1215* (Woodbridge: Boydell, 2003).

Bak, J., 'Hungary and crusading in the fifteenth century', in *CFCMI*, 116–27, 224–7.

Balard, M., 'Latins in the Aegean and the Balkans in the fourteenth century', in M. Jones, ed., *NCMH, VI, c. 1300–c. 1415* (Cambridge: Cambridge University Press, 2000), 825–38.

Barber, M., 'The Albigensian Crusades: wars like any other?', in *DGF*, 45–55.

Barber, M., *The Cathars. Dualist Heretics in Languedoc in the High Middle Ages* (Harlow: Longman, 2000).

Barber, M., 'The crusade of the shepherds in 1251', in J. F. Sweets, ed., *Proceedings of the Tenth Annual Meeting of the Western Society for French History* (Lawrence, KS: Western Society for French History, 1984), 1–23.

Barber, M., *The New Knighthood. A History of the Order of the Temple* (Cambridge: Cambridge University Press, 1994).

Barber, M., 'The pastoureaux of 1320', *JEH* 32 (1981), 143–66.

Barthélemy, D., *L'An mil et la paix de Dieu: la France chrétienne et féodale, 980–1060* (Paris: Fayard, 1999).

Barthélemy, D., *L'Ordre seigneuriale XIe–XIIe siècle* (Paris: Seuil, 1990).

Bartlett, R., *The Making of Europe. Conquest, Colonization and Cultural Change 950–1350* (London: Allen Lane, 1993).

Barton, S., 'Traitors to the faith? Christian mercenaries in al-Andalus and the Maghreb, c. 1100–1300', in R. Collins and A. Goodman, eds, *Medieval Spain. Culture, Conflict and Coexistence. Studies in Honour of Angus MacKay* (Basingstoke: Palgrave Macmillan, 2002), 23–45.

Bauer, D., K. Herbers and N. Jaspert, eds, *Jerusalem im Hoch- und Spätmittelalter. Konflikte und Konfliktbewältigung – Vorstellungen und Vergegenwärtigungen* (Frankfurt: Campus, 2001).

Beaune, C., *The Birth of an Ideology. Myths and Symbols of Nation in Late-Medieval France*, trans. S. R. Huston, ed. F. L. Cheyette (Berkeley: University of California Press, 1991).

Becker, A., *Papst Urban II* (2 vols, Stuttgart: A. Hiersemann, 1964–88).

Beebe, B., 'The English baronage and the crusade of 1270', *BIHR* 48 (1975), 127–49.

Berry, V. G., 'The Second Crusade', in *HC* 1: 463–512.

Bird, J., 'Reform or crusade? Anti-usury and crusade preaching during the pontificate of Innocent III', in *PIW*, 165–85.

Bisaha, N., *Creating East and West. Renaissance Humanists and the Ottoman Turks* (Philadelphia: University of Pennsylvania Press, 2004).

Bisaha, N., 'Petrarch's vision of the Muslim and Byzantine east', *Speculum* 76 (2001), 284–314.

Bisaha, N., 'Pope Pius II and the crusade', in *CFCMI*, 39–52, 188–91.

Bisaha, N., 'Pope Pius II's letter to Sultan Mehmed II: A reexamination', *Crusades* 1 (2002), 183–200.

Black, R., *Benedetto Accolti and the Florentine Renaissance* (Cambridge: Cambridge University Press, 1985).

Blake, E. O., 'The formation of the "crusade idea" ', *JEH* 21 (1970), 11–31.

Blake, E. O., and C. Morris, 'A hermit goes to war: Peter and the origins of the First Crusade', *SCH* 22 (1985), 79–107.

Bloch, M., *Feudal Society*, trans. L. A. Manyon (London: Routledge, 1961).

Bolton, B., 'The Cistercians and the Aftermath of the Second Crusade', in *SCC*, 131–40.

Bolton, B., ' "Serpent in the dust, sparrow on the housetop": attitudes to Jerusalem and the Holy Land in the circle of Innocent III', in *HLHL*, 154–80.

Bonney, R., *Jihād. From Qur'ān to bin Lāden* (Basingstoke: Palgrave Macmillan, 2004).

Boockmann, H., *Der Deutsche Orden. Zwölf Kapitel aus seiner Geschichte* (3rd edn, Munich: C. H. Beck, 1989).

Boulton, D'A. J. D., *The Knights of the Crown. The Monarchical Orders of Knighthood in Later Medieval Europe, 1325–1520* (Woodbridge: Boydell, 1987).

Bracewell, C. W., *The Uskoks of Senj. Piracy, Banditry, and Holy War in the Sixteenth-Century Adriatic* (Ithaca, NY: Cornell University Press, 1992).

Bredero, A. H., 'Jérusalem dans l'occident médiévale', in P. Gallais and Y.-J. Riou, eds, *Mélanges offerts à René Crozet* (2 vols, Poitiers: Société d'études médiévales, 1966), 1: 259–71.

Brett, M., ''Abbasids, Fatimids and Seljuqs', in D. Luscombe and J. Riley-Smith, eds, *NCMH, IV, c.1024–c.1198, Part Two*, 675–720.

Brett, M., 'The Near East on the eve of the crusades', in *PCNAD*, 119–36.

Brooke, C., *Europe in the Central Middle Ages, 962–1154* (2nd edn, London: Longman, 1987).

Brundage, J. A., 'Adhemar of Puy: the bishop and his critics', *Speculum* 34 (1959), 201–12.

Brundage, J. A., 'Crusades, clerics and violence: reflections on a canonical theme', in *EC*, 147–56.

Brundage, J. A., 'Holy war and the medieval lawyers', in T. P. Murphy, ed., *The Holy War* (Columbus: Ohio State University Press, 1976), 99–140.

Brundage, J. A., 'Immortalizing the crusades: law and institutions', in *MSCH*, 251–60.

Brundage, J. A., *Medieval Canon Law* (Longman: London, 1995).

Brundage, J. A., *Medieval Canon Law and the Crusader* (Madison: University of Wisconsin Press, 1969).

Brundage, J. A., 'Prostitution, miscegenation and sexual purity in the First Crusade', in *CS*, 57–65.

Brundage, J. A., 'St. Bernard and the jurists', in *SCC*, 25–33.

BIBLIOGRAPHY

Bull, M., 'The diplomatic of the First Crusade', in *FCOI*, 35–54.

Bull, M., ed., *France in the Central Middle Ages* (Oxford: Oxford University Press, 2002).

Bull, M., *Knightly Piety and the Lay Response to the First Crusade. The Limousin and Gascony, c.970–c.1130* (Oxford: Oxford University Press, 1993).

Bull, M., 'Origins', in *OIHC*, 13–33.

Bull, M., 'The roots of lay enthusiasm for the First Crusade', *History* 78 (1993), 353–72.

Bull, M., 'Views of Muslims and of Jerusalem in miracle stories, c. 1000 – c. 1200: Reflections on the study of first crusaders' motivations', in *EC*, 13–38.

Burns, R. I., *Muslims, Christians, and Jews in the Crusader Kingdom of Valencia. Societies in Symbiosis* (Cambridge: Cambridge University Press, 1984).

Cahen, C., 'An introduction to the First Crusade', *P&P* 6 (1954), 6–29.

Cardini, F., 'I costi della crociata. L'aspetto economico del progetto di Marin Sanudo il Vecchio (1312–1321', in *Studi in memoria di Federigo Melis* (5 vols, Naples: Giannini, 1978), 2: 179–210.

Cardini, F., 'La société italienne et les croisades', *CCM* 28 (1985), 19–33.

Cardini, F., 'La società lucchese e la prima crociata', *Actum Luce. Rivista di studi lucchesi* 8 (1979), 7–29.

Cardini, F., 'L'inizio del movimento crociato in Toscana', in *Studi di storia medievale e moderna per Ernesto Sestan, 1* (Florence: Leo S. Olschki, 1980), 135–57.

Caron, M.-T., and D. Clauzel, eds, *Le Banquet du faisan* (Arras: Artois Presses Université, 1997).

Caspi-Reisfeld, K., 'Women warriors during the crusades, 1095–1254', in S. B. Edgington and S. Lambert, eds, *Gendering the Crusades* (Cardiff: University of Wales Press, 2001), 94–107.

Cate, J. L., 'The crusade of 1101', in *HC* 1: 343–67.

Cazel, F. A., 'Financing the crusades', in *HC* 6: 116–49.

Chazan, R., *European Jewry and the First Crusade* (Berkeley: University of California Press, 1987).

Chazan, R., *God, Humanity, and History. The Hebrew First Crusade Narratives* (Berkeley: University of California Press, 2000).

Cheynet, J.-C., 'Mantzikert. Un désastre militaire?' *Byzantion* 50 (1980), 410–38.

Christiansen, E., *The Northern Crusades. The Baltic and the Catholic Frontier 1100–1525* (London: Macmillan, 1980).

Cohen, J., *Sanctifying the Name of God. Jewish Martyrs and Jewish Memories of the First Crusade* (Philadelphia: University of Pennsylvania Press, 2004).

Cohn, N., *The Pursuit of the Millennium. Revolutionary Millenarians and Mystical Anarchists of the Middle Ages*, revd edn (New York: Oxford University Press, 1970).

Cole, P., 'Humbert of Romans and the crusade', in *EC*, 157–74.

Cole, P., ' "O God, the heathen have come into your inheritance" (Ps. 78.1). The theme of religious pollution in crusade documents, 1095–1188', in *CMTCS*, 84–111.

Cole, P. J., *The Preaching of the Crusades to the Holy Land, 1095–1270* (Cambridge, MA: Medieval Academy of America, 1991).

Constable, G., 'The crusading project of 1150', in *MSCH*, 67–75.

Constable, G., 'The financing of the crusades in the twelfth century', in *OSHCKJ*, 64–88.

Constable, G., 'The historiography of the crusades', in A. E. Laiou and R. P. Mottahedeh, eds, *The Crusades from the Perspective of Byzantium and the Muslim World* (Washington, DC: Dumbarton Oaks Research Library and Collection, 2001), 1–22.

Constable, G., 'Medieval charters as a source for the history of the crusades', in *CS*, 73–89.

Constable, G., 'Opposition to pilgrimage in the Middle Ages', *Studia Gratiana* 19 (1976), 123–46.

Constable, G., 'The place of the crusader in medieval society', *Viator* 29 (1998), 377–403.

Constable, G., 'The Second Crusade as seen by contemporaries', *Traditio* 9 (1953), 213–79.

Contamine, P., *War in the Middle Ages*, trans. M. Jones (Oxford: Blackwell, 1984).

Coupe, M. D., 'Peter the Hermit – a reassessment', *Nottingham Medieval Studies* 31 (1987), 37–45.

Coureas, N., 'Cyprus and the naval leagues, 1333–1358', in N. Coureas and J. Riley-Smith, eds, *Cyprus and the Crusades* (Nicosia: Society for the Study of the Crusades and the Latin East and Cyprus Research Centre, 1995), 107–24.

Cowdrey, H. E. J., 'Christianity and the morality of warfare during the first century of crusading', in *EC*, 175–92.

Cowdrey, H. E. J., 'Cluny and the First Crusade', *Revue Bénédictine* 83 (1973), 285–311, repr. in *PMC*, study XV.

Cowdrey, H. E. J., 'From the peace of God to the First Crusade', in *PCNAD*, 51–61.

Cowdrey, H. E. J., 'The genesis of the crusades: the springs of western ideas of the holy war', in T. P. Murphy, ed., *The Holy War* (Columbus: Ohio State University Press, 1976), 9–32, repr. in *PMC*, study XIII.

Cowdrey, H. E. J., 'The Mahdia campaign of 1087', *EHR* 92 (1977), 1–29, repr. in *PMC*, study XII.

Cowdrey, H. E. J., 'Martyrdom and the First Crusade', in *CS*, 46–56.

Cowdrey, H. E. J., 'The peace and truce of God in the eleventh century', *P&P* 46 (1970), 42–67.

Cowdrey, H. E. J., *Pope Gregory VII 1073–1085* (Oxford: Oxford University Press, 1998).

Cowdrey, H. E. J., 'Pope Gregory VII's "crusading" plans of 1074', in *OSHCKJ*, 27–40, repr. in *PMC*, study X.

Crouzet, D., *Les Guerriers de Dieu. La violence au temps des troubles de religion vers 1525– vers 1610* (2 vols, Seyssel: Champ Vallon, 1990).

Daly, W. M., 'Christian fraternity, the crusades and the security of Constantinople', *Medieval Studies* 22 (1960), 43–91.

Daniel, N., *The Arabs and Medieval Europe* (2nd edn, London: Longman, 1979).

Daniel, N., *Heroes and Saracens. An Interpretation of the Chansons de geste* (Edinburgh: Edinburgh University Press, 1984).

Defourneaux, M., *Les Français en Espagne aux XIe et XIIe siècles* (Paris: Presses universitaires de France, 1949).

Delaruelle, E., *L'Idée de croisade au moyen âge* (Turin, 1980).

Delaville le Roulx, J., *La France en orient au XIVe siècle: expéditions du maréchal Boucicaut* (2 vols, Paris: Ernest Thorin, 1886).

Demurger, A., 'Le pape Clément VI et l'Orient: ligue ou croisade?', in J. Paviot and J. Verger, eds, *Guerre, pouvoir et noblesse au Moyen Âge. Mélanges en l'honneur de Philippe Contamine* (Paris: Presses de l'Université de Paris-Sorbonne, 2000), 207–14.

Demurger, A., 'Le Religieux de Saint-Denis et la croisade', in F. Autrand, C. Gauvard and J.-M. Moeglin, eds, *Saint Denis et la royauté: études offertes à Bernard Guenée* (Paris: Publications de la Sorbonne, 1999), 181–96.

Dickson, G., 'The advent of the *pastores* (1251)', *RBPH* 66 (1988), 249–67.

Dickson, G., 'La genèse de la croisade des enfants (1212)', *BEC* 153 (1995), 54–102 [English version as 'The genesis of the Children's Crusade (1212)', in his *Religious Enthusiasm in the Medieval West: Revivals, Crusades, Saints* (Aldershot: Ashgate Variorum, 2000), study IV].

Dickson, G., 'Revivalism as a medieval religious genre', *JEH* 51 (2000), 473–96.

Dickson, G., 'Stephen of Cloyes, Philip Augustus, and the Children's Crusade of 1212', in B. N. Sargent-Baur, ed., *Journeys Towards God. Pilgrimage and Crusade* (Kalamazoo: Medieval Institute Publications, Western Michigan University, 1992), 83–105.

Dijkstra, C. T. J., *La Chanson de croisade. Étude thématique d'un genre hybride* (Amsterdam, 1995).

Donovan, J., *Pelagius and the Fifth Crusade* (Philadelphia: University of Pennsylvania Press, 1950).

Douglas, D. C., *The Norman Achievement 1050–1100* (London: Eyre and Spottiswoode, 1969).

Duby, G., 'Laity and the peace of God', in *The Chivalrous Society*, trans. C. Postan (London: Edward Arnold, 1977), 123–33.

Dufournet, J., and L. Harf, eds, *Le Prince et son historien. La vie de saint Louis de Joinville* (Paris: Honoré Champion Éditeur, 1997).

Duncalf, F., 'The Peasants' Crusade', *AHR* 26 (1921), 440–54.

Dupront, A., *Du sacré: croisades et pèlerinages, images et langages* (Paris: Gallimard, 1987).

Edbury, P. W., 'Christians and Muslims in the eastern Mediterranean', in M. Jones, ed., *NCMH, VI, c. 1300–c. 1415* (Cambridge: Cambridge University Press, 2000), 864–84.

Edbury, P. W., *The Kingdom of Cyprus and the Crusades, 1191–1374* (Cambridge: Cambridge University Press, 1991).

Edbury, P. W., 'Preaching the crusade in Wales', in A. Haverkamp and H. Vollrath, eds, *England and Germany in the High Middle Ages* (Oxford: Oxford University Press, 1996), 221–33.

Edbury, P. W., and J. G. Rowe, *William of Tyre. Historian of the Latin East* (Cambridge: Cambridge University Press, 1988).

Edgington, S. B., 'Albert of Aachen reappraised', in *FCJ*, 55–67.

Edgington, S. B., 'Albert of Aachen, St Bernard and the Second Crusade', in *SCSC*, 54–70.

Edgington, S. B., 'The First Crusade: reviewing the evidence', in *FCOI*, 55–77.

Edson, E., 'Reviving the crusade: Sanudo's schemes and Vesconte's maps', in R. Allen, ed., *Eastward Bound. Travel and Travellers, 1050–1550* (Manchester: Manchester University Press, 2004), 131–55.

Edwards, J., '*Reconquista* and crusade in fifteenth-century Spain', in *CFCMI*, 163–81, 235–7.

Ehlers, A., 'The crusade of the Teutonic Knights against Lithuania reconsidered', in *CCBF*, 21–44.

Elm, K., 'Die Eroberung Jerusalems in Jahre 1099. Ihre Darstellung, Beurteilung und Deutung in den Quellen zur Geschichte des Ersten Kreuzzugs', in Bauer, Herbers and Jaspert, eds, *Jerusalem*, 31–54.

Epstein, S. A., 'Genoa and the crusades. Piety, credit, and the fiscal-military state', in L. Balletto, ed., *Oriente e occidente tra medioevo ed età moderna. Studi in onore di Geo Pistarino* (Genoa: Glauco Brigati, 1997), 245–59.

Erdmann, C., *The Origin of the Idea of Crusade*, trans. M. W. Baldwin and W. Goffart (Princeton, NJ: Princeton University Press, 1977).

Evans, A. P., 'The Albigensian crusade', in *HC* 2: 277–324.

Favreau-Lilie, M.-L., *Die Italiener im Heiligen Land vom ersten Kreuzzug bis zum Tode Heinrichs von Champagne (1098–1197)* (Amsterdam: Adolf M. Hakkert, 1989).

Fernández-Armesto, F., *Before Columbus: Exploration and Colonisation from the Mediterranean to the Atlantic, 1229–1492* (Basingstoke: Macmillan, 1987).

Fernández-Armesto, F., *Columbus* (Oxford: Oxford University Press, 1991).

Fernández-Armesto, F., *The Spanish Armada. The Experience of War in 1588* (Oxford: Oxford University Press, 1989).

Ferreiro, A., 'The siege of Barbastro 1064–65: a reassessment', *JMH* 9 (1983), 129–44.

Flahiff, G. B., 'Deus non vult: a critic of the Third Crusade', *Mediaeval Studies* 9 (1947), 162–88.

Fletcher, R. A., 'Reconquest and crusade in Spain c. 1050–1150', *TRHS* 5th ser. 37 (1987), 31–47.

Fletcher, R. A., *Saint James's Catapult. The Life and Times of Diego Gelmírez of Santiago de Compostela* (Oxford: Oxford University Press, 1984).

Flori, J., 'De Clermont à Jérusalem. La première croisade dans l'historiographie récente (1995–1999)', *Le Moyen Age* 105 (1999), 439–55.

Flori, J., 'De la paix de Dieu à la croisade? Un réexamen', *Crusades* 2 (2003), 1–23.

Flori, J., *La Guerre sainte. La formation de l'idée de croisade dans l'Occident chrétien* (Paris: Aubier, 2001).

Flori, J., *Pierre l'Ermite et la première croisade* (Paris: Fayard, 1999).

Flori, J., 'Pour une redéfinition de la croisade', *CCM* 47 (2004), 329–50.

Flori, J., 'Réforme, *reconquista*, croisade. L'idée de reconquête dans la correspondance pontificale d'Alexandre II à Urbain II', *CCM* 40 (1997), 317–35.

Flori, J., 'Un problème de méthodologie: la valeur des nombres chez les chroniqueurs du moyen âge. À propos des effectifs de la première croisade', *Le Moyen Age* 99 (1993), 399–422.

Flori, J., 'Une ou plusieurs "première croisade"? Le message d'Urbain II et les plus anciens pogroms d'Occident', *RH* 285 (1991), 3–27.

Forey, A. J., 'The crusading vows of the English King Henry III', *Durham University Journal* 65 (1973), 229–47.

Forey, A. J., 'The failure of the siege of Damascus in 1148', *JMH* 10 (1984), 13–25.

Forey, A. J., 'The military orders, 1120–1312', in *OIHC*, 184–216.

Forey, A. J., *The Military Orders from the Twelfth to the Early Fourteenth Centuries* (Basingstoke: Macmillan, 1992).

Fossier, R., 'The rural economy and demographic growth', in D. Luscombe and J. Riley-Smith, eds, *NCMH, IV, c.1024–c.1198, Part One* (Cambridge: Cambridge University Press, 2004), 11–46.

France, J., 'Anna Comnena, the Alexiad and the First Crusade', *Reading Medieval Studies* 10 (1984), 20–38.

France, J., 'The crisis of the First Crusade: from the defeat of Kerbogah to the departure from Arqa', *Byzantion* 40 (1970), 276–308.

France, J., 'The departure of Tatikios from the army of the First Crusade', *BIHR* 44 (1971), 131–47.

France, J., 'The election and title of Godfrey de Bouillon', *Canadian Journal of History* 18 (1983), 321–9.

France, J., 'Holy war and holy men: Erdmann and the lives of the saints', in *EC*, 193–208.

France, J., 'Patronage and the appeal of the First Crusade', in *FCOI*, 5–20.

France, J., 'The use of the anonymous *Gesta Francorum* in the early twelfth-century sources for the First Crusade', in *FCJ*, 29–42.

France, J., *Victory in the East. A Military History of the First Crusade* (Cambridge: Cambridge University Press, 1996).

France, J., *Western Warfare in the Age of the Crusades, 1000–1300* (London: UCL Press, 1999).

Frassetto, M., and D. R. Blanks, eds, *Western Views of Islam in Medieval and Early Modern Europe* (Basingstoke: Palgrave, 2000).

Freedman, P., and G. M. Spiegel, 'Medievalisms old and new: the rediscovery of alterity in North American medieval studies', *AHR* 103 (1998), 677–704.

Friedman, Y., *Encounters between Enemies. Captivity and Ransom in the Latin Kingdom of Jerusalem* (Leiden: Brill, 2002).

Fudge, T. A., ed. and trans., *The Crusade against Heretics in Bohemia, 1418–1437. Sources and Documents for the Hussite Crusades* (Aldershot: Ashgate, 2002).

Fudge, T. A., *The Magnificent Ride. The First Reformation in Hussite Bohemia* (Aldershot: Ashgate, 1998).

García, J. M. R., 'Henry III, Alfonso X of Castile and the crusading plans of the thirteenth century', in B. Weiler and I. Rowlands, eds, *England and Europe in the Reign of Henry III (1216–72)* (Aldershot: Ashgate, 2002), 99–120.

García, J. M. R., 'Historiografía de las Cruzadas', *Espacio, Tiempo y Forma*, serie 3, *Historia Medieval* 13 (2000), 341–95.

García-Guijarro Ramos, L., 'Expansión económica medieval y cruzadas', in *PCNAD*, 155–66.

Geary, P. J., *Furta sacra. Thefts of Relics in the Central Middle Ages* (Princeton, NJ: Princeton University Press, 1988).

Geldsetzer, S., *Frauen auf Kreuzzügen 1096–1291* (Darmstadt: Wissenschaftliche Buchgesellschaft, 2003).

Giese, W., 'Die "lancea Domini" von Antiochia (1098/99)', in W. Setz, ed., *Fälschungen im Mittelalter. Internationaler Kongress der Monumenta Germaniae Historica 16.–19. September 1986* (6 vols, Hannover: Hahn, 1988–90), 5: 485–504.

Gilchrist, J., 'The Erdmann thesis and the canon law, 1083–1141', in *CS*, 37–45.

Gilchrist, J., 'The Lord's war as the proving ground of faith: Pope Innocent III and the propagation of violence (1198–1216)', in *CMTCS*, 65–83.

Gillingham, J., 'Richard I and the science of war in the Middle Ages', in *WGMA*, 78–91.

Gillingham, J., *Richard the Lionheart* (London: Weidenfeld and Nicolson, 1978).

Gillingham, J., 'Roger of Howden on crusade', in D. O. Morgan, ed., *Medieval Historical Writing in the Christian and Islamic Worlds* (London: School of Oriental and African Studies, 1982), 60–75.

Godfrey, J., *1204: The Unholy Crusade* (Oxford: Oxford University Press, 1980).

Goez, W., 'Wandlungen des Kreuzzugsgedankens im Hoch- und Spätmittelalter', in W. Fischer and J. Schneider, eds, *Das Heilige Land im Mittelalter. Begegnungsraum zwischen Orient und Okzident* (Neustadt an der Aisch: Verlag Degener, 1982), 33–44.

Goñi Gaztambide, J., *Historia de la bula de la cruzada en España* (Vitoria: Editorial del Seminario, 1958).

Goodman, J. R., *Chivalry and Exploration 1298–1630* (Woodbridge: Boydell, 1998).

Gordon, D., *Making and Meaning: The Wilton Diptych* (London: National Gallery Publications, 1993).

Grabois, A., 'The crusade of Louis VII: a reconsideration', in *CS*, 94–104.

Grabois, A., '*Militia* and *Malitia*: the Bernardine vision of chivalry', in *SCC*, 49–56.

Grousset, R., *Histoire des croisades et du royaume franc de Jérusalem* (3 vols, Paris: Plon, 1934–6).

Guidi, P., et al., eds, *Rationes decimarum Italiae nei secoli XIII e XIV* (13 vols, Rome: Vatican City, 1932–52).

Hagenmeyer, H., *Chronologie de la première croisade (1094–1100)* (Paris: Ernest Leroux, 1902).

Hagenmeyer, H., *Peter der Eremite: ein kritischer Beitrag zur Geschichte des ersten Kreuzzuges* (Leipzig: Harrassowitz, 1879).

Hamilton, B., 'The impact of crusader Jerusalem on western Christendom', *CHR* 80 (1994), 695–713.

Hamilton, B., 'Rebuilding Zion: the holy places of Jerusalem in the twelfth century', *SCH* 14 (1977), 105–16.

Hankins, J., 'Renaissance crusaders: humanist crusade literature in the age of Mehmed II', *Dumbarton Oaks Papers* 49 (1995), 111–207.

Harris, J., *Byzantium and the Crusades* (London: Hambledon, 2003).

Hay, D., 'Gender bias and religious intolerance in accounts of the "massacres" of the First Crusade', in *TISCAC*, 3–10, 135–9.

Hehl, E.-D., *Kirche und Krieg im 12. Jahrhundert. Studien zu kanonischem Recht und politicher Wirklichkeit* (Stuttgart: A. Hiersemann, 1980).

Hehl, E.-D., 'War, peace and the Christian order', in D. Luscombe and J. Riley-Smith, eds, *NCMH, IV, c.1024–c.1198, Part One*, 185–228.

Hehl, E.-D., 'Was ist eigentlich ein Kreuzzug?' *Historische Zeitschrift* 259 (1994), 297–336.

Helmrath, J., 'The German *Reichstage* and the crusade', in *CFCMI*, 53–69, 191–203.

Heymann, F. G., 'The crusades against the Hussites', in *HC* 3: 586–646.

Hiestand, R., 'Friedrich II. und der Kreuzzug', in A. Esch and N. Kamp, eds, *Friedrich II. Tagung des Deutschen Historischen Instituts in Rom in Gedenkjahr 1994* (Tübingen: Max Niemeyer Verlag, 1996), 128–49.

Hiestand, R., 'Juden und Christen in der Kreuzzugspropaganda und bei den Kreuzzugspredigern', in *JCZK*, 153–208.

Hiestand, R., 'Kingship and crusade in twelfth-century Germany', in A. Haverkamp and H. Vollrath, eds, *England and Germany in the High Middle Ages* (Oxford: Oxford University Press, 1996), 235–65.

Hiestand, R., 'The papacy and the Second Crusade', in *SCSC*, 32–53.

Hiestand, R., ' "Precipua tocius christianismi columpna". Barbarossa und der Kreuzzug', in A. Haverkamp, ed., *Friedrich Barbarossa. Handlungsspielräume und Wirkungsweisen des Staufischen Kaisers* (Sigmaringen: Jan Thorbecke Verlag, 1992), 51–108.

Hiestand, R., 'Reconquista, Kreuzzug und heiliges Grab: die Eroberung von Tortosa 1148 im Lichte eines neuen Zeugnisses', *Gesammelte Aufsätze zur Kulturgeschichte Spaniens* 31 (1984), 136–57.

Hill, G., *A History of Cyprus* (4 vols, Cambridge: Cambridge University Press, 1940–52).

Hill, J. H. and L. L., 'The convention of Alexius Comnenus and Raymond of St Gilles', *AHR* 58 (1953), 322–7.

Hill, J. H. and L. L., 'Justification historique du titre de Raymond de St Gilles, "Christiane milicie excellentissimus princeps" ', *Annales du Midi* 66 (1954), 101–12.

Hill, J. H. and L. L., *Raymond IV, Count of Toulouse* (Syracuse, NY: Syracuse University Press, 1962).

Hillenbrand, C., *The Crusades. Islamic Perspectives* (Edinburgh: Edinburgh University Press, 1999).

Hillenbrand, C., 'The First Crusade: the Muslim perspective', in *FCOI*, 130–41.

Hillgarth, J. N., *Ramon Lull and Lullism in Fourteenth-Century France* (Oxford: Oxford University Press, 1971).

Hillgarth, J. N., *The Spanish Kingdoms 1250–1516* (2 vols, Oxford: Oxford University Press, 1976–8).

Hilton, R., *Bond Men Made Free. Medieval Peasant Movements and the English Rising of 1381* (repr. London: Routledge, 1986).

Hoch, M., 'The choice of Damascus as the objective of the Second Crusade', in *APC*, 359–70.

Hoch, M., 'The price of failure: the Second Crusade as a turning-point in the history of the Latin East?' in *SCSC*, 180–200.

Holmes, G., 'Cardinal Beaufort and the crusade against the Hussites', *EHR* 88 (1973), 721–50.

Housley, N., 'A necessary evil? Erasmus, the crusade, and war against the Turks', in *CTS*, 259–80.

Housley, N., *The Avignon Papacy and the Crusades, 1305–1378* (Oxford: Oxford University Press, 1986).

Housley, N., 'Costing the crusade: budgeting for crusading activity in the fourteenth century', in *EC*, 45–59.

Housley, N., *The Crusaders* (Stroud: Tempus, 2002).

Housley, N., 'Crusades against Christians: their origins and early development, c. 1000–1216', in *CS*, 17–36.

Housley, N., 'The crusading movement, 1274–1700', in *OIHC*, 260–93.

Housley, N., 'Giovanni da Capistrano and the crusade of 1456', in *CFCMI*, 94–115, 215–24.

Housley, N., *The Italian Crusades. The Papal–Angevin Alliance and the Crusades against Christian Lay Powers, 1254–1343* (Oxford: Oxford University Press, 1982).

Housley, N., 'Jerusalem and the development of the crusade idea, 1095–1128', in *HH*, 27–40.

Housley, N., *The Later Crusades, 1274–1580. From Lyons to Alcazar* (Oxford: Oxford University Press, 1992).

Housley, N., 'Le maréchal Boucicaut à Nicopolis', *Annales de Bourgogne* 68 (1996), 85–99.

Housley, N., 'One man and his wars: the depiction of warfare by Marshal Boucicaut's biographer', *JMH* 29 (2003), 27–40.

Housley, N., '*Pro deo et patria mori*: sanctified patriotism in Europe, 1400–1600', in P. Contamine, ed., *War and Competition between States* (Oxford: Oxford University Press, 2000), 221–48.

Housley, N., *Religious Warfare in Europe, 1400–1536* (Oxford: Oxford University Press, 2002).

Housley, N., 'The thirteenth-century crusades in the Mediterranean', in D. Abulafia, ed., *NCMH, V, c. 1198–c. 1300* (Cambridge: Cambridge University Press, 1999), 569–89.

Housley, N., with M. Bull, 'Jonathan Riley-Smith, the crusades and the military orders: an appreciation', in *EC*, 1–10.

Il concilio di Piacenza e le crociate (Piacenza: Fida Custodia, 1996).

Irwin, R., *The Middle East in the Middle Ages. The Early Mamluk Sultanate 1250–1382* (London: Croom Helm, 1986).

Jackson, J., 'The crusades of 1239–41 and their aftermath', *Bulletin of the School of Oriental and African Studies* 50 (1987), 32–60.

Jaspert, N., '*Capta est Dertosa, clavis Christianorum*: Tortosa and the crusades', in *SCSC*, 90–110.

Jensen, C. S., 'Urban life and the crusades in northern Germany and the Baltic lands in the early thirteenth century', in *CCBF*, 75–94.

Jensen, J. M., '*Sclavorum expugnator*: conquest, crusade, and Danish royal ideology in the twelfth century', *Crusades* 2 (2003), 55–81.

Jensen, K. V., 'Denmark and the Second Crusade: the formation of a crusader state?' in *SCSC*, 164–79.

Jensen, K. V., 'Introduction', in *CCBF*, xvii–xxv.

Johnson, E. N., 'The German crusade on the Baltic', *HC* 3: 545–85.

Jones, T., *Chaucer's Knight. The Portrait of a Medieval Mercenary* (revd edn, London: Methuen, 1994).

Jordan, W. C., *Louis IX and the Challenge of the Crusade. A Study in Rulership* (Princeton, NJ: Princeton University Press, 1979).

Jordan, W. C., 'The representation of the crusades in the songs attributed to Thibaud, count palatine of Champagne', *JMH* 25 (1999), 27–34.

Kahl, H.-D., 'Crusade eschatology as seen by St Bernard in the years 1146 to 1148', in *SCC*, 35–47.

Kantorowicz, E. H., '*Pro patria mori* in mediaeval political thought', *AHR* 56 (1950–1), 472–92.

Katzenellenbogen, A., 'The central tympanum at Vézelay, its encyclopaedic meaning and its relation to the First Crusade', *Art Bulletin* (1944), 141–51.

Kedar, B. Z., *Crusade and Mission. European Approaches toward the Muslims* (Princeton, NJ: Princeton University Press, 1984).

Kedar, B. Z., 'Crusade historians and the massacres of 1096', *Jewish History* 12 (1998), 11–31.

Kedar, B. Z., 'The forcible baptisms of 1096: history and historiography', in K. Borchardt and E. Bünz, eds, *Forschungen zur Reichs-, Papst- und Landesgeschichte. Peter Herde zum 65. Geburtstag* (2 vols, Stuttgart: Hiersemann, 1998), 1: 187–200.

Kedar, B. Z., 'The Jerusalem massacre of July 1099 in the western historiography of the crusades', *Crusades* 3 (2004), 15–75.

Kedar, B. Z., 'The passenger list of a crusader ship, 1250: towards the history of the popular element on the Seventh Crusade', *Studi medievali*, 3rd ser. 13 (1972), 267–79.

Keen, M., *Chivalry* (New Haven, CT: Yale University Press, 1984).

Keene, D., 'Towns and the growth of trade', in D. Luscombe and J. Riley-Smith, eds, *NCMH, IV, c.1024–c.1198, Part One* (Cambridge: Cambridge University Press, 2004), 47–85.

Kenaan-Kedar, N., and B. Kedar, 'The significance of a twelfth-century sculptural group: le retour du croisé', in *DGF*, 29–44.

Kennan, E., 'Innocent III and the first political crusade: a comment on the limitations of papal power', *Traditio* 27 (1971), 231–49.

Kennan, E., 'Innocent III, Gregory IX and political crusades: a study in the disintegration of papal power', in G. F. Lytle, ed., *Reform and Authority in the Medieval and Reformation Church* (Washington, DC: Catholic University of America, 1981), 15–35.

Kennedy, H., *Crusader Castles* (Cambridge: Cambridge University Press, 1994).

Knoch, P., 'Kreuzzug und Siedlung: Studien zum Aufruf der Magdeburger Kirche vom 1108', *Jahrbuch für die Geschichte Mittel- und Ostdeutschlands* 23 (1974), 1–33.

Krueger, H. C., 'The crusades and European expansion', in J. A. Brundage, ed., *The Crusades. Motives and Achievements* (Boston, MA: D. C. Heath, 1964), 59–62.

Krueger, H. C., 'The Italian cities and the Arabs before 1095', *HC* 1: 40–53.

Kugler, B., *Studien zur Geschichte des zweiten Kreuzzuges* (Stuttgart, 1866).

Kunt, I. M., 'The rise of the Ottomans', in M. Jones, ed., *NCMH, VI, c. 1300–c. 1415* (Cambridge: Cambridge University Press, 2000), 839–63.

Lacaze, Y., 'Philippe le Bon et le problème hussite: Un projet de croisade bourguignon en 1428–1429', *RH* 241 (1969), 69–98.

Laurent, V., 'La Croisade et la question d'orient sous le pontificat de Grégoire X (1272–1276)', *Revue historique du sud-est européen* 22 (1945), 105–37.

Leclercq, J., 'Gratien, Pierre de Troyes et la seconde croisade', *Studia Gratiana* 2 (1954), 583–93.

Leclercq, J., 'Pour l'histoire de l'encyclique de S. Bernard sur la croisade', in *Études de civilisation médiévale, IXe–XIIe siècles. Mélanges Edmond-René Labande* (Poitiers: CESCM, 1974), 479–94.

Leclercq, J., ed., 'Un document sur les débuts des Templiers', *Revue d'histoire ecclésiastique* 52 (1957), 81–91.

Le Concile de Clermont de 1095 et l'appel à la croisade (Rome: École française de Rome, 1997).

Le Goff, J., *Saint Louis*, Bibliothèque des histoires (Paris: Gallimard, 1996).

Leopold, A., *How to Recover the Holy Land. The Crusade Proposals of the Late Thirteenth and Early Fourteenth Centuries* (Aldershot: Ashgate, 2000).

Ligato, G., 'Fra Ordini Cavallereschi e crociata: "milites ad terminum" e "confraternitates" armate', in *'Militia Christi' e crociata nei secoli XI–XIII* (Milan: Vita e pensiero, 1992), 645–97.

Lilie, R.-J., *Byzantium and the Crusader States, 1095–1204*, trans. J. C. Morris and J. C. Ridings (Oxford: Oxford University Press, 1993).

Lilie, R.-J., *Byzanz und die Kreuzzüge* (Stuttgart: Kohlhammer, 2004).

Lilie, R.J., 'Der erster Kreuzzug in der Darstellung Anna Komnenes', in *Varia II: Beiträge von A. Berger et al.* (Bonn: R. Habelt, 1987), 49–148.

Linder, A., *Raising Arms. Liturgy in the Struggle to Liberate Jerusalem in the Late Middle Ages* (Turnhout: Brepols, 2003).

Lindkvist, T., 'Crusades and crusading ideology in the political history of Sweden, 1140–1500', in *CCBF*, 119–30.

Linehan, P., *History and the Historians of Medieval Spain* (Oxford: Oxford University Press, 1993).

Linehan, P., *The Spanish Church and the Papacy in the Thirteenth Century* (Cambridge: Cambridge University Press, 1971).

Livermore, H. V., 'The "conquest of Lisbon" and its author', *Portuguese Studies* 6 (1990), 1–16.

Lloyd, S., 'The crusading movement, 1096–1274', in *OIHC*, 34–65.

Lloyd, S., *English Society and the Crusade, 1216–1307* (Oxford: Clarendon Press, 1988).

Lloyd, S., 'The Lord Edward's crusade, 1270–2: its setting and significance', in *WGMA*, 120–33.

Lloyd, S., 'William Longespee II: the making of an English crusading hero', *Nottingham Medieval Studies* 35 (1991), 41–69; 36 (1992), 79–125.

Lock, P., *The Franks in the Aegean, 1204–1500* (London: Longman, 1995).

Lomax, D. W., *The Reconquest of Spain* (London: Longman, 1978).

Longnon, J., 'Les Vues de Charles d'Anjou pour la deuxième croisade de Saint-Louis: Tunis ou Constantinople?' *Septième centenaire de la mort de Saint-Louis. Actes des colloques de Royaumont et de Paris* (Paris, 1976), 183–95.

Lopez, R. S., 'The Norman conquest of Sicily', *HC* 1: 54–67.

Lotter, F., 'The crusading idea and the conquest of the region east of the Elbe', in *MFS*, 267–306.

Lotter, F., *Die Konzeption des Wendenkreuzzugs: ideengeschichtliche, kirchenrechtliche und historisch-politische Voraussetzungen der Missionierung von Elb- und Ostseeslawen um die Mitte des 12. Jahrhunderts* (Sigmaringen: Thorbecke, 1977).

Loutchitskaja, S., 'L'Image des musulmans dans les chroniques des croisades', *Le Moyen Age* 105 (1999), 717–35.

Lunt, W. E., *Financial Relations of the Papacy with England* (2 vols, Cambridge, MA: Mediaeval Academy of America, 1939–62).

Lunt, W. E., *Papal Revenues in the Middle Ages* (2 vols, New York: Columbia University Press, 1934).

Luttrell, A. T., 'The crusade in the fourteenth century', in J. Hale, R. Highfield and B. Smalley, eds, *Europe in the Late Middle Ages* (London: Faber and Faber, 1965), 122–54.

Luttrell, A. T., 'Gregory XI and the Turks: 1370–1378', *Orientalia Christiana periodica* 46 (1980), 391–417.

Luttrell, A. T., 'The Hospitallers at Rhodes, 1306–1421', in *HC* 3: 278–313.

Luttrell, A. T., 'Interessi fiorentini nell'economia e nella politica dei Cavalieri Ospedalieri di Rodi nel trecento', *Annali della Scuola normale superiore di Pisa*, 2nd ser: *Lettere, storia e filosofia* 28 (1959), 317–26.

Lyons, M. C., and D. E. P. Jackson, *Saladin. The Politics of the Holy War* (Cambridge: Cambridge University Press, 1982).

McGinn, B, 'Iter sancti sepulchri. The piety of the first crusaders', in B. K. Lackner and K. R. Philip, eds, *Essays in Medieval Civilisation* (Austin: University of Texas Press, 1978), 33–72.

McGinn, B., ed., *Visions of the End. Apocalyptic Traditions in the Middle Ages* (new edn, New York: Columbia University Press, 1998).

MacKay, A., 'Religion, culture, and ideology on the late medieval Castilian-Granadan frontier', in *MFS*, 217–43.

Madden, T., *Enrico Dandolo and the Rise of Venice* (Baltimore, MD: Johns Hopkins University Press, 2003).

Madden, T., 'Outside and inside the Fourth Crusade', *IHR* 17 (1995), 726–43.

Madden, T., 'Vows and contracts in the Fourth Crusade: the treaty of Zara and the attack on Constantinople in 1204', *IHR* 15 (1993), 441–68.

Magee, J., 'Crusading at the court of Charles VI, 1388–1396', *French History* 12 (1998), 367–83.

Maier, C. T., 'The *bible moralisée* and the crusades', in *EC*, 209–22.

Maier, C. T., 'Crisis, liturgy and the crusade in the twelfth and thirteenth centuries', *JEH* 48 (1997), 628–57.

Maier, C. T., 'Crusade and rhetoric against the Muslim colony of Lucera: Eudes of Châteauroux's *Sermones de rebellione Sarracenorum in Apulia*', *JMH* 21 (1995), 343–85.

Maier, C. T., ed., *Crusade Propaganda and Ideology. Model Sermons for the Preaching of the Cross* (Cambridge: Cambridge University Press, 2000).

Maier, C. T., 'Mass, the eucharist and the cross: Innocent III and the relocation of the crusade', in *PIW*, 351–60.

Maier, C. T., *Preaching the Crusades. Mendicant Friars and the Cross in the Thirteenth Century* (Cambridge: Cambridge University Press, 1994).

Malkiel, A., 'The underclass in the First Crusade: a historiographical trend', *JMH* 28 (2002), 169–97.

Markowski, M., 'Peter of Blois and the conception of the Third Crusade', in *HH*, 261–9.

Markowski, M., 'Richard Lionheart: bad king, bad crusader?' *JMH* 23 (1997), 351–65.

Marshall, C., 'The crusading motivation of the Italian city republics in the Latin East, 1096–1104', in *EC*, 60–79.

Mastnak, T., *Crusading Peace. Christendom, the Muslim World, and Western Political Order* (Berkeley: University of California Press, 2002).

Matuzova, V. I., 'Mental frontiers: Prussians as seen by Peter von Dusburg', in *CCBF*, 253–9.

Mayer, H. E., *The Crusades*, trans. J. Gillingham (Oxford: Oxford University Press, 1972, 2nd edn 1988).

Mayer, H. E., *Mélanges sur l'histoire du royaume latin de Jérusalem* (Paris: Imprimerie nationale, 1984).

Mentgen, G., 'Kreuzzugsmentalität bei antijüdischen Aktionen nach 1190', in *JCZK*, 287–326.

Menzel, M., 'Kreuzzugsideologie unter Innocenz III', *Historisches Jahrbuch* 120 (2000), 39–79.

Meserve, M., 'Italian humanists and the problem of the crusade', in *CFCMI*, 13–38, 183–8.

BIBLIOGRAPHY

Milhou, A., *Colón y su mentalidad mesiánica en el ambiente franciscanista español* (Valladolid: Casa-Museo de Colón Seminario Americanista de la Universidad de Valladolid, 1983).

'Militia Christi' e crociata nei secoli XI–XIII (Milan: Vita e pensiero, 1992).

Mitchell, P. D., *Medicine in the Crusades. Warfare, Wounds and the Medieval Surgeon* (Cambridge: Cambridge University Press, 2004).

Moore, J. C., *Pope Innocent III (1160/61–1216): To Root Up and to Plant* (Leiden: Brill, 2003).

Moore, R. I., *The Formation of a Persecuting Society. Power and Deviance in Western Europe, 950–1250* (Oxford: Blackwell, 1987).

Morris, C., 'Geoffrey of Villehardouin and the Conquest of Constantinople', *History* 53 (1968), 24–34.

Morris, C., *The Papal Monarchy. The Western Church from 1050 to 1250* (Oxford: Oxford University Press, 1989).

Morris, C., 'Picturing the crusades: the uses of visual propaganda, c. 1095–1250', in *CTS*, 195–209.

Morris, C., 'Policy and visions: the case of the holy lance at Antioch', in *WGMA*, 33–45.

Muldoon, J., *Popes, Lawyers, and Infidels. The Church and the Non-Christian World 1250–1550* (Liverpool: Liverpool University Press, 1979).

Mulinder, A., 'Albert of Aachen and the crusade of 1101', in *FCJ*, 69–77.

Murray, A. V., 'The army of Godfrey of Bouillon, 1096–1099: structure and dynamics of a contingent on the First Crusade', *RBPH* 70 (1992), 301–29.

Murray, A. V., comp., 'Bibliography of the First Crusade', in *FCJ*, 267–310.

Murray, A. V., comp., 'Crusade and conversion on the Baltic frontier 1150–1550: a bibliography of publications in English', in *CCBF*, 277–85.

Murray, A. V., 'The title of Godfrey of Bouillon as ruler of Jersualem', *Collegium Medievale: Interdisciplinary Journal of Medieval Research* 3 (1990), 163–78.

Nelson, J. A., and E. J. Mickel, eds, *The Old French Crusade Cycle* (11 vols, Tuscaloosa: University of Alabama Press, 1977–2003).

Nicholson, H. J., 'Women on the Third Crusade', *JMH* 23 (1997), 335–49.

Nicol, D. M., *Byzantium and Venice. A Study in Diplomatic and Cultural Relations* (Cambridge: Cambridge University Press, 1988).

Nicol, D. M., *The Last Centuries of Byzantium 1261–1453* (London: Rupert Hart-Davis, 1972).

Nielsen, T. K., 'The missionary man: Archbishop Anders Sunesen and the Baltic crusade, 1206–21', in *CCBF*, 95–117.

Nirenberg, D., *Communities of Violence. Persecution of Minorities in the Middle Ages* (Princeton, NJ: Princeton University Press, 1996).

Noble, P., 'The importance of Old French chronicles as historical sources of the Fourth Crusade and the early Latin empire of Constantinople', *JMH* 27 (2001), 399–416.

Nowakowska, N., 'Poland and the crusade in the reign of King Jan Olbracht, 1492–1501', in *CFCMI*, 128–47, 227–31.

O'Callaghan, J. F., *Reconquest and Crusade in Medieval Spain* (Philadelphia: University of Pennsylvania Press, 2003).

Painter, S., 'The crusade of Theobald of Champagne and Richard of Cornwall, 1239–1241', in *HC* 2: 463–85.

Palmer, J. J. N., *England, France and Christendom, 1377–99* (London: Routledge and Kegan Paul, 1972).

Paravicini, W., *Die Preussenreisen des europäischen Adels* (2 vols, Sigmaringen: Jan Thorbecke, 1989–95).

Patschovsky, A., 'Feindbilder der Kirche: Juden und Ketzer im Vergleich (11.–13. Jahrhundert)', in *JCZK*, 327–587.

Paviot, J., *Les Ducs de Bourgogne, la croisade et l'orient (fin xive siècle – xve siècle)* (Paris: Presses de l'Université de Paris-Sorbonne, 2003).

Petkov, K., 'The rotten apple and the good apples: Orthodox, Catholics, and Turks in Philippe de Mézières' crusading propaganda', *JMH* 23 (1997), 255–70.

Phillips, J., *Defenders of the Holy Land. Relations between the Latin East and the West, 1119–1187* (Oxford: Oxford University Press, 1996).

Phillips, J., 'Ideas of crusade and holy war in *De expugnatione lyxbonensi* (*The conquest of Lisbon*)', in *HLHL*, 123–41.

Phillips, J., 'Odo of Deuil's *De profectione Ludovici VII in Orientem* as a source for the Second Crusade', in *EC*, 80–95.

Phillips, J., 'Papacy, empire and the Second Crusade', in *SCSC*, 15–31.

Phillips, J., 'Saint Bernard of Clairvaux, the Low Countries and the Lisbon letter of the Second Crusade', *JEH* 48 (1997), 485–97.

Porges, W., 'The clergy, the poor and the non-combatants on the First Crusade', *Speculum* 21 (1946), 1–23.

Poumarède, G., *Pour en finir avec la croisade. Mythes et réalités de la lutte contre les Turcs aux xvie et xviie siècles* (Paris: Presses universitaires de France, 2004).

Powell, J. M., *Anatomy of a Crusade 1213–1221* (Philadelphia: University of Pennsylvania Press, 1986).

Powell, J. M., 'Crusading by royal command: monarchy and crusade in the kingdom of Sicily', in *Potere, società e popolo tra età normanna ed età sveva (1187–1230)* (Bari: Centro di studi normanno-svevi, University of Bari, 1983), 131–46.

Powell, J. M., ed., *Innocent III, Vicar of Christ or Lord of the World?* (revd edn, Washington, DC: Catholic University of America Press, 1994).

Powell, J. M., 'Myth, legend, propaganda, history: the First Crusade, 1140–ca. 1300', in *APC*, 127–41.

Prawer, J., 'Jerusalem in the Christian and Jewish perspectives of the early Middle Ages', *Settimane di studio del Centro italiano di studi sull'alto medioevo, 26. Gli Ebrei nell'alto medioevo* (Spoleto: Centro italiano di studi sull'alto medioevo, 1980), 739–95.

Prawer, J., *The Latin Kingdom of Jerusalem. European Colonialism in the Middle Ages* (London: Weidenfeld and Nicolson, 1972).

Pryor, J. H., *Geography, Technology, and War. Studies in the Maritime History of the Mediterranean, 649–1571* (Cambridge: Cambridge University Press, 1988).

Pryor, J. H., 'The oaths of the leaders of the First Crusade to Emperor Alexius I Comnenus', *Parergon. Bulletin of the Australian and New Zealand Association for Medieval and Renaissance Studies*, ns 2 (1984), 111–41.

Pryor, J. H., 'The Venetian fleet for the Fourth Crusade and the diversion of the crusade to Constantinople', in *EC*, 103–23.

Purcell, M., *Papal Crusading Policy 1244–1291. The Chief Instruments of Papal Crusading Policy and Crusade to the Holy Land from the Final Loss of Jerusalem to the Fall of Acre* (Leiden: Brill, 1975).

Queller, D. E., and T. F. Madden, *The Fourth Crusade. The Conquest of Constantinople* (2nd edn, Philadelphia: University of Pennsylvania Press, 1997).

Racaut, L., 'The polemical use of the Albigensian Crusade during the French Wars of Religion', *French History* 13 (1999), 261–79.

Racine, P., ed., *Piacenza e la prima crociata* (Reggio Emilia: Diabasis, 1995).

Raedts, P., 'The Children's Crusade of 1212', *JMH* 3 (1977), 279–323.

Renouard, Y., *Les Relations des papes d'Avignon et des compagnies commerciales et bancaires de 1316 à 1378* (Paris, 1941).

Renouard, Y., *Recherches sur les compagnies commerciales et bancaires utilisées par les papes d'Avignon avant le Grand Schisme* (Paris, 1942).

Reuter, T., 'The "non-crusade" of 1149–50', in *SCSC*, 150–63.

Rey-Delqué, M., ed., *Les Croisades, l'orient et l'occident d'Urbain II à Saint-Louis (1096–1270)* (Milan: Electa, 1997).

Richard, J., *Histoire des croisades* (Paris: Fayard, 1996).

Richard, J., 'La Fondation d'une église latine en Orient par saint Louis: Damiette', *BEC* 120 (1962), 39–54.

Richard, J., *Saint Louis. Crusader King of France*, trans. J. Birrell (Cambridge: Cambridge University Press, 1992).

Richard, J., '1187: Point de départ pour une nouvelle forme de la croisade', in *HH*, 250–60.

Riley-Smith, J., 'Casualties and the number of knights on the First Crusade', *Crusades* 1 (2002), 13–28.

Riley-Smith, J., 'The crown of France and Acre, 1254–1291', in D. H. Weiss and L. Mahoney, eds, *France and the Holy Land. Frankish Culture at the End of the Crusades* (Baltimore, MD: Johns Hopkins University Press, 2004), 45–62.

Riley-Smith, J., *The Crusades. A Short History* (London: Athlone Press, 1987, 2nd edn forthcoming).

Riley-Smith, J., 'Crusading as an act of love', *History* 65 (1980), 177–92.

Riley-Smith, J., 'The crusading movement and historians', in *OIHC*, 1–12.

Riley-Smith, J., 'Early crusaders to the east and the costs of crusading 1095–1130', in *CCCCP*, 237–57.

Riley-Smith, J., 'Erdmann and the historiography of the crusades, 1935–1995', in *PCNAD*, 17–29.

Riley-Smith, J., 'The First Crusade and St Peter', in *OSHCKJ*, 41–63.

Riley-Smith, J., *The First Crusade and the Idea of Crusading* (London: Athlone Press, 1986).

Riley-Smith, J., 'The First Crusade and the persecution of the Jews', *SCH* 21 (1984), 51–72.

Riley-Smith, J., 'Government in Latin Syria and the commercial privileges of foreign merchants', in D. Baker, *Relations between East and West in the Middle Ages* (Edinburgh: Edinburgh University Press, 1973), 109–32.

Riley-Smith, J., 'History, the crusades and the Latin East, 1095–1204: a personal view', in *CMTCS*, 1–17.

Riley-Smith, J., 'Islam and the crusades in history and imagination, 8 November 1898 – 11 September 2001', *Crusades*, 2 (2003), 151–67.

Riley-Smith, J., 'The motives of the earliest crusaders and the settlement of Latin Palestine', *EHR* 98 (1983), 721–36.

Riley-Smith, J., 'The state of mind of crusaders to the east, 1095–1300', in *OIHC*, 66–90.

Riley-Smith, J., 'The structure of the orders of the Temple and the Hospital in c. 1291', in *MC*, 125–43.

Riley-Smith, J., 'The title of Godfrey of Bouillon', *BIHR* 52 (1979), 83–6.

Riley-Smith, J., 'The Venetian crusade of 1122–1124', in *CIRCG*, 337–50.

Riley-Smith, J., 'Were the Templars guilty?' in *MC*, 107–124.

Riley-Smith, J., *What were the Crusades?* (3rd edn, Basingstoke: Palgrave Macmillan, 2002).

Rist, R., 'Papal policy and the Albigensian Crusades: continuity or change?' *Crusades* 2 (2003), 99–108.

Robbert, L. B., 'Venice and the crusades', in *HC* 5: 379–451.

Robinson, I. S., 'Gregory VII and the soldiers of Christ', *History* 58 (1973), 161–92.

Robinson, I. S., *The Papacy 1073–1198. Continuity and Innovation* (Cambridge: Cambridge University Press, 1990).

Rogers, R., 'Peter Bartholomew and the role of "the poor" in the First Crusade', in T. Reuter, ed., *Warriors and Churchmen in the High Middle Ages. Essays presented to Karl Leyser* (London: Hambledon, 1992), 109–22.

Roscher, H., *Papst Innocenz III. und die Kreuzzüge* (Göttingen: Vandenhoeck and Ruprecht, 1969).

Rouche, M., 'Cannibalisme sacré chez les croisés populaires', in Y.-M. Hilaire, ed., *La Religion populaire. Aspects du Christianisme populaire à travers l'histoire* (Lille: Centre interdisciplinaire d'études des religions de l'Université de Lille III, 1981), 29–41.

Rousset, P., *Les Origines et les caractères de la première croisade* (Neuchatel: La Baconnière, 1945).

Routledge, M., 'Songs', in *OIHC*, 91–111.

Rowe, J. G., 'Alexander III and the Jerusalem crusade: an overview of problems and failures', in *CMTCS*, 112–32.

Rowe, J. G., 'The origins of the Second Crusade: Pope Eugenius III, Bernard of Clairvaux and Louis VII of France', in *SCC*, 79–89.

Rowe, J. G., 'Paschal II, Bohemund of Antioch and the Byzantine empire', *Bulletin of the John Rylands Library* 49 (1966), 165–202.

Rowell, S. C., *Lithuania Ascending. A Pagan Empire within East-Central Europe, 1295–1345* (Cambridge: Cambridge University Press, 1994).

Rubinstein, J., 'How, or how much, to reevaluate Peter the Hermit', in *MC*, 53–69.

Ruiz, T. F., 'Unsacred monarchy: the kings of Castile in the late Middle Ages', in S. Wilentz, ed., *Rites of Power. Symbolism, Ritual, and Politics since the Middle Ages* (Philadelphia: University of Pennsylvania Press, 1985), 109–44.

Runciman, S., *A History of the Crusades* (3 vols, Cambridge: Cambridge University Press, 1951–4).

Russell, F. H., *The Just War in the Middle Ages* (Cambridge: Cambridge University Press, 1975).

Russell, P., *Prince Henry 'the Navigator'. A Life* (New Haven, CT: Yale University Press, 2000).

Schein, S., *Fideles Crucis. The Papacy, the West, and the Recovery of the Holy Land 1274–1314* (Oxford: Oxford University Press, 1991).

Schein, S., 'From "milites Christi" to "mali Christiani". The Italian communes in western historical literature', in *CIRCG*, 679–89.

Schein, S., 'Philip IV and the crusade: a reconsideration', in *CS*, 121–6.

Schmandt, R., 'The Fourth Crusade and the just war theory', *CHR* 61 (1975), 191–221.

Schwinges, R. C., *Kreuzzugsideologie und Toleranz. Studien zu Wilhelm von Tyrus* (Stuttgart: A. Hiersemann, 1977).

Schwinges, R. C., 'William of Tyre, the Muslim enemy, and the problem of tolerance', in *TISCAC*, 124–32, 173–6.

Setton, K. M., *The Papacy and the Levant (1204–1571)* (4 vols, Philadelphia: American Philosophical Society, 1978–84).

Setton, K. M., *Venice, Austria, and the Turks in the Seventeenth Century* (Philadelphia: American Philosophical Society, 1991).

Sheils, W. J., ed., *The Church and War, SCH 20* (Oxford: Blackwell, 1983).

Siberry, E., *Criticism of Crusading, 1095–1274* (Oxford: Oxford University Press, 1985).

Siberry, E., 'Images of the crusades in the nineteenth and twentieth centuries', in *OIHC*, 365–85.

Siberry, E., *The New Crusaders. Images of the Crusades in the Nineteenth and Early-Twentieth Centuries* (Basingstoke: Ashgate, 2000).

Siberry, E., 'Nineteenth-century perspectives of the First Crusade', in *EC*, 281–93.

Sieber-Lehmann, C., 'An obscure but powerful pattern: crusading, nationalism and the Swiss confederation in the late Middle Ages', in *CFCMI*, 81–93, 208–15.

Šmahel, F., *Die Hussitische Revolution* (3 vols, Hannover: Hahnsche Buchhandlung, 2002).

Smail, R. C., *Crusading Warfare (1097–1193)* (Cambridge: Cambridge University Press, 1956).

Smail, R. C., 'Latin Syria and the west, 1149–1187', *TRHS* ser. 5, 19 (1969), 1–20.

Somerville, R., 'Clermont 1095: crusade and canons', in *PCNAD*, 63–77.

Southern, R. W., *Western Views of Islam in the Middle Ages* (Cambridge, MA: Harvard University Press, 1962).

Stacey, R. C., 'Crusades, martyrdoms, and the Jews of Norman England', in *JCZK*, 233–51.

Strayer, J. R., 'The crusades of Louis IX', in *HC* 2: 487–518.

Strayer, J. R., 'France: the Holy Land, the Chosen People, and the Most Christian King', in J. F. Benton and T. N. Bisson, eds, *Medieval Statecraft and the Perspectives of History. Essays by Joseph R. Strayer* (Princeton, NJ: Princeton University Press, 1971), 300–14.

Strayer, J. R., 'The political crusades of the thirteenth century', in *HC* 2: 343–75.

Strayer, J. R., *The Reign of Philip the Fair* (Princeton, NJ: Princeton University Press, 1980).

Sumberg, L. A. M., 'The "Tafurs" and the First Crusade', *Mediaeval Studies* 21 (1959), 224–46.

Swanson, R. N., *Religion and Devotion in Europe, c. 1215–c. 1515* (Cambridge: Cambridge University Press, 1995).

Taylor, J., *Muslims in Medieval Italy: The Colony at Lucera* (Lanham, MD: Lexington Books, 2003).

Thorau, P., *The Lion of Egypt. Sultan Baybars I and the Near East in the Thirteenth Century*, trans. P. M. Holt (London: Longman, 1987).

Throop, P. A., *Criticism of the Crusade: A Study of Public Opinion and Crusade Propaganda* (Amsterdam: N. V. Swets and Zeitlinger, 1940, repr. Philadelphia: Porcupine Press, 1975).

Tolan, J. V., *Saracens: Islam in the Medieval European Imagination* (New York: Columbia University Press, 2002).

Toubert, P., 'Les Déviations de la croisade au milieu du xiiie siècle: Alexandre IV contre Manfred', *Le Moyen Age* 69 (1963), 391–9.

Trenchs Odena, J., '"De Alexandrinis" (El comercio prohibido con los musulmanes y el papado de Aviñón durante la primera mitad de siglo XIV)', *Anuario de estudios medievales* 10 (1980), 237–320.

Trotter, D. A., *Medieval French Literature and the Crusades* (Geneva: Droz, 1988).

Tyerman, C. J., *England and the Crusades 1095–1588* (Chicago: University of Chicago Press, 1988).

Tyerman, C. J., 'The Holy Land and the crusades of the thirteenth and fourteenth centuries', in *CS*, 105–12.

Tyerman, C., *The Invention of the Crusades* (Basingstoke: Macmillan, 1998).

Tyerman, C. J., 'Marino Sanudo Torsello and the lost crusade: lobbying in the fourteenth century', *TRHS* 32 (1982), 57–73.

Tyerman, C. J., 'Philip V of France, the assemblies of 1319–20 and the crusade', *BIHR* 57 (1984), 15–34.

Tyerman, C. J., 'Philip VI and the recovery of the Holy Land', *EHR* 100 (1985), 25–51.

Tyerman, C. J., 'Sed nihil fecit? The last Capetians and the recovery of the Holy Land', in *WGMA*, 170–81.

Tyerman, C. J., 'What the crusades meant to Europe', in P. Linehan and J. L. Nelson, eds, *The Medieval World* (London: Routledge, 2001), 131–45.

Tyerman, C. J., 'Who went on Crusades to the Holy Land?' in *HH*, 13–26.

BIBLIOGRAPHY

Urban, W., *The Baltic Crusade* (2nd edn, Chicago: Lithuanian Research and Studies Center, 1994).

Urban, W., *The Livonian Crusade* (Washington, DC: University Press of America, 1981).

Urban W., *The Prussian Crusade* (Lanham, MD: University Press of America, 1980).

Urban, W., *The Samogitian Crusade* (Chicago: Lithuanian Research and Studies Center, 1989).

Vaughan, R., *Philip the Bold. The Formation of the Burgundian State* (London: Longman, 1962).

Waeger, G., *Gottfried von Bouillon in der Historiographie* (Zurich: Fretz und Wasmuth, 1969).

Watt, J. A., 'The crusades and the persecution of the Jews', in P. Linehan and J. L. Nelson, eds, *The Medieval World* (London: Routledge, 2001), 146–62.

Webb, D., *Medieval European Pilgrimage, c. 700–c. 1500* (Basingstoke: Palgrave, 2002).

Weiler, B., 'The *Negotium Terrae Sanctae* in the political discourse of Latin Christendom, 1215–1311', *IHR* 25 (2003), 1–36.

Williams, J. B., 'The making of a crusade: the Genoese anti-Muslim attacks in Spain, 1146–1148', *JMH* 23 (1997), 29–53.

Woehl, C., *Volo vincere cum meis vel occumbere cum eisdem. Studien zu Simon von Montfort und seinen nordfranzösischen Gefolgsleuten während des Albigenserkreuzzugs (1209 bis 1218)* (Frankfurt am Main: Peter Lang, 2001).

Wood, D., *Clement VI. The Pontificate and Ideas of an Avignon Pope* (Cambridge: Cambridge University Press, 1989).

Yewdale, R. B., *Bohemond I, Prince of Antioch* (Princeton, NJ: n.p., 1924).

Zachariadou, E., 'Holy war in the Aegean during the fourteenth century', in B. Arbel and others, eds, *Latins and Greeks in the Eastern Mediterranean after 1204* (London: Frank Cass, 1989), 212–25.

Index

The following abbreviations are used:

a   archbishop
b   bishop
c   count
d   duke
e   emperor
k   king
p   pope
s   sultan